HUNTS' GUIDE TO

WEST
MICHIGAN

By Mary and Don Hunt

MIDWESTERN GUIDES

Midwestern Guides
506 Linden
Albion, Michigan 49224
Telephone: (517) 629-4494

ISBN 0-9623499-1-7

A Midwestern Guides Book

Other Midwestern Guides titles:

Hunts' Highlights of Michigan

Michigan Fresh: A food-lovers' guide to growers & bakeries

*Hunts' Getaways on the Upper Mississippi
between Chicago & the Twin Cities*

Hunts' Guide to Southeast Michigan

Cover designer & design consultant: Christine Golus

Printing: Malloy Lithographing, Ann Arbor, Michigan

Illustrations:
Marge Bronsink: pages 203, 208, 212
Victor Casenelli: pages 171, 177
Gillette Visitor Center, pages 89, 191
Michigan Travel Commission: pages 8, 28, 31, 65, 83,
102, 118, 128, 131, 135, 138, 158
Courtesy of Rollamd Peterson: pages 91, 100
Merle Proctor: pages 179, 189, 195
State Archives of Michigan: pages 50, 64, 66, 81, 82, 112, 121, 148
Tri-Cities Historical Museum: pages 157, 164

ABOUT USING THIS 1993 UPDATE:
Changes have been made to reflect business closings,
new locations, some new businesses, and other major changes. Most
entries reflect 1990 prices and hours. Calling ahead to confirm hours is
always a good idea, since hours change frequently. In this case it's even
more important. Most prices are only slightly higher than they were in
1990; some are even lower.

Contents

To our readers

This guide to west Michigan is part of a series of Michigan guides. Our philosophy of guidebook writing is to find and report on a large variety of interesting things to experience in an area. You'll find a lot more here than just the obvious sights that a AAA or Mobil Guide includes. Each place included in this book was personally visited. A good many places we visited were not included because we didn't find them interesting enough.

A great deal of time and energy went into surveying the region to find the most interesting places to visit. To be of maxiumum usefulness to the traveler, much effort has also gone into providing directions, seasons, hours of operation, and specific prices. We have sought out not only the very best lodgings and restaurants in an area, but also affordable places to eat and sleep for families on a budget. Independent motels have been visited and screened, and campgrounds have been evaluated.

No charge for inclusion. Places that appear were selected because of their interest value. There is absolutely no charge. In fact, many owners or managers have no idea their businesses were selected. Our interest is not in promoting the region, but providing you with good advice on what's of interest.

About stars ★★. While every point of interest and restaurant in this book has been judged of special interest, some entries are more noteworthy than others, worth a considerable detour. Stars flag places of unusual interest. Three stars is the highest possible rating.

Call to confirm hours. Some hours stay the same for years, others change. If you're counting on a business being open, call to confirm. (We've provided the telephone numbers of every entry.) On holidays in resort areas businesses are almost always open. In non-resort areas, they may well be closed.

About prices. A great many prices are quoted in this book. Whether for the cost of a motel room, a meal, or a piece of pottery, they are intended only to be an relative guide. Prices change frequently. Hotel rates go up and down with changing market conditions. It always pays to comparison shop and call for special hotel packages.

Motels and hotels are air-conditioned with private phones unless otherwise noted.

Bed and breakfasts are usually but not always air-conditioned in lakeshore areas. Rates given are for double occupancy; rooms typically have one double bed. Most don't have private phones or T.V.s. Nearly all prohibit smoking in guest rooms, and often in the entire house. Many can be rented by groups in the off-season for seminars and meetings. In busy resort areas, especially the New Buffalo area, South Haven, and Grand Haven, a two-night minimum is usually required on weekends.

We welcome suggestions for new entries and feedback on current entries. Contact us at Midwestern Guides, 506 Linden, Albion, Michigan 49224, or call (517) 629-4494.

ABOUT USING THIS 1993 UPDATE:

Changes have been made to reflect business closings, new locations, some new businesses, and other major changes. Most entries reflect 1990 prices and hours. Calling ahead to confirm hours is always a good idea, since hours change frequently. In this case it's even more important. Most prices are only slightly higher than they were in 1990; some are even lower.

Michigan State Parks charge more for everything, however. The yearly sticker is now $18, for seniors $4.50. Daily admission is $3.50 per vehicle. Camping at modern campgrounds is $14 a night.Advance reservations are $4 extra.

New Buffalo and vicinity

"Harbor Country" is the new, promotion-minded name for the stretch of summer resorts between Lake Michigan and the Red Arrow Highway. It extends fifteen miles from Michiana and Grand Beach on the Indiana line and New Buffalo on the south, through Union Pier, Lakeside, and Harbert, to Sawyer and Warren Dunes State Park to the north.

Until just a few years ago it was a quiet, neglected place, and New Buffalo was its commercial center. But today four-story condo developments cluster around the largest full-service marina on Lake Michigan. Sprouting up on every scrap of available property all along the lake are new vacation houses, including some by Chicago's most famous architects. Rundown cottages along Lake Shore Drive in Union Pier, a resort town with a trailer camp near its center, are being transformed into elaborately landscaped summer homes and mini-condo complexes. On Whittaker Street in New Buffalo, chic resortwear shops face Scotty's Roller Bowl and other vestiges of the recent past, when New Buffalo was a somnolent blue-collar town.

Boom times from lumber and railroading

The area was first developed as a string of lumber piers and sawmills for shipping the wood products of southwest Michigan's great hardwood forests to Chicago. A remnant of virgin timberland survives in nearby **Warren Woods**.

New Buffalo itself was platted in 1835 by land speculators who dreamed it would become an important lake port. The name honors the New York hometown of an original settler, who first found the site when shipwrecked there. For a few lucrative years from 1849 to 1853, New Buffalo was the western terminus of the Michigan Central Railroad. Passengers, lumber, and other freight went to Chicago on the rail line's ships. But this brief boom ended when the railroad's route to Chicago was completed.

Sawmills were built in the 1850s, and piers for loading lumber schooners were extended out into Lake Michigan at **Lakeside** and **Union Pier**. Lakeside was then called Wilkinson; the name was changed after the Civil War.

But by the turn of the century, the lumber was mostly gone. Benton Harbor and St. Joseph had come

Modest 1920s cottages a block from the beach in Union Pier have been gutted, restored outside with added porches and decks, and landscaped in an "old-fashioned" style. Marketed as condos in 1989, the Shore Line Resort Cottages were "affordably priced" from $160,000 to $195,000.

*Interesting histories of Harbor Country communities, from hometown pioneers to celebrated vacationers, appear in the topnotch **Harbor Country Guide,** along with a map, events calendar, special attractions, and helpful ads. Get it at the participating advertisers or the Chamber of Commerce, 3 W. Buffalo, in New Buffalo, MI 49117. (616) 469-5409.*

to dominate shipping in southwest Michigan. New Buffalo's future as a vacation getaway and commercial center for the surrounding resorts was set.

Each resort had a station on the Pere Marquette Railroad, now the Chesapeake & Ohio, which roughly paralleled the Red Arrow Highway. Amtrak's Chicago to Grand Rapids train still stops at New Buffalo, in fact. The first decade of the 20th century saw camps, estates and summer homes, private and rental cottages, and small resort hotels built all along the lakeshore. In the 1920s, when automobiles were first in widespread use and the highway was paved, the area boomed, albeit in a fairly low-key way. Recognizing the huge impact of Chicago vacationers, the State of Michigan highway department opened the first roadside tourist information center in the United States on U.S. 12 outside New Buffalo in 1934.

Resorts reflected the ethnic makeup of Chicago's south side

Ethnic patterns established early in the century tend to persist today, to the extent that cottages remain in the same families for generations. For many families, the summer place is the only constant in a rapidly changing world of job-related transfers and moves. Beautiful **Grand Beach**, with its private park and winding drives, was favored by Irish Catholics. Its Golfmore resort hotel was quite a glamorous spot in the 1920s. Mayor Daley's summer place was here; so is theologian/novelist Father Andrew Greeley's today.

Lakeside, genteel and quiet, was the domain of University of Chicago faculty and "old" (by Chicago standards) meat-packing families. Orthodox Jews formed an enclave on some of Lakeside's smaller, interior lots between Schaffner and Kruse. But restrictive real estate covenants prevented Jews from owning lakefront property here.

Union Pier, however, was largely Jewish. Chicago Bohemians and Lithuanians had resorts and individual cottages here, too, and made up a large part of the year-round population of **New Buffalo** itself. Swedes clustered farther north, in **Sawyer** and in **Harbert**, home of the Bethany Beach Swedish Christian summer community and a substantial year-round Swedish

Some 2,000 condos now cluster around the New Buffalo harbor, and more are on the way. South Cove (left), Michigan's first condo-dock project, was designed by Harry Weese, one of several famous Chicago architects contributing to Harbor Country's luxury boom. (The model on Harbor Isle Drive is open daily except Monday, 11-6.) Stanley Tigerman, who has a home in the area, has designed an entire subdivision near Sawyer.

*Organized tourism — water parks, band concerts, summer theater — is in short supply in Harbor Country, where summer is more about getting away from it all. Look to St. Joe and Saugatuck for **summer concerts,** Saugatuck and Holland for **the-ater,** and Muskegon and Whitehall and the Blue Lake Fine Arts camp the biggest range of **family activities** and **music,** and the best, least crowded **beaches.** For **nature** and **bird-watching,** Benton Harbor, Berrien Springs, and Muskegon are tops.*

population. The Harbert Swedish Bakery is still going strong 80 years later (p. 16). The area has enough year-round Greeks, often connected with restaurants and truck stops, to have their own cultural center.

Not all land near the lakes was intensely developed as lakeside property. Carl Sandburg had his famous goat farm near Harbert, where he bred and sold goats and wrote most of his biography of Abraham Lincoln.

Preservation through benign neglect

The eccentric charm of the Red Arrow Highway comes from the fact that its 1950s roadside kitsch survived, unaltered, long enough to be appreciated. That was because a generation of vacationers was skipped in the 1960s. People who always used to spend the summer here had more options by then. Air-conditioning made city summers more tolerable. Jets and interstates made it less of an ordeal to go farther north, to New England or northern Michigan, even for short vacations. The action in vacation homes and boating was farther north, at Macatawa and Castle Park near Holland, at Leland and Harbor Springs, and in Door County and Lake Geneva, Wisconsin.

Development and updating in the New Buffalo area was pretty much put on hold. Upkeep of many rental properties declined, and old resorts fell out of favor. Areas of large family summer homes continued to be well maintained; old money wasn't as likely to lose the taste for slow-paced vacations. But vacation rentals dwindled.

Local men mostly commuted to industrial jobs in Indiana, in Michigan City and LaPorte. With the decline of heavy industry, local kids mainly moved away after high school. New Buffalo's simple, close-in housing stock went downhill.

An improved harbor stimulated change

The foundations of modern New Buffalo, its luxury condos and glitz, were laid when a boat club in Gary, Indiana, was displaced by a new steel mill in the late 1960s and moved to the New Buffalo Harbor. Boaters, along with local construction firm owner Paul Oselka, lobbied for large-scale harbor improvements. Oselka had dredged out the sandy harbor each year. Improvements came in 1976, when the Corps of Engineers created a harbor of refuge in New Buffalo. By then Oselka was in the marina and boat business and gradually buying up a good deal of harborfront property. Waves of marina-building followed suit. Today Oselka's huge Snug Harbor marina is the largest full-service marina on Lake Michigan, with sales, service, condos, dockominiums, and three pools for boaters. Within a few years it looks as if it will be encircled by a virtual wall of condominiums.

Indiana Dune Country is experiencing a similar boom to Harbor Country's, on top of a much larger population base. Michigan City is almost 40,000, La Porte and Valparaiso are over 20,000, and Chesterton is nearly 10,000. That means museums, a zoo, and more tourist destinations. Find out more at the Lighthouse Place visitor center, (219) 879-6506.

Lighthouse Place, less than 15 miles from New Buffalo in Michigan City, Indiana, is a two-floor discount mall with some uncommon pluses: for example, Dansk, Ralph Lauren, Anne Klein, Benetton, Royal Doulton, and Capezio, in addition to most of the outlets found in Michigan Marketplace malls in Michigan, such as Bass, Manhattan, Van Heusen, Socks Galore, Maidenform, Harve Benard, and The Paper Works. It's right downtown at 6th and Wabash, just a block south of U.S. 12. Hours (Central Standard Time, an hour later than Michigan Time) are March-Dec: Mon-Sat 9-8, Sun 10-6. Jan & Feb: Mon-Sat 9-6, Sun 10-6.

Fishing, for years a mainstay of New Buffalo tourism, is still good, though now overshadowed by new glitz. For charter and fishing information, contact the Harbor Country Chamber of Commerce, (616) 469-54509.

In 1984 and 1985, things started heating up away from the harbor as well. As some popular northern resorts became overcrowded and uncomfortably glitzy, the pokey, convenient New Buffalo area, not two hours from Chicago's Loop, began to look pretty good to affluent, over-stressed Baby Boomers — even some from the North Shore. They enjoyed the simple pleasures of bowling and hanging out. The area was rediscovered by urbanites who came here as kids in the Fifties and are seeking to recapture that experience for their kids. Several bed and breakfasts were started by Chicago-area women; often their husbands spent the work week in the city and came out for long weekends. Dennis and Connie Brennen moved to Lakeside from suburban Chicago, where he still teaches, and started Brennen's Bookstore in New Buffalo. Chicago decorator Ken Gosh started coming on weekends and soon decided to stay and rehab older buildings. In 1988 he and his brother opened Rabbit Run, a folk art and antique gallery. Barbara Barickman and her husband bought a 1950s motel in Grand Beach.

Mayor Byrne's pivotal loss

These do-it-yourself pioneer entrepreneurs soon set off a great chain migration from Chicago. The single pivotal event in New Buffalo's transformation into a chic, creative hot spot may well have been when Chicago mayor Jane Byrne lost the mayoral nomination to Harold Washington. That meant that Byrne's gifted press agent, Karen Conner, was out of a job. She followed her friends to New Buffalo and started a deli. A natural promoter, she talked up the deli — and New Buffalo — to her friends in politics and the media. Soon she was writing articles about the area for Chicago publications, and selling real estate, too.

Before long, movie critic Gene Siskel had bought a house in Michiana. And Siskel's partner, Roger Ebert, went together with *Sun-Times* reporter Robert Zonka on a house in Union Pier. Zonka proceeded to buy the *New Buffalo Times.*. "We had some great, life-changing conversations in my living room here," recalls Barickman. "Then we'd hear that one person after another had kicked their jobs, changed careers, dropped out. It all happened when we reached 40."

The Brennens tell the same story about an evening in film critic Roger Ebert's cottage, when the talk was dominated with fantasies about dropping out and starting over. Former ABC News reporter Ron Miller and his wife, Chris, sunk almost half a million dollars into refurbishing a 1920s resort and dance hall into a restaurant serving California-style food at close-to-Chicago prices. They added a takeout in the adjacent Art Deco gas station.

Bottlenecks and big-money interests

New Buffalo became a hot topic in the Chicago press. "Now all of Chicago is right here," says one disappointed pioneer/refugee. "Old cliques have been re-formulated. You can't get away from it all anymore. I now have to put on makeup just to go to the drugstore."

All this development has had its costs. Without a city planning and review process, New Buffalo is experiencing huge bottlenecks at the marina, which is alongside the only road to the area's only public beach. Yet two hotels are going up in that area. Residents worry about the danger of fire from the marina's concentration of boats and fuel. And the creative pioneer entrepreneurs who helped launch the boom with low-budget sweat equity have been outvoted on the Chamber of Commerce by big-money business interests, local and out-of-town, who promote large-scale development. Some of the people who rehabbed lakeside cottages five years ago are now thinking about moving to the rural area near Three Oaks.

Nevertheless, Harbor Country at this moment offers quite a fascinating mix of sophistication and ungentrified folksiness.

Michigan time is Eastern Standard Time, which means all stated times are an hour later than Chicago time. Being on the far western fringe of the time zone has its advantages (longer daylight in the evening) and disadvantages (school kids wait for the morning bus in the dark).

Lake levels have been low and beaches have widened for the past few years. Building up and down the Lake Michigan shore has resumed at a furious pace. Little thought is paid to recent disasters, when high lake levels combined with big winter storms to chew up beach frontage like this in Michiana, near the border. Buildings too close to the lake have toppled up and down the shore.

If you don't like the crowds, you can go to peaceful Three Oaks for supplies, as many Lakeside summer people do. "A lot of Three Oaks people belong to the Chickaming Golf Club in Lakeside, and it is fascinating for some summer people who've spent their lives in Chicago suburbs to get to know small-town life," says a third-generation Lakeside summer resident.

Anyway, New Buffalo is only "a ten-week boom town," one resident says. Fall is beautiful on any of the shady drives along the lake, holiday shopping is terrific and unhurried, and in winter, Lakeshore Road is so quiet, it makes for wonderful cross-country ski jaunts, framed with snowy branches arching overhead.

POINTS OF INTEREST

New Buffalo Beach

At the end of North Whittaker between U.S. 12 and Lake Michigan. $4/car/day. Closes at 11 p.m.

The main public beach between here and the spectacular, huge Warren Dunes State Park is right at the busy outlet of the Galien River and the harbor. The swimming area here is more protected from the boating traffic than it at first seems, and the public beach is longer. There are **restrooms**, a **refreshment stand**, a small **play area** for children, and a dune **stairway** and longish **overlook and boardwalk** atop the dunes.

Lakeshore Road/ Riviera Road ★★

Along Lake Michigan from New Buffalo Beach to Harbert, where it joins the Red Arrow Hwy. It's called Riviera Rd. until it enters Union Pier.

The **lakeshore road** to Union Pier and Lakeside passes a big variety of vacation homes, from boldly contemporary designs toward New Buffalo to some plain and occasionally tumbledown resorts and cottages in Union Pier on to the gracious, sedate lakefront estates in Lakeside. Nowhere is the contrast between the area's declining past and booming present more dramatic

than in Union Pier, where some modest properties owned by generations of Lithuanian and Bohemian families from Chicago have been gutted and jazzed up for affluent new buyers.

The shady road is ideal for bicycling. It is especially beautiful in fall and in winter after it has snowed.

If you look carefully, you can see gated roads every three or four blocks leading down to the beach. Unless signs are posted to indicate private property, these are **public township beaches** which anyone can use. No resident identification system has been introduced. You'll need to find a parking spot on nearby residential streets.

Downtown New Buffalo

Centered on Whittaker between U.S. 12 and the harbor. Shops open 7 days in summer; almost all remain open from Thursday through Monday in spring and fall and on weekends throughout the year.

Until recently downtown New Buffalo was a pokey, humdrum little place. Now it has been mostly taken over by upscale shops that are especially strong in women's clothing, home accessories, and the predictable beach and surf shops and frozen yogurt stores. The main business section is on North Whittaker between U.S. 12 (in town it's called Buffalo Street) and the harbor and beach. But there is a growing num-

er of shops and galleries in houses along Buffalo and scattered side streets. The most interesting stores are those in which mid-life career-changers have fled Chicago's intensity and decided to fulfill their dreams at a more relaxed pace. shops of the Pere Marquette Railroad (p. 8-9). This area is *hot* (you can begin to become infected with real estate hype here) and constantly evolving — until the next recession, anyway — so ask around to find out what's new. The most interesting stores are those in which mid-life career-changers have decided to fulfill their dreams.

Off South Whittaker between U.S. 12 and the train tracks, an ambitious retail project remodeled the former roundhouse and train repair shops of the Pere Marquette Railroad. The railroad shops had been the lifeblood of the local economy for many years. Retailing in the renovated Roundhouse never really got off the ground — it opened just as the 1991 recession put the brakes on the hot Harbor Country real estate scene. As of 1993 the space is occupied only by an antiques mall.

Despite the changes, the **V & S Variety Store** at Buffalo and Whittaker (also known as Buffalo Drugs) is where everybody, old-timers and summer residents, city-stylish and workaday plain, comes together. (Casey's Pub and Rosie's café serve the same function.) **Barbie's,** the old small-town department store on

New Buffalo's unremarkable downtown consists of two blocks of North Whittaker.

North Whittaker at Merchant, has upscaled its merchandise but continues to offer small-town service and "a little bit of everything" for all the family.

Here is a selection of shops that really stand out in merchandise or atmosphere:

Whittaker House
126 N. Whittaker. (616) 429-0220. Open daily, year-round 10-6.

Relaxed, contemporary classic clothing in beautiful fabrics of excellent quality. Also carries accessories for the home.

Hearthwoods ★★
116 1/2 N. Whittaker, off a pedestrial alleyway between Lyssa and a silkscreen shop. (616) 469-5551. Mem.-Labor Day: daily 10-6. Labor Day-Xmas and March 15- Mem. Day: Fri-Mon 10-6. Otherwise Sat & Sun only.

Rustic furniture made of branches and twigs is more than just a trend with owner/craftsman Andrew Brown, and it shows in this unusual studio/shop. A full range of quaint and picturesque stuff is here, from Adirondack chairs and birchbark birdhouses to burl bowls and simple homemade chests decorated with a kind of applied marquetry of half-round twigs. The price range is tremendous. A coffee table could cost from $75 to $800.

Brown recreates folk styles and

invents his own original styles, like four-poster beds in which a top canopy is formed by a sort of lattice of thin branches that sprouted directly from thick, chunky trees. They look good in many settings, from white-walls contemporary to the rich, warm look of English paisleys and chintzes.

Some pieces incorporate plain boards painted by artists Brown works with and are then trimmed with twigs. Nancy Drew (of The Fine Line cartoon fame) uses bright, strong yellows and limes in childlike designs; Kris Hosbine's unusual potato-print decorations are more muted pastels. Painted coffee tables run $350-$450; a Nancy Drew armoire is $1,600.

Growing up in Quebec, Brown learned how to make twig furniture from his history teacher. Two years ago he quit a job in advertising sales to pursue his hobby full-time. He doesn't bend willow or hickory in the popular style of interconnected loops done by the Amish, but prefers to look through quantities of trees and limbs cut by municipal and utility crews to find interesting natural branching patterns.

Lyssa
116 N. Whittaker. (616) 469-1162. May-Dec. open daily 11-5, until 9 on Saturdays in July & August. Jan-April: Thurs-Sun 11-5.

Unusual, sometimes whimsical jewelry from Europe, Africa, and the U.S. is played off against generally classic clothing, mostly for women but with cashmere, wool, and cotton sweaters from Scotland for men as well.

Country Mates
120 W. Buffalo between Barton and Barker. (616) 469-2890. Mon-Sat 10-6, Sun 12-6. Sat until 9 in July & Aug.

The country look, replete with long skirts, geese, and teddy bears, reigns supreme at this big, rambling, hugely successful gift shop with a separate large **Christmas shop**. Country basics like simple painted

furniture, salt glaze pottery, wood toys, and handwoven rugs among all the collectibles and myriad accessories. Some people come just for the **dried flowers and herbs**, largely grown by the owners and custom-arranged to suit customers' decor. An unusual variety of ornamental and culinary herbs is for sale in spring.

Brennen's Bookstore
44 S. Whittaker, south of U.S. 12 and across from Hannah's. June-Sept: open daily 10-6 except Tues. otherwise open 11-5.

A wide range of vacation reading for all tastes — from bestsellers, romances, and westerns to classics, celebrity biographies, and teen novels — is the stock in trade at this simple, charming bookshop. It's in an 1836 house originally built as the stable of New Buffalo's founder, Captain Whittaker. There's also a great selection of greeting cards, gift items, and Dover paper construction projects. Most interesting is the section of local authors, with books by the many Chicago-area writers who have vacation homes and year-round residences here. Autograph parties on Saturday are a regular summer event.

La Grand Trunk
447 S. Whittaker at the train tracks, 12 blocks south of U.S. 12 in New Buffalo. (616) 469-2122. Summer hours: 11-7 daily, except Sun until 5 and Sat in July & August until 9. Winter: 11-5 daily, sometimes closed Mon.

There's big-city fashion excitement in these unusually dramatic contemporary clothes, accessories, and beachwear, sometimes served up with ethnic, gypsyish touches. The painted floor is a knockout. Just next door is the delightful outdoor **Food Gallery Cafe**, with salads, sandwiches, pastries, and Ben and Jerry's ice cream.

New Buffalo Railroad Museum

530 S. Whittaker just south of the tracks. (616) 469-3166. Sat & Sun 12-5. Closed January thru April.

The railroad did much to develop New Buffalo — first from 1849 to 1853, during its brief boom as the western terminus of Michigan's principal railroad, the Michigan Central. A second boom began in the 1920s, when the Pere Marquette Railroad built its main repair shops and yard here. It ran between Chicago and northern Michigan, 2/3 of the way up Lake Michigan's eastern shore. The repair shops, which survived in diminished form until 1985, were the main local employer. Railroad crews stayed at the Pere Marquette's hotel by the yards.

The developers of The Roundhouse shopping complex next door decided to ornament their project with this museum. Using the original plans of the circa-1920 depot that once stood across the way east of Whittaker, they have reconstructed the depot on this site, next to the remnant of the old roundhouse. Many former railroad employees have contributed time, artifacts, and information to the project.

The waiting room, ticket office, and freight room have been faithfully reproduced. The first displays of uniforms and rail memorabilia were not yet installed as this book went to press. The museum centerpiece is the model railroad layout of the neighboring Pere Marquette roundhouse and yards as they probably looked in the 1920s.

The Roundhouse ★

530 S. Whittaker just south of the tracks. Open daily except Wednesday 11-6. (616) 469-3166.

The Pere Marquette Railroad's high brick repair shops (see preceding entry) have been turned into an attractive, two-level retail complex that failed to thrive after it opened in 1990. Today in 1993 it is occupied by an **antiques mall.**

Of the original 16-stall roundhouse, three stalls remain. It's easy to look out from the big windows of the central court onto the original turntable in the rail yard and get a sense of the scale of locomotive repair shops. Enlarged photographs and occasional tools, pulleys, and doors serve as historical accents.

Rainbow's End Antiques ★

On Lakeside Rd. south of Wilson right on the Michigan-Indiana border. From Lakeside and the Red Arrow Hwy., take Lakeside Rd. 6 miles south. From I-94 exit 1, go right to Wilson, then left (east) 3 miles, turn right (south) to 4th house. (616) 756-9291. Year-round, daily and Sun 9-5.

Since 1967 this antique-lovers' farm has been an area draw, despite its location off the beaten path. The big barn, chicken coop, and pig shed have been given over to quality antiques: finished furniture, glassware, china, ivory, jewelry, oil and watercolor paintings, and primitives.

Rabbit Run ★★

15460 Red Arrow Hwy. in Lakeside. (616) 469-0468. Year-round, daily and Sun 10-6.

When Chicago people like decorator Ken Gosh do country, it has a fresh, witty, comfortable look, never saccharine, and nary a goose or duck in sight. Gosh, an early emigrée to Harbor Country, sets a tone that you see a lot around here. There are bright, rich colors of Amish quilts; lots of old and new folk art; dune country primitives; twig crafts, Turkish kilims; antique English and Irish scrubbed pine chests, cupboards, and tables that really anchor a room; along with new, often whimsical china and accessories from England and Brazil.

Local Color

16187 Red Arrow Hwy., south of the light at the Unior Pier. (616) 469-5332. Mem.-Labor Day: daily 12-5. Fall: 6 days/week until Christmas. Winter: weekends only.

Works by 80 artists and craftspeople from the area, including ceramics by co-owner Rita Cochran, are attractively displayed in this big space. Some are whimsical, some are serious, all are contemporary in mood, and the effect comes off well. Many media are represented, and there's a good deal of hand-decorated clothing presented as wearable art.

Antique Mall and Village

9300 Union Pier Rd. just west of the I-94 Union Pier exit and almost a mile east of the Red Arrow Hwy. (616) 469-2555. 10-6 daily, year-round.

An appealingly fanciful "village" in the woods. The mall features dozens of interesting dealers, mainly from Chicago — much higher quality that typical malls. Don't miss the interesting primitive and Indian things in the log cabin, or the stained glass windows in the church. A produce market, gift shop, and outdoor cafe are also on the premises.

Lakeside Gallery

15486 Red Arrow Hwy. at Warren Woods Rd. (616) 469-3022. Fri-Sun 10-6. Closed Jan & Feb.

Here in the sales gallery of the nearby Lakeside Center for the Arts, art comes alive as an exciting process of exploration and experiment. Both the center and gallery were started by John Wilson, the artist and print dealer who organized Chicago's influential Art Expo at Navy Pier. The center, in an old Lakeside summer hotel, is a working artists' retreat that furthers artistic and cultural exchange among artists from around the world, mainly the U.S.,

the nations of the former Soviet Union, and China. Artists donate half the work they create there to support the center; it's sold in this gallery. Works are produced under conditions of unusual freedom.

About half the artists are American; others are largely Soviet (from the Baltic nations to Soviet Georgia and central Asia) and Chinese. They are selected after submitting proposals for projects. Sales from their works help support the center. Prices range from $20 for small prints to $20,000 and up.

Gallery windows look out on a yard provocatively studded with sculptures. If most art galleries leave you feeling cynical and manipulated, this may prove different.

The Silver Crane Gallery ★

On Lakeside Rd. in the center of Lakeside. From the Red Arrow Hwy., turn west onto Lakeside at the half-timbered gazebo and park. (616) 469-4000. Year-round, daily & Sun: 11-6.

Striking silver jewelry — many cases of it, by various craftsmen — is what stands out in this new shop. Owners are Herb and Joann ("Butch") Crane claim to have the Midwest's largest collection of sterling silver (mostly jewelry, with some vases and bowls). She used to wholesale silver. They import direct from workshops in Taxco, Mexico, which makes for outstanding values on mostly hand-crafted Mexican silver. There's a wide selection of pins and earrings between $20 and $40, on up to $800 or so for collectors' necklaces of turquoise and sterling made by American Indians.

The Los Castillo workshop in Taxco, Mexico, makes simple, smooth vases and bowls strikingly embellished with sinuous animal forms. Antonio Castillo, the preeminent Mexican silversmith, was an early student of William Spratling, who introduced a new, nontraditional style of work to Taxco silversmiths. In one memorable Castillo piece, lizards inlaid with malachite form the handle of a $710 pitcher made of silver over copper.

The Cranes also represent Indian silver craftsmen from the American Southwest. They now work in contemporary styles — not all that different from the classic modern work of Georg Jensen — as well as traditional styles with turquoise and Indian motifs.

The Silver Crane Gallery is prominently located in a picturesque brick and half-timber building, once the general store and post office of this cultivated summer resort. It's one of many buildings in and around Lakeside built in a neo-Elizabethan style. An antique shop, takeout deli, and neo-impressionist art gallery are nearby.

East Road Gallery

14906 Red Arrow Hwy. just south of East Rd. in Lakeside. (616) 469-5995. Open year-round Sat & Sun 12-5, otherwise by chance or appt.

Turning a 1912 Craftsman-style resort in Lakeside into The Pebble House bed & breakfast introduced Jean and Ed Lawrence to the Arts & Crafts furniture that the old place seemed to want. Now they hold seminars on the Arts & Crafts movement and write guides to antiquing. Their new shop here features generic Mission and related styles, never low-end but not signed Stickley, either. Room settings are fully accessorized with the likes of copper lamps, etchings, old Craftsman-style books, and some compatible paintings by living artists.

Lakeside Antiques

14866 Red Arrow Hwy. just north of East Rd. in Lakeside. (616) 469-4467. Spring thru Xmas: open Fri-Mon 11-6. Winter: Sat & Sun only.

Two buildings are filled with quality pieces, including some uncommon specialties: 1950s; folk art (both antique and by living art-

ists); bamboo, wicker, and painted furniture, plus primitive and country. Different dealers run a shop and mall next door.

Lakeside Center for the Arts ★

15251 Lakeshore Rd. (616) 469-1377.

Visitors are welcome to tour the studios at this international artists' retreat. Artists stay in the simple old inn and use the studios (painting, printmaking, ceramics, and sculpture) in the rear of the eight-acre property. It's sort of a sharecropping arrangement, in which artists give half the work made here to the center. It is sold in the Lakeside Gallery, 15486 Red Arrow Highway in Lakeside. Rooms not used by artists are rented to the general public at $60/night and up, including kitchen privileges.

Theatrical performances by the Chicago professional theater group Pendragon are held on summer weekends in the ballroom. Call for details.

The East Road Gallery has pieces like this library table from the Grand Rapids Bookcase and Chair Company.

Filoni Vestimenti ★

15300 Red Arrow Hwy. in Wilkenson Village, Lakeside, next to Panozzo's Cafe. (616) 469-4944. Mem.-Labor Day: Mon-Fri 11-5, Sat &Sun 10-5.

Despite the name, this is not an Italian designer boutique. True, the clothing (for women and men) is fashion-forward, contemporary, and unusual, but most of it is American, and many outfits are in the $100 range. Owner-buyer Shari Filoni reps for 15 designers in Chicago; here she has assembled her favorites, along with interesting jewelry and accessories, including some nifty old watches.

In the adjacent space, open the same hours, is the **Wilkinson Heritage Museum**, devoted to Lakeside history. It perpetuates the village's original name, after the family who purchased 2,500 acres of timberland, built a pier for shipping lumber, and started a trading post. When a post office was established here, it is said that the post office department pushed for a different name because of the Wilkinson family's alleged Southern sympathies during the Civil War.

The one-room museum was established by the landlady, Realtor Nadra Kissman, a Wilkinson descendant. It has a spare, somber, elegant look, with black dresses, hair lock remembrances, and carefully organized documents that make it like looking through a meticulously arranged desk and closet.

Harbert Swedish Bakery ★

13746 Red Arrow Hwy. in Harbert. (616) 469-1777. Easter-Mem. Day Fri-Sun 7:30-6, until 4:30 Sun. June; Thurs-Sun. July 4-Labor Day: Wed-Sun. Fall up to Thanksgiving: Fri-Sun. Closed until Easter.

This popular institution looks and feels like it's been around for a long, long time. It's housed in an addition to the owner's home that's paneled in knotty pine with that 1950s rustic look. Lace curtains are at the windows.

There are a few inside tables for coffee drinkers. The bakery cases are full of baked goods that are strong on traditional Swedish breads and cakes: round limpa bread, Swedish rye, sesame poppyseed, cardamom. In addition, there are other white and rye breads, Danish pastries, many kinds of sweet rolls, soft pretzels, donuts, kaiser rolls, coffee cakes, bran muffins, eclairs, 12 kinds of cookies plus Bohemian kolachys, tortes, and pies. Prices start at $1.40 for a 1 1/2 lb. loaf of Swedish rye bread; Danish pastries are 85¢.

Picnic tables outside are welcomed by bicyclists and families.

There's been a bakery here for 80 years. The current baker-owner, a former Chicago upholsterer of Swedish descent, fulfilled his dreams when he moved out here eight years ago and became a baker as a sort of a pre-retirement business.

Judith Racht Gallery ★★

On Prairie Rd. just east of the Red Arrow Hwy., in Harbert. Turn opposite the Harbert Swedish Bakery. (616) 683-9527. Open 10-5 daily from Mem. to Labor Day. Otherwise weekends only. Closed Jan-March except by appt.

The area's top gallery shows "young, upcoming artists — people who will rock and shake you," says co-owner Doug Stock. A quilt collector, he mounts an October quilt show augmented by tramp art and outsider art. Contemporary crafts and new folk art by naive painters are also big at this always-interesting gallery in the old Harbert schoolhouse. Racht is a protegee of John Wilson, who started the Lakeside Center for the Arts. (See above.)

RESTAURANTS

Rosie's ★

128 N. Whittaker in downtown New Buffalo. (616) 469-4382. Open 7-2 daily including Sun. Breakfast available all day; lunch 11-2. Breakfasts average $3.50-$4, lunches $3.50-$5. No alcohol or credit cards.

So much excitement was stirred up with the terrific, low-cost food here after two Czech-speaking cooks took over this simple family restaurant last year that the place threatened to be undone by its own success. So the new owners scrapped dinner altogether to keep things manageable. $4.95 buys you Bohemian-style roast pork with juice, dumplings or potatoes, sauerkraut, red cabbage or applesauce, bread and dessert. Big fruit dumplings, served with cottage cheese, soup, and dessert is $4.50. A farmer's omelet is a big hit at breakfast, when you see quite a cross-section of local society.

Casey's Pub & BBQ

136 N. Whittaker. (616) 469-9885. Open 11 a.m.-midnight daily. Full bar. No credit cards.

The popular pork barbecue ribs ($5.25 a dinner), smoked on the premises, are a big draw at this 35-year-old bar with a family atmosphere. Another specialty is the broasted chicken dinner ($4.50); even people who can't digest greasy food enjoy it. Sides include baked beans, potato and macaroni salads, and cole slaw. Locals and Chicago people love the worn wood floors and unfussed-over atmosphere — the way New Buffalo used to be before it was discovered.

The Lighthouse

244 N. Whittaker on the harbor in downtown New Buffalo. (616) 469-5489. Tues-Sat lunch 11-4, dinner 4-10 (later on weekends). Sun brunch 11-3, dinner 4-10. Full bar. Visa, MC, AmEx.

The only area restaurant with a water view (of the harbor *and* the lake) offers a varied menu, with salads, soups, pastas, and a popular wet burrito ($6.25). Appetizers include the pizza-like Lighthouse Lahvosh ($5.25). Burgers and sandwiches on homemade buns ($4.75-$6.95) include a side. Big dinner favorites are prime rib ($12.95/ $15.95) and perch ($11.95), with soup or salad, starch, and bread.

Fatouros' Greek Harbor ★

105 E. Buffalo (U.S.12) just east of Whittaker. (616) 469-2511. 7:30 a.m.-11 p.m. daily. Lunches average $5, dinners $6 to $7. No alcohol or credit cards.

Breakfast, lunch, and dinner dishes are available any time at this old Greek-run soda and sandwich shoppe. It's been here since 1922 and there's still an old fortune-telling machine at the counter, but the interior is vintage 1960s at its worst — lots of dark paneling and violent orange plastic. Fountain treats (malts, sodas, etc.) and burgers are standard fare, but Mama Fatouros's Greek specialties win raves. Movie critic Roger Ebert has her cook regularly for his friends. Some say the gyros here is the best they've ever had. For $3.75 you can get a good Greek salad with two small pieces of fabulously tender and lemony spinach pie. Roast lamb is $7, stuffed grape leaves $5.50, and souvlaki $7.95. Carryout available — consider eating at the beach overlook (p. 10) or the pond at The Roundhouse (p. 13).

Hannah's

115 S. Whittaker 1 block south of U. S. 12 in New Buffalo. (616) 469-1440. Sun-Thurs 11:30-10:30, Fri & Sat 11:30-11:30. Lunches average $7; dinners average $12-$13. Full bar. Visa, AmEx, MC.

For years this much-expanded large house was the Little Bohemia restaurant, and some menu items still reflect New Buffalo's Bohemian background. Remodeled as Hannah's, the place seats 250 while managing to retain a spare but comfortable 1950ish charm. Lately Hannah's has been hot, more for the convivial atmosphere than the food, which is good but not great. There's a piano player Wednesday-Sunday. (For real Bohemian cooking, have lunch at Rosie's.)

For lunch, crab meat in wonton-like wrappers deep fried ($5.95) is popular, as is the crab salad ($5.25). The favorite sandwich is the Canadian jack chicken sandwich ($5.95). For dinner, the duck and roast pork loin (both $11.95) are popular. Prime rib is available in four different cuts ($12.95-$25.95) and can be blackened on request.

Redamak's

616 E. Buffalo. (616) 469-4522. Mon-Thurs, 11-10:30, Fri 11-11, Sat & Sun 12-11. Full bar. No credit cards. Carryout burger hotline: 469-4522.

"The hamburger that made New Buffalo famous" got its start in 1950, when Redamak's on U.S. 12 was a convenient stop for vacationing Chicagoans. This simple, old-fashioned burger bar has become one of those must-visit places for anyone in the area. It's a dark, cool, old-timey bar with a lot of old wood and beer signs. The hamburger (made of 5 1/3 ounces of beef cut and ground fresh each day) is very good. Local tradespeople take advantage of the $2 working person's special, with a hamburger or cheeseburger and fries. (Available Monday-Friday 11 a.m.-3 p.m.) Otherwise hamburgers are $2.25, with cheese 25¢ and grilled onions 50¢ extra. The rest of a huge menu consists mostly of baskets of fried food, from three pieces of chicken ($4.75) and shrimp to ravioli and mozzarella sticks ($3.50), the most popular appetizer. Soups are artifi-

cially thickened and disappointing.

With numerous additions, Redamak's now seats 200 indoors and another 130 on an adjacent patio, but don't be surprised if you have to wait in the summer.

J & J Family Restaurant

East U.S. 12 at the Red Arrow Hwy., 1 mile east of New Buffalo. (616) 469-3171. Open 24 hours between 5 a.m. Mon and 8 p.m. Sat. On Sun open 6 a.m.-8 p.m. No bar.

For good diner fare virtually round the clock, this busy truck stop is just the place. Cops from the nearby State Police post, salesmen, truck drivers, and various locals congregate (and smoke) at the counter and in booths. Decorator touches are Greek religious pictures, a bottle collection, and an elaborate copper urn. The big menu includes three-egg omelets with excellent American fries and toast for $2.85 and up; the usual burgers and sandwiches (1/3 lb. burgers are $1.80 and up, a gyros sandwich $3.10); sauerkraut and sausage; spinach pie; rice pudding; and half a fried chicken with soup or salad, a vegetable, potato and roll for $5.85.

Beyond the Sea Crab House

16036 Red Arrow Hwy., Union Pier. I-94 exit 6 to Red Arrow. (616) 469-0200. Open Fri-Sun year round. Mem. Day-Labor Day: Mon-Fri 3-10, Sat & Sun 3-11. Dinners average $10. Full bar. MC & Visa..

Fresh, good blue-claw Maryland crab cakes ($10.95 as a dinner, $5.95 as a sandwich) are the favorite at this popular, utterly plain place, an authentic Maryland crab house. Other specialties include cajun squid, lightly floured and deep fired with a remoulade sauce ($8.50) and battered fried shrimp ($10.95). Dinners come with potatoes and undistinguished cole slaw; the side of green beans is blah. There's a big sandwich menu (chicken breast or fish $4.95, soft shell crab $6.95, peanut butter and jelly with milk for kids $2.95).

Miller's Country House

16409 Red Arrow Hwy. in Union Pier, 3 miles north of New Buffalo. (616) 469-5950. Open daily including Sun. Lunch 12-5, dinner 5-10, until 11 on Fri & Sat. Closed Tues from Labor Day through June. Lunch entrees average $8, dinners $12. Full bar, take-out deli. AmEx, Visa, Diners, MC.

The restaurant and dance hall of a 1920s resort has become a chic but casual 250-seat restaurant with fresh, California-style food and a good list of Michigan wines — the kind of place that had crayons for drawing on paper tablecloths two years ago. Miller's is the likely spot to run into Chicago-area celebrities. The main dining area overlooks a rear garden area and woods, as does an outdoor deck seating another 40.

Entrees are surprisingly conventional. Grilled Norwegian salmon ($16.95), fresh perch ($13.95), chicken breast ($11.95) and rack of lamb ($18.95) are favorites, served with potato, chef's choice of vegetable, and great French bread. You can also get char-grilled duck confit, steaks, pasta specialties, and (any night but Saturday) burgers. Desserts like gelato, sorbets, chocolate strawberries, flourless chocolate cake $3 and up. Espresso, cappucino. Some locals prefer to enjoy the sophisticated, fun atmosphere for less by ordering off the bar menu.

Red Arrow Roadhouse

15710 Red Arrow Hwy., Union Pier. Take exit 6 from I-94. (616) 469-3939. Mon-Thurs 11-10, Fri-Sun 11-11. Lunch entrees average $4-$4.50; dinners $10-$11. Full bar. MC and Visa.

It really is an old roadhouse, turned into a comfortably casual 85-seat restaurant geared to affluent Chicago baby boomers. Vintage touches — pine paneling, a rainbow-

glowing jukebox —are cultivated. The big draw weekdays is the 16-oz. T-bone steak ($9.95). In addition, 3 to 4 dinner specials are offered weekdays ($8-$14). On Friday night the breaded lake perch ($10.50) is also a specialty. Weekends the emphasis is fresh seafood, with broiled or sauteed swordfish and walleye leading the list. Accompanying sides of coleslaw and potato salad is made on the premises (no MSG). Sandwiches (like the $5.25 chicken sautée with spinach and mushrooms and one side) are available throughout the day. Desserts include cheesecake ($2.50-$3), brownies with vanilla ice cream and hot fudge sauce ($2.50), and chocolate mud pie ($3.25).

Panozzo's Cafe

15300 Red Arrow Hwy. at Sunset, Lakeside. (616) 469-2370. Summer hours : usually 9-3 daily, 9-2 Sun, plus Fri night pasta buffet 6-9. Open Fri-Sun from Easter to end of year. Closing time varies; call ahead. No credit cards or alcohol.

Overstressed Chicagoans rave over the relaxing, healthy breakfasts at Patty Panozzo's woodsy little (35 seat) garden cafe. A Kankakee produce dealer's daughter, she cooks creatively with lots of fresh fruit in season, and the presentation is inspired. An engaging new cookbook, **Breakfast at Panozzo's**, shares her ideas and recipes for a large and changing variety of pancakes with fruit sauces and fillings, versions of French toast, egg dishes, cereals, muffins, and breads. Cappuccino, espresso, and desserts are new additions. Breakfasts average $4 to $5. Come before 10 to avoid a wait. Sunday brunch ($8.95) and the Friday evening pasta buffet are *very* popular.

LODGINGS

Comfort Inn
(616) 469-4440. 1-800-228-5150.
11539 Wilson Rd. at I-94 exit 1., 2
miles from downtown New Buffalo.
96 rooms on 2 floors. Double room
$67.95 weekends, $54.95 weekdays.
Suites (includes jacuzzi, microwave,
wet bar, refrigerator) $89.95 week-
ends, $69.95 weekdays. 2-bedroom
suite $130/night. Free continental
breakfast. Outdoor pool.

Grand Beach Motel
(616) 469-1555.
U.S 12 at Wilson Rd., 2 1/2 miles west
of New Buffalo.
13 rooms, 1 floor. $40-$45 Mem.-
Labor Day, $30-$35 otherwise.
Closed Nov. 1-March 31. Heated pool
screened from highway. No phones in
rooms; pay phone outside. Color TV.
Simple rooms, very tastefully decorated, with extra table and desk. Superior tile bathrooms. Continental
breakfast on weekends. Friendly,
knowledgeable proprietors make this
more like a low-cost bed-and-breakfast than an ordinary older motel.

Tall Oaks Inn
(616) 469-0097.
In Grand Beach on Ravine at
Pinewood. From Grand Ave. entrance
off U.S. 12, turn left onto Grand Beach
Rd., right onto Royal, left onto Station
Rd. continue to Ravine. Write: Box 6,
New Buffalo, MI 49117.
8 suites, 3 rooms all on 2nd floor.
Rooms $65 (share bath) and $95
(private bath). Suites $140 (with 2-
person jacuzzi, sitting room, fireplace
and/or deck), $190 (2 bedrooms). 2-
night weekend minimum. Full breakfast. Off-season midweek rates are
$20, $30, and $40 off.
    A rather plain 1920s inn has been
plushly remodeled and furnished
rather formally (mahogany furniture,
oriental rugs in large living area with
rustic stone fireplace) except for oc-

casional stuffed ducks and bears.
Room decor varies; some is wicker.
Large sun porch, dining room, front
porch, big trees. Outdoor hot tub,
barbecue pit, cross-country ski
equipment, bicycles. Walking distance to public Grand Beach golf
course. Free soft drinks, pastries. 10-
15 minute walk through a neighborhood to beach. Grand Beach has big
trees, many stately homes, nice
walks.

The Inn at Union Pier
(616) 469-4700.
9708 Berrien St. 1/2 block from
Lakeshore Dr. in Unior Pier. Write:
Box 222, Union Pier, MI 49129.
15 rooms, all with baths. 5 rooms in
the main house mostly $98; 4 in one
outbuilding $85; 6 with private bal-
conies in another building $110.
    What was built as Karonsky's
Jewish resort retains a pleasantly
unpretentious simplicity despite the
fancy plumbing and beautiful landscaping. The inspiration is the light,
colorful, comfortable Old Country
look popularized by Swedish painter
Carl Larsson's turn-of-the-century

**Swedish fireplaces and an airy country
look at the Inn at Union Pier.**

watercolors. Most rooms have pretty Swedish ceramic fireplaces. Guests gather in a huge great room (with lots of games to play), sunporch, patios, and even the kitchen. Croquet, bocci. Year-round hot tub and sauna. Short walk to a township beach. Full breakfast, afternoon snacks, evening wine, popcorn. Inquire on midweek off-season prices.

Pine Garth Inn
(616) 469-1642.
15790 Lakeshore Rd. on Lake Michigan in Union Pier. Write: Box 347, Union Pier, MI 49129.
7 rooms, all but one with lake views. 5 larger rooms with whirlpool baths, private decks $125-$130. Smaller rooms $105-$115. 2-night weekend minimum. Full breakfast buffet 9-11 a.m. Call for lower off-season midweek rates.

A beautiful big yard and stunning lakefront location with three private lookout decks makes this justify the prices. Rooms have rustic furniture, rich floral wallpapers, and VCRs hidden in armoires. Hundreds of good old movie cassettes are downstairs in library with fireplace, where afternoon tea or wine and cheese is served. Sunporch and patio overlook lake. Pretty setting on Lakeshore Rd.

Lakeside Studio Hotel
(616) 469-1377
15251 Lakeshore Rd. in Lakeside.
Open May through Sept.
This unrestored old summer hotel provides rustic accommodations for artists in residence working in the studios in back (p. 15). The general public can rent extra rooms for from $60 (for a double bed) to $80 for sitting-room suites. No phones or TVs in rooms. Shared baths are down the hall. Guests can use the kitchen (continental breakfast provided), lobby and sunporch with old wicker furniture, and the beach house.

The Pebble House
(616) 469-1416
15093 Lake Shore Rd. in Lakeside.
7 rooms in main house and 2 cottages, connected by boardwalks and pergolas. 5 rooms are $90 and $96, one with kitchen is $106, bi-level apartment (sleeps 2) is $130.

This large and deliberately plain 1912 summer retreat offers guests a most unusual opportunity to sample the simple, refined Arts and Crafts style of home furnishings that took hold among many reform-minded Americans of the Progressive Era in the early 20th century. It was a reaction to material excess, ostentation, and the mock-aristocratic design of the Gilded Age. Here furniture by leading Arts & Crafts manufacturers has been authentically accessorized with hand-hammered copper bowls, and with dried flowers, lovely linens, and subdued pastel accents for a warmer, softer look than this style sometimes has. Even the beautiful flower garden is of the period. Tennis court. Beach across the street. Scandinavian-style breakfast buffet. Several common rooms. Good reading on architecture and design in the sunporch-library.

Three Oaks

In a summer weekend, Three Oaks, a village of 1,800, is an oasis of small-town calm in comparison with the resort crowds along Lake Michigan five miles to the west. But Three Oaks, too, owes a lot to Chicago visitors for helping keep the town alive as a pleasant, low-key shopping destination and retirement haven. The old, sprawling Featherbone factory complex that dominates the entire west side of town is now abandoned. But tourism has taken up some of the slack caused by the decline and subsequent move of the Warren Featherbone Company, the homegrown firm that turned Three Oaks from an unimportant village into a prosperous small town in the late 19th century.

The tight-laced corsets that gave Victorian women their hourglass figures were stiffened with stays inserted in vertical seams. E. K. Warren's superior "Featherbone" stays were promoted with testimonials from celebrities, including actress Sarah Bernhardt. "I have always used Warren's Featherbone in my costumes," she wrote, "for I believe it to be the best dress boning material in existence."

How a better corset stay boomed Three Oaks

As a Three Oaks storekeeper in the 1870s, E. K. Warren heard customers complain that women's whalebone corset stays became brittle with age and snapped — sometimes to great embarrassment. To make matters worse, whalebone was becoming scarce and expensive.

Warren got the idea for an improved corset stay on a visit to a Chicago factory making feather dusters. The manufacturer burned big piles of useless turkey feathers that had plumage on only one side. Waste like that bothered Warren, a Congregational minister's son whose ecological thinking was way ahead of his time in other ways. (See pp. 26 and 51.) A year later it occurred to him to use the springy, elastic turkey quills as a sub-stitute for whalebone in corset stays. Coming up with a name — "Featherbone" — was easy. But it took years of work with a machinist in nearby Michigan City, Indi-ana, to devise a patentable machine to turn turkey feathers into corset stays.

In November, 1883, the Warren Featherbone Company opened in a small factory on North Elm. Skeptical locals derided the venture. But orders flooded in. At first the firm's supply of feathers and labor was taxed. "By May 1884, Warren was desperately advertising in neighboring towns for additional workers," writes popular historian Larry Massie in *Voyages into Michigan's Past*. "Townspeople gazed in awe as long lines of boxcars loaded with turkey quills and passenger cars carrying rosy-cheeked misses who had left the farm for the featherbone factory lumbered into Three Oaks." Soon spare rooms throughout the vicinity were rented

to new Featherbone employees. Warren started producing buggy whips with springy Featherbone filler, and cities all over Michigan competed to win Featherbone's new factory. Three Oaks citizens, no longer derisive, won out by putting up $10,000 worth of stock.

By 1900, E. K. Warren owned the Bank of Three Oaks and the *Three Oaks Acorn*, the town's only newspaper. He also held the saloon license allotted to Three Oaks, but didn't operate a saloon in order to promote a wholesome working and living environment. In addition, Warren purchased and preserved two important natural areas, now called Warren Dunes and Warren Woods, a virgin forest west of Three Oaks.

Warren died in 1919, as the winds of fashion were changing to make corsets passé. The Warren Featherbone Company survived through the Depression, reduced in size, by making other dressmaker supplies. Today the extensive brick factory buildings of the Featherbone empire on the west side of North Elm are impressive, even romantic, in their decline. They are being divided up and sold. Boat lifts are made in one section, industrial soap in another. Architects are thinking about constructing 40 condos in part of the complex. And in a wing that comes out to the street, across from the Three Oaks Bicycle Museum, the **Featherbone Pottery Outlet** sells terra cotta planters and other garden ware daily from May to October.

The unexpected benefits of low-key tourism

At Drier's Meat Market, Three Oaks' most famous attraction, the ring bologna and liverwurst that once fed factory hands has now found an upscale market in Chicago visitors. Vacationers and day-trippers also support the fruit farms and wineries that keep nearby Baroda, Berrien Springs, and Eau Claire from falling victim to the vicissitudes of American agriculture.

Two blocks down Elm, Three Oaks' main street, is the interesting, information-packed **Bicycle Museum** and tourist information center started by bicycling promoter Brian Volstorff. Now he's Three Oaks' mayor. He has big hopes for an industrial park to revive the local manufacturing economy "so we won't lose our kids." And now, as if to confirm Three Oaks' newly

The handsome train station across from the Dewey Cannon Park was built in 1899 especially for President McKinley's presentation of the cannon. Today it has become the attractive Art & Clock Depot 616-756-5811) with grandfather clocks; mantel, wall, ship and cuckoo clocks,wildlife art, handhooked rugs, and a nifty souvenir wood whistle (under $3) that sounds just like a train whistle.

The pride of Three Oaks is the Dewey Cannon, in the park north of the tracks and just east of the business block. It was the first cannon captured by Admiral George Dewey in the Battle of Manila Bay during the hysterically popular Spanish-American War of 1898, the United States's first chance to play imperial power. In a campaign to raise money for a war monument in Washington, the cannon was to be awarded to the city that raised the most money on a per-capita basis. Three Oaks was spurred on by E. K. Warren and headlines in his newspaper that pitted "Three Oaks Against the World." The town raised an average of $1.44 for each of its approximately 1,500 residents to win the cannon. The flat, grassy **park** here has playground equipment, shade trees, and picnic tables.

emerging status as a homey but desirable period piece, Oprah Winfrey has purchased a millionaire's lavish country retreat south of town. True, it's actually just across the Indiana border, but it's definitely within greater Three Oaks. Magazine articles at supermarket checkout stands throughout the country report her delight in jogging along country roads and getting to know her rural neighbors.

Three Oaks' two-block downtown along Elm Street runs perpendicular to U.S. 12. It has a vast and complete variety store, mis-named **Downtown Drugs**, in an old, creaky-floored department store; **Marie's**, a good diner; the **Village Pump**, a widely popular bar with good Mexican food; a nice little bowling alley with pizza; and **Ramberg's Bakery and Ice Cream**, which caters to visitors and cyclists. The movie theater closed down when its manager, Marie Gillem, had a chance to take over the diner.

Drier's customers in the old days were plain folks with lunchpails who worked in the Featherbone factory. "A ring of baloney was a T.V. dinner, long before T.V. " explains philosopher-sausage maker Ed Drier. "People stopped by to pick up their instant supper so they could have time to work in the garden." Trains stopped longer in Three Oaks so passengers could get a ring of Drier's famous baloney.

POINTS OF INTEREST

Drier's Butcher Shop ★★

14 S. Elm in downtown Three Oaks, about a block north of U.S. 12. (Elm intersects with 12.) (616) 756-3101. Closed Jan. 1 until 2 weeks before Easter. Mon-Sat 9-5:30. The funny branch store on U.S. 12 east of town is open Sat & Sun 9:30-5, also closed in winter.

It's easy to assume that Drier's is "the way it used to be." There's sawdust on the floor, old tools, and a meat rack with ornamental cows that may go all the way back to 1875, when the building was converted from a wagon repair shop to a butcher shop. The four-paned windows that pre-date plate glass were installed then. Plain but corny signs like "This baloney cuts the mustard" tap into the Burma-Shave folk tradition of advertising.

Actually, Drier's today is one astute man's business response to changing times, cleverly crafted in favor of preserving quality of life — his own, and his employees' and customers'. Drier's today offers what second-generation owner-sausage maker Ed Drier calls "a limited

menu": hot dogs, Polish sausage, ring bologna at $3.75 a pound ("all beef, less fat, no belching," a sign points out), liver sausage, and cheese that has been made elsewhere. Bologna, hams, and bacon is smoked on the premises. Choice meat justifies the premium prices.

What Drier's doesn't sell, ever since shortly after Ed Drier's dad died, is fresh meat of any kind. "We quit slaughtering in '65," says Drier. "Smartest thing we ever did. We would have spend $100,000 to fulfill government regulations."

Antiques and art make Drier's today a lot more interesting than the plain place depicted in a historical photo postcard given away here. Now you'll find three massive marble butcher's tables from France, picked up on Drier's midwinter travels around the world. There's a deer head, family memorabilia, signs like "Nicht auf den Boden spucken" ("no spitting on the floor" in German, a reminder that this place is quintessentially German in its earthy,

unassuming style), and caricatures — frequently of Ed Drier, like the portrait of him as a grumpy-looking knight, done in magazine-cover style by a *Time* cover artist who was a customer.

All this stuff launches conversations with customers. "That's part of the deal — the dog and pony show," says Drier, who relishes the personal side of the business and the nice letters that come with orders for holiday hams.

In pre-med classes at the University of Michigan, Drier says, a professor told him he'd be better off making baloney than pursuing a medical degree. After finishing college and getting out of the service, he went back to work with his dad in 1945. "We always enjoyed our work," he says. Drier also enjoys living two minutes from his shop and playing tennis with old college chums.

Ed Drier has relied on his family, especially his daughter, Carolyn, and about a dozen young men from the area to help. Even when they've gone out into the work world to become teachers, dentists, engineers, and the like, some come back to the shop to help out on their vacations. "This hooey about what's the matter with young people is mostly what's the matter with the old people," comments Drier. "It's not how many mistakes are made, it's how they are corrected."

Three Oaks Bicycle Museum & Info. Center ★

110 N. Elm. (616) 756-3361. Write: Box 5000, Three Oaks, MI 49128. 9-5 daily, year-round. Call to confirm in winter.

This remarkable little institution is the result of one gung-ho guy and the phenomenal unplanned success of the Apple Cider Century, the 100-mile bicycling tour he started. Within five years of its haphazard inception by Bryan Volstorf, then a computer operator at Clark Equipment, the

Brian Volstorf has parlayed the Apple Cider Century Ride into a job as the director of a year-round bicycle museum and information center and a position of leadership as the improvement-minded mayor of Three Oaks. "Backroads Bikeways," a map of signed bike routes (20-60 miles) radiating out from Three Oaks, is yours for the asking from the museum.

Apple Cider Century was attracting 1,300 cyclists. That made the ride, held in beautiful Berrien County on the third Sunday in September, America's most popular century tour — a distinction it continues to hold.

Fees from the ride's current 6,500 participants fund the museum. It has loads of free visitor information about sights, bed and breakfasts, and such throughout west Michigan, plus county maps showing paved and unpaved roads and regional information about bicycling. Principal staffers are Volstorf himself and in summer his two teenage children.

This spiffily renovated museum also contains a collection of unusual bicycles (from a high-wheeler to a modern recumbent bicycle, in which the cyclist sits near the ground with legs and pedals in front); a top-notch exhibit on the early history of cycling and the Good Roads movement; and videos on bicycle safety and the Apple Cider Century itself, which is headquartered here. Well-designed T-shirts promoting the Apple Cider Century and Three Oaks are for sale.

The museum is also the meeting place of the Three Oaks Spokes, a Michiana bicycling club. In back there is a **picnic table** and **bicycle stands** for cyclists.

Bicycle rentals are $1 an hour after the first $5 hour, or $10/day, $49/week. Bikes are recent-model, single-speed Schwinns with balloon tires for adults and children. A Cannondale bugger attachment for small children is also available. Call to reserve.

Brian Volstorf is an improbable success story. Today he's the mayor of Three Oaks, the founder and operator of the nation's most popular century bicycle ride, and a one-man economic development whirlwind for this town of 1,800 which last prospered during the glory days of the Warren Featherbone Company. He says he·was a shy person until he invented a game called Rainy Day Golf in the Air Force. Promoting it, he hit his stride, discovered he enjoyed public speaking, and was transformed into an outgoing promoter. Volstorf started bicycling for exercise in 1971. He plunged into the sport with characteristic intensity, made a 700-mile tour, formed the Three Oaks Spokes cycling club, and sponsored a Heart Association Bike-A-Thon which left the club $300 in debt. The first Apple Cider Century was held in fall, 1974 to replenish the treasury after that fiasco.

By 1979 the ride had grown to 1,800 riders. But the club's 18 members, who handled the sag wagon, refreshment stand, spaghetti dinner, security, publicity, church sleepover, and cleanup, were approaching burnout. When community organizations took over the support services, they found themselves earning what now amounts to $13,000 a year. Merchants and restaurants finally woke up to the bonanza and started staying open all night for the weekend.

Today, Volstorf reports, the event grosses $220,000 a year and fills every motel room for 30 miles around. Volstorf is now applying his

Featherbone's glory days have been revived in a small way by the attractive renovation of the handsome Roman brick building housing the Bank of Three Oaks, newly renamed Harbor Country Bank. E. K. Warren built it in 1905 for his bank and Warren Featherbone company offices. The bank president today has duplicated Warren's office. Visitors may enjoy looking inside at the bank's original marble-paneled foyer with murals depicting three spreading oaks and a log cabin ("Home 1858-1864") in the subdued, sentimental style of the early 20th century.

promotional skills to selling Three Oaks, not just as mayor, but as a a real estate agent and the driving force behind its Downtown Development Authority that recently installed sidewalk and streetscape improvements on Elm.

Warren Woods Natural Area ★★

Entrances on Elm Valley Rd. and Warren Woods Rd. about a mile west of Three Oaks Rd., which is the north-south extension of Three Oaks' main street between U.S. 12 and the Red Arrow Hwy. From I-94 south of Warren Dunes State Park, take exit 12 (Sawyer Rd.). Go west 1/2 mile to Three Oaks Rd. and turn south onto it. In 3 miles, Warren Woods Rd. leads west to the north entrance. In another mile you would get to Elm Valley Rd., which leads west to the south entrance. For more information, contact Warren Dunes State Park, (616) 426-4013. Open all the time, year-round. State park sticker required ($3/day, $15/year).

These 200 acres comprise one of Michigan's few remaining virgin beech-maple climax forests. That they were preserved at all is due to the remarkable foresight of E. K. Warren, the Three Oaks storekeeper who made a fortune by inventing a better, cheaper corset stay made of turkey feathers. Over a hundred years ago, when most good businessmen were figuring out how to exploit natural resources, he decided to buy this virgin timberland in order to preserve it.

There's parking, a **picnic table**, and **restrooms** at the end of a drive off Elm Valley Rd. The woods you see from the car don't look different from a hundred other places. But if you take the foot trail across the Galien River to the loop that largely parallels the river, you'll see some enormous, majestic beech trees, along with maples and hemlocks. The gravel-surfaced **trails** (3 1/2 miles in all) are flat except for rolling terrain along the river. For **cross-country skiing**, they're rated novice.

The damp soil here makes for a jungly, humid, environment that's sunnier and quite unlike the stand of virgin oaks and hickories at Russ Forest, another piece of southwest Michigan virgin forest on Marcellus Highway (M-216) between Dowagiac and Marcellus.

"Warren Woods is also one of the state's premier birding sites," notes Tom Powers in *Michigan State and National Parks: A Complete Guide.* "During spring migrations the woods attract numerous warblers, many of them uncommon to Michigan and usually only seen much farther south [Acadian Flycatchers and Louisiana Waterthrushes, for instance]." Woodpeckers abound.

Watkins Park/ Hoadley Trail

Behind Harding's supermarket on U.S. 12 a few blocks west of the light in Three Oaks. Enter via drive between Harding's & laundromat.

Exercise course and park on the property where Bicycle Museum and Apple Cider Century founder Brian Volstorf is saving and planning to built a community center with indoor track and pool. Proceeds from the enormously popular century ride are going to build the center. Of the 23 exercise stations, half are in the open area behind Harding's, and half in the woods behind that. Picnic tables, playground equipment, and a volleyball court have already been built.

RESTAURANTS

Village Pump

13 S. Elm in downtown Three Oaks. (616) 756-9132. 11 a.m.-midnight daily. Full bar. Visa, AmEx, MC.

This popular local bar is known for its American-Mexican fare. Wet burritos, tostadas, and taco salads are all $4.35. The reuben sandwich ($4.95) is popular, as is the Cheese Pump Platter ($4.95), a cheeseburger with fries.

Berrien Springs and vicinity

Vineyards and orchards cover rolling hills and high glacial moraines in most of central Berrien County. It's a beautiful, orderly, highly cultivated landscape, sprinkled with villages. The area looks much more like Europe than most of the American Midwest.

The scenery, the wineries, the abundant farm stands, and the natural beauty of the St. Joseph River Valley all make for delightful outings by car or bicycle, especially in spring (fruit trees blossom in very early May) and in fall. Even in winter, the patterns of pruned fruit trees against the snow are a beautiful sight.

Contrasted with the fruitful landscape is the sense of hard times that hangs over most all the towns inland from the booming Lake Michigan coast. Falling fruit prices have meant that nearly all fruit farms depend on second incomes and farm stands to survive. It was a big blow to the fragile area economy when Clark Equipment, founded and headquartered in Buchanan, virtually shut down Michigan operations, taking away thousands of jobs here.

A sleepy village

Berrien Springs, perched above the beautiful St. Joseph River in the exact center of the county, still has the sleepy look of a mid-19th-century rural village. In

Muhammed Ali lives outside Berrien Springs with his wife and family on an 80-acre estate that was long the center of much local rumor and conjecture. The opulent spread, where the guest house has 8 bedrooms, was built by Louis Campagna, thought to be in cahoots with Al Capone. The famous Chicago gang kingpin was said to use Campagna's place as a hideout, in fact. Campagna was eventually imprisoned for extortion and died in 1955.

White blossoms and spring-green grass make for lovely drives and bike rides through Berrien County in late April and early May.

most southern Michigan towns of this size (its 1880 population was about 1,000), a railroad arrived to develop industry and commerce in the post Civil War boom. That enabled business districts to rebuild in brick buildings with round-arched Italianate windows — the quintessentially small town look. Berrien Springs missed out on that handsome architectural era. Its wooden 19th-century storefronts survived into the early 20th century, to be replaced by mostly dull squat, utilitarian brick buildings.

Two blocks from downtown, the old courthouse survives as a museum. It's not one of the Victorian wedding cakes considered classic old courthouses today. Rather, it's one of the last of an earlier generation of plain Greek Revival frame courthouses built in the 1830s and 1840s, in which a single courtroom occupies the entire upper floor.

An entirely different era marks the northwest side of town, along U.S. 31/33 — the auto-oriented 1960s, during which the Emmanuel Missionary College established here by the Seventh-Day Adventists in 1901 blossomed into Andrews University, with some 3,000 students today. There are even traffic jams by the

Carbon's famous malted pancake and waffle mix, made right in Buchanan, is sold mainly to restaurants, along with their line of custom waffle and ice cream cone bakers. The company blends nutritious malt with flour for a distinctive, somewhat nutty crunch. It is distributed locally, for instance, at Harding's Market, 714 E. Front, where a 20 oz. package is $1.79; 60 oz. $4.79.

MICHIGAN PRODUCE	JUNE	JULY	AUG.	SEPT.	OCT.
APPLES					
ASPARAGUS					
BEANS (GREEN)					
BEETS					
BLACKBERRIES					
BLUEBERRIES					
RASPBERRIES (BLACK)					
RASPBERRIES (RED)					
STRAWBERRIES					
OTHER BERRIES					
BROCCOLI					
CABBAGE					
CANTALOUPE					
CARROTS					
CAULIFLOWER					
CHERRIES (SWEET)					
CHERRIES (TART)					
CELERY					
CORN (INDIAN)					
CORN (SWEET)					
CUCUMBERS					
EGGPLANT					
GOURDS					
GRAPES					
ONIONS					
PEACHES					
PEARS					
PEPPERS (GREEN)					
PICKLES					
PLUMS					
POTATOES					
SQUASH					
TOMATOES					
TURNIPS					

A U-Pick Guide and 3 nifty **backroads maps** featuring southwest Michigan attractions and events for spring, fall, and winter can be had for the asking from Southwestern Michigan Tourist Council, Benton Harbor, MI 49022. (616) 925-6301.

university along the highway. The Andrews campus
has the flat-topped, practical brick dorms and in-
structional buildings typical of the 1960s. Apple
Valley, a large vegetarian supermarket and natural
foods store run by Adventists, is a visitor attraction in
the area (p. 32).

Steamboat resort

Berrien Springs dramatically illustrates the effect
of transportation on development. Its central location
in Berrien County led it to be named the county seat of
an unusual county whose main towns and transportation routes are along its edges: Benton Harbor/St. Joseph and the old Territorial Road (now the I-94 corridor) along the north, Lake Michigan to the west, and
the Michigan Central Railroad and Niles to the east.
Legislators traveled to Berrien Springs by stagecoach.
A daily steamboat plied the St. Joseph River between
St. Joseph and Berrien Springs. The steamboat, along
with the town's attractive river location amidst fruit
farms, led to Berrien Springs' brief status as a summer
resort after the Civil War.

But reliable rail connections escaped the county
seat, a great embarrassment to progress-minded
county leaders. "This is too fast an age to travel by
horsepower," complained one newspaper. In 1894
Berrien County voters voted by a narrow margin to
move the county seat to St. Joseph.

A rural refuge for Adventists

Loss of the county seat sent the village into an economic torpor. The Seventh-Day Adventists were looking for just such a backwater in which to relocate their
college and missionary school. The denomination had
been centered in Battle Creek for the past half-cen-
tury. During that time Battle Creek had grown from a
village that was remarkably receptive to all sorts of
alternative belief systems, from Quakers and
Adventists to spiritualists and phrenologists, into a
booming industrial center. By 1900, Battle Creek had
become all too worldly, what with its amazing break-
fast-cereal boom and associated advertising hype and
get-rich-quick schemes. Adventist prophetess Ellen
White had an ominous vision of a flaming sword
hanging over the city.

Adventists investigated many towns in southwest
Michigan (South Haven and Benton Harbor were
strong candidates), but two farms outside Berrien
Springs seemed more appropriate. Battle Creek
College moved here in 1901 and became Emmanuel
Missionary College. The denomination headquarters
moved to near Washington, D. C., where it established
a theological seminary. The seminary and associated
graduate school moved to Berrien Springs in 1960, and
the college became Andrews University.

Niles,
the historic old town
just 5 miles east of
Buchanan, is worth a
visit for the high-
*quality **Michiana***
***Antiques Mall** on U/*
S. 33 and the very
special Indian things
*in its **Fort St. Joseph***
***Museum**, behind the*
fabulous Queen Anne
mansion at 508 E.
Main that's today the
***city hall**. (Visitors are*
welcome to look
around.) Across the
street, get a fresh
*ginger beer at **Mamie's***
***Jamaican BBQ**. For*
more on Niles, contact
the Four Flags Area
Tourist Council, 321 E.
Main, Box 1300, Niles
49120. (616) 683-3720.
Read all about Niles in
upcoming volumes of
Hunts' Guides to
Michigan.

The dam across the St. Joseph River at Berrien Springs is a favorite fishing spot.

Students and faculty come from all over the world. The denomination is strong in Africa, and many Africans are here studying mostly education and theology. If you go into the slick, contemporary Apple Valley supermarket for a club sandwich, you may encounter stately African women in vivid robes and headwraps, speaking French to their children.

A visit to Berrien Springs puts you in an odd place in time and space. First you feel like you're revisiting 19th-century rural America. Then you run into a suburban version of a multi-cultural Christian utopia.

Backroads Bikeways , a full-color map and guide to recommended marked bicycle routes around beautiful Berrien County, is available for free from The Bicycle Museum, 110 N. Elm, Three Oaks, MI 49128. Open 9-5 daily year 'round, it's a great place to pick up ideas about interesting bicycling destinations.

POINTS OF INTEREST

1839 Courthouse Museum and Courthouse Square ★★

On U.S. 31 (Cass) at Union St., 3 blocks north of Shawnee and downtown Berrien Springs. (616) 471-1202. Tues-Fri 9-4, Sat & Sun 1-5. Closed holidays. Free admission.

An outstanding small **local history museum** is in the lower level of this trim Greek Revival courthouse, Michigan's oldest county government building. Well-written, clearly presented displays of select artifacts illuminate key events and trends in area history, from Native Americans and early French forts to hardwood lumbering, railroads, and Berrien's enthusiasm for the Civil War. Some important parts of Berrien County history — fruit, wine, Adventists here

in Berrien Springs, Southern black and white migration to World War II war production plants — are missing. But the museum is still young and developing. The displays tell important stories here; in many museums, they never do.

Renovation work prompted by a 1989 fire has rearranged many areas and displays. The expanded **gift shop** has an unusually good selection of publications on regional and local history.

The spare, dignified, light-filled **courtroom** upstairs has been meticulously restored and furnished. It also served as a community center, the scene of temperance and religious meetings, village Christmas parties, and the like. Architects and builders may enjoy the cut-away views of how the wall was constructed.

Next door, the **1870 sheriff's**

The Berrien Springs courthouse and a similar one in Lapeer are the sole survivors of the first generation of Michigan courthouses built in the Greek Revival style shortly after statehood in 1837. Here the old courthouse forms the centerpiece of an interesting museum complex.

house features a gallery for adroitly presented **changing exhibits** (currently on St. Joseph River steamboats) and the **restored sheriff's office.** An unusually large, two-story **log house,** authentically furnished, is also open to the public. The museum's knowledgeable director and curator are happy to answer questions; don't hesitate to ask to talk to them.

In 1907 the old courthouse became the first permanent home of the Seventh-Day Adventists' Emmanuel Missionary College, now Andrews University. Threatened with demolition in 1967, it was purchased by the county for use by the Berrien County Historical Association.

Wild Birds Unlimited   ★

109 N. Main just north of Ferry in downtown Berrien Springs. (616) 471-4031. Mon-Fri 9-5, Sat 9-1.

This attractive little shop carries a nearly complete range of bird-feeding supplies: feeders, birdbaths,

and seed. Ask for the free catalog; it'll teach you a lot. For instance, birds prefer oily black sunflower seeds to the messier, more expensive striped sunflower seeds commonly available.

There's also a wonderful variety of bird-related stuff, from books and binoculars to jewelry and T-shirts. "Winter is for the birds" is the caption on a T-shirt with a snow scene at a bird feeder. To sharpen bird-identification skills, there are bird-watching videos and birdsong audio tapes. Prices are standard, and the selection is tremendous.

Owner Richard Schinkel was a naturalist at Sarett Nature Center near Benton Harbor when he came up with the idea for a bird specialty store with merchandise selected by a knowledgeable bird specialist. A partner developed Wild Birds Unlimited into a small midwestern franchise chain. Now Schinkel spends most of his time here (his bird-feeder wholesaling business is behind the store) when he's not leading worldwide bird-watching expeditions for Sarett.

Apple Valley

U. S. 31 at the Andrews campus, 2 miles northwest of downtown Berrien Springs. (616) 471-2324. Sun-Thurs 8 a.m.-11 p.m., Fri until 6, closed Sat.

Run by Adventists, this large vegetarian supermarket resembles a big, state-of-the-art supermarket with deli, bakery, salad bar, and snack shop — everything but meat. That's fake bacon, cleverly made of vegetarian ingredients, in the refrigerator case, and fake turkey in the club sandwich. (It doesn't have much taste, but then, neither does most turkey.) The natural foods section is extensive, though there's not much you couldn't get in a good co-op or health food store. The produce is terrific. So is the bakery. You can sit down there and have sweet rolls and not coffee but Postum cereal beverage. (Adventists discourage caffeine and other stimulants along with alcohol and smoking.) That famous coffee substitute, which launched the Post food empire, was first devised by Ella Kellogg, wife of famed Adventist doctor John Harvey Kellogg, to serve at his internationally known Battle Creek Sanatarium.

The Seventh-Day Adventists' espousal of a vegetarian diet goes back to the visions of prophetess Ellen White, which incorporated many principles of health reform current in the mid-19th century. The denomination founded the Sanatarium, where the Kelloggs devised many of the meat substitutes like Protose, a soybean mix used like hamburger, that can be found on Apple Valley's shelves today. A more out-front grain-based diet would have seemed too austere to meatloving middle-class Americans of the late 19th century.

A good many customers are foreigners, sometimes in native dress, who come from all over the world to study at the Adventists' Andrews University adjacent to Apple Valley Plaza. Adventists observe the sabbath on Saturday, the seventh day, and Apple Valley is closed then.

Andrews University Horn Archaeological Museum

In a small, square building near the main circular intersection near the campus entrance. The campus is off U.S. 31/33 2 miles northwest of Berrien Springs. From I-94 and Benton Harbor, take U.S. 31/33 past Redbud Trail and Lemon Creek Rd. look for Andrews' sign. (616) 471-3273. Open during the school year Tues-Thurs 9-5, Sat & Sun 2-5. Other times by appt.; staff is usually there.

Biblical archaeology is a subject of special interest to Adventists. The Siegfried Horn Museum is connected with the Andrews Institute of Archaeology. They focus on Biblical archaeology, that is, on artifacts from Biblical periods and from the land of Palestine. Museum artifacts are shown in historical context provided by color murals depicting scenes from everyday life from the early bronze age of the Egyptian dynasties into the Islamic period. The collection of cuneiform tablets is one of the largest in the U.S.

Andrews archaeologists, like all Andrews faculty, are Adventists. Adventists' conservative theological beliefs (that the world was created in seven days, and not too terribly long before the beginning of recorded history) do not interfere with their scholarly status with secular scholars in the field of Biblical archaeology, which is limited to accepted historical periods.

The Andrews natural history museum, with a fine reconstructed mammoth excavated nearby, is also open to the public. Ask for directions at the Horn Museum.

Love Creek County Park & Nature Center ★

9228 Huckleberry Rd., about 2 miles east of Berrien Springs. From U.S. 31/33 just east of town, turn east onto Pokagon Rd. In 1 1/2 miles, turn north onto Huckleberry Rd. (616) 471-2617. Trails open dawn to dusk daily. Interpretive center open Wed-Sun 10-5. $3/car, $2 for Berrien Co. residents.

Berrien County is replete with wonderful natural areas, and its three nature centers all set a high standard for beauty and user-friendliness. This 100-acre county park and wildlife sanctuary along pretty Love Creek is almost in the same league with nature centers as the generously endowed Fernwood and Sarett.

Love Creek's 100 acres are to the rear of the county hospital and onetime poor farm on Dean's Hill Road. They include a marsh, open meadows, wet forests, and a beech-maple climax forest, plus the creek valley and bottomland.

Five miles of **hiking trails** are laid out in interconnecting loops, mostly along the creek and bottomland, ranging from 1/2 mile to 3 miles in length. Wooden bridges, trailside benches, and a marsh observation tower encourage visitors to stop and open their eyes and ears to all the little sights and sounds around them.

The spring woodland wildflower show is "unbeatable," according to naturalist Kip Miller. The **interpretive building** has an informal exhibit area and a very effective wildlife observation window that lets you get up close to many birds and animals. Love Creek's two naturalists welcome visitors' questions. **Free programs,** offered on most weekends, include nature walks (on foot or skis) and field trips. All are free. Write the park (9228 Huckleberry Rd., Berrien Center, MI 49102) for a complete **schedule** of nature programs, ski lessons, and torch-lit ski evenings.

Cross-country skiing is very popular on six miles of groomed and track-set trails, some open and easy, and some wooded, with challenging turns. Trail fees are $2/person/day; rentals are $6/2 hours. Daytime lessons and torch-lit evening skis ($2 trail fee) are offered weekends in January and February. **Snowshoes** may be rented for $2 for use on trails maintained for that purpose, or made at a January workshop. Ski and snowshoe rental hours in season: Wed-Fri 1-4, weekends 10-4.

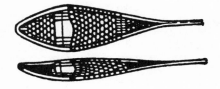

Tree-Mendus Fruit ★★

*On E. Eureka Rd. off M-62, 2 miles due east of Eau Claire and 5 miles northeast of Berrien Springs. From I-94 and the east, take M-140 (Watervliet exit 41) south about 14 miles to M-62, go east 1/4 mile and look for signs. From Niles, take M-140 north 11 miles, see above. From I-94 and the west, take U.S. 31/33 (exit 27) from St. Joseph or take Shawnee Rd. north of exit 16 at Bridgman, go east to Berrien Springs, stay on 31 east of town, turn after crossing the river onto Pokagon Rd. In 2 1/2 miles, go north on M-140. At M-140 and M-62, turn east and look for signs. (616) 782-7101. Write for **newsletter:** East Eureka Road, Eau Claire, MI 49111. Last week in June-Labor Day: daily except Tues 10-6. After Labor Day through 3rd week in Oct: Fri-Mon 10-6. Group tours by appt. any day begin in blossomtime (early May).*

During the 1960s, fruit farmers began to find it hard to make a profit simply selling their fruit wholesale. Trucking strikes, farm labor boycotts, and erratic prices led far-sighted growers to think about diversifying. The most successful grape- and apple-growers have succeeded by combining direct-to-consumer sales with recreation.

No one has done this better than Herb Teichman of Tree-Mendus Fruit. He has transformed his father's Skyline Orchards, tucked away on a scenic, hilly road west of Indian Lake, into a well-organized, aggressively promoted visitor destination, the home of the **International Cherry Pit Spitting Championship** held July 4.

Tree-Mendus Fruit artfully provides a pleasant day in the country for a generation of Americans who no longer have relatives down on the farm. In addition to 560 acres of U-pick orchards, there's a big **picnic area** and 120-acre **nature park** with **hiking trails** through wooded wildlife areas with ponds. Visitors can fill **water jugs** at their deep

Antique apples are a specialty at Tree-Mendus Fruit. 50 varieties of fruit are for sale and 300 trees are in the "apple museum." Much stock came from GM attorney Robert Nitschke, an avid fan who collected and propagated many kinds in his Birmingham back yard. To order scions of his trees, write for the catalog of Southmeadow Fruit Gardens, 15310 Red Arrow Hwy., Lakeside, MI 49116.

country well. There's even a **Chapel in the Wildwood,** promoted as "a breathtaking setting for weddings, retreats, sunrise services or vespers." On busy weekends ushers are on hand to direct visitors to all parts of the farm. School and senior bus tours, company picnics, and family reunions are all popular. The picking, picnicking, and touring is all very well organized, and the place has a nice, rural atmosphere.

Teichman manages to focus on fruit and teach visitors a lot about it. He doesn't run a carnival, as some well-known cider mills and orchards do. We met a man from Grosse Pointe who drives over each fall to play golf (the excellent Indian Hills public course is just half a mile away), get together with his children and grandchildren who live within a two-hour radius, and pick their family tree (rented for $50 a year on the average). Compared to the cost and trouble of spraying a few fruit trees, renting a tree makes sense.

Teichman himself is a font of interesting information on fruit, and he loves to talk to customers when it's not too hectic. His **orchard tours** cover the evolution of fruit varieties and a first-hand look at cultivation techniques from grafting and pruning to harvesting, depending on the season. **One-hour tours** ($4/person, with a $40 minimum) are given by appointment, on short notice when possible.

Teichman's **"old-time apple museum"** has grown from a few dozen antique apple trees that interested his dad to a remarkable collection of over 300 varieties from around the world, including the Spitzbergen (Thomas Jefferson's favorite), the Westfield Seek-No-Further, and the tasty, tart, crisp Calville Blanc, which goes back to 1627. Modern fruit-picking and marketing demands apples that look uniform and attractive, ship well, and can be picked at once. Such requirements have eliminated many old favorites, but about 50 old apple varieties are sold here for $1 a pound. On orchard tours, visitors can sample antique apples and purchase ones they like.

Measured by the pound, Tree-mendus Fruit isn't exactly cheap. Apples you pick yourself easily cost about what they'd cost at the supermarket. But then, Teichman doesn't charge for admission to his private park.

Jams, apple butter, frozen peaches and cherries, and the farm's distinctive varieties of cider and cherry cider are for sale in the **Tree House Country Store.** Waffle boat desserts with peaches, cherries, or apples in season and lots of whipped cream are cooked and served on the premises. On crisp fall days, pickers can warm themselves by the big fireplace.

Cherries ripen in July, followed by peaches, apricots, plums, nectarines, apples, pears, and pumpkins, all grown on the farm and sold U-pick or picked. Recently the Teichmans have gotten into experimental vegetables, traditional and exotic, for sale as available: gobo, Chinese artichokes, echayote, and yard-long beans, for example. Herb's son Bill is improving strains of paw-paws, and elderberries are a new crop.

Wicks Apple House   ★

52281 Indian Lake Rd. about 8 miles northeast of Berrien Springs and 6 miles northwest of Dowagiac. See directions for Tree-Mendus Fruit, but stay on M-62 about 2 1/2 miles east to Indian Lake Rd., turn north. Wicks is in about 3 miles. (616)782-6822. Open Memorial Day weekend to Nov. 1. Tues-Sun 8-6. Full breakfast served 8-11 through Labor Day (continental breakfast in fall), lunch 11:30-5 through fall.

This rambling, attractive farm market plus cider mill (1960) plus bakery (1969) plus gift shop (1973) plus restaurant (1988) grew from a front-yard apple stand (1950). Now it's a three-generation family business employing 25 non-family members as well. Prices are competitive, and there's quite a bit to do even on rainy days. Through glass walls you can **see cider being made** on weekends from the end of September on (good explanatory signs help); the **bakery** is visible, too. Customers can pick their own apples (big and small, as they like) from big orchard-run boxes.

The simple, cheery **Orchard View Room restaurant** serves good, reasonably priced homemade soup, sandwiches and hot dogs, baked goods, and pies ($1.45/slice) made from founding mother Marian Wicks' recipes. Favorite meals include a Reuben ($3, or $4.50 for the Monster), a Philly beef and cheese with lots of grilled peppers and onions ($3.85), and quiche with fresh fruit and homemade apple bread ($4).

It's a treat to feel the hands-on energy and community involvement in family enterprises like this, where

neighbors help out on the weekends and kids home from college get dressed up like apples for the fall **Cider Fest** (2nd weekend of October). It features live country music and other entertainment, square dancing, and horse-drawn wagon tours of the farm.

The **farm market** features Michigan produce whenever possible, from mid-June on. The Wicks raise their own asparagus, tart cherries, Stanley plums, apples, and Concord grapes. Daughter-in-law Sue Wicks helped found Women for the Survival of Agriculture in Michigan a decade ago. Her father worked in the institutional food business in Chicago; her marketing savvy, joined with a century of Wicks family farming commitment, have made Wicks Apple House the popular rural attraction it is today.

Lemon Creek Fruit Farms, Vineyards & Winery   ★★

533 Lemon Creek Rd. east of Baroda, 7 miles west of Berrien Springs and 5 miles east of Bridgman. From I-94, take the Bridgman exit (16), go north on Red Arrow Hwy. 2 miles to Lemon Creek Rd., then east 5 miles. From U.S. 31/33 2 miles northwest of Berrien Springs, take Lemon Creek Rd. west 5 miles. (616) 471-1321. Open regularly May-Dec: Mon-Sat 9-6, Sun 12-6. Other times by appointment. Bus tours by appointment only.

This small, family-owned winery and fruit farm offers a rare opportunity to taste a good variety of medium-priced Michigan wines (including many award-winners), buy fresh fruit, and see most aspects of wine production, from growing grapes to fermentation and bottling, all in a scenic rural setting. (Only crushing and pressing is done off the premises, at St. Julian Winery, which also buys grapes from Lemon Creek.) Your tour guide is one of the owners, not hired part-time help.

The Lemon family has grown fruit and grapes here, in the beautiful, rolling fruit-growing area between

orchards with wine grapes. Prices fell dramatically as a result. The Lemons, like an increasing number of fruit and vegetable producers, realized they'd be more secure financially if they marketed their own produce and added value to it in the production process.

They continued supplying Tabor Hill, St. Julian, and Good Harbor with wine grapes but also opened their own winery in 1984. For newcomers to the tricky business of winemaking, they've been extraordinarily successful, with 37 awards for their wines thus far. Cathy Lemon says being small and family-run has its advantages: better quality control from using only their own grapes, and greater commitment from having a staff comprised only of family-owners. "We don't distribute a lot," she says. "There's no money in it unless you do a large volume. 85% of our sales are right here, 75% from the Chicago area."

Wine prices run from $4.50 a bottle for Baco Rose (a fruity, crisp semi-sweet Michigan State Fair gold medal winner) to $7.95 for dry or semi-sweet Johannisberg Riesling and $8.95 for Vidal Blanc champagne. Lemon Creek's three Vidal wines (dry, semi-sec, and semi-sweet; $5.95 each) have won the most awards and are big sellers. Sparkling juice (grape, red raspberry, and peach) is $3.50. Mail orders welcome; 10% case discount.

Fruits for sale (packaged or U-pick) include raspberries, four kinds of sweet cherries, tart cherries, three varieties of peach, nectarines, plums, pears, and eight kinds of apples.

A June **festival** each Father's Day weekend includes hayrides, games for kids, arts and crafts booths, and live music.

Baroda and Berrien Springs, since the 1850s. Between the farmhouse and orchards is a metal building housing the winery, fruit sales room, and tasting room, run by the personable Cathy Lemon. She is happy to give visitors an informal tour of the adjacent wine-making facilities. Just outside, you can see the vines, neatly labeled by variety, and the tall mechanical picker that straddles the rows of vines and harvests the grapes. Visitors can **picnic** at tables outside the tasting room.

Winemakers can purchase grapes already picked or pick them themselves. Varieties include Concord, several French hybrids (Chamborsin, Baco, Vignole, and Vidal), and Riesling, the viniferous variety that does best in Michigan. Thick-skinned and hardy, Vidal is their leading planting stock.

Brothers Tim, Jeff, and Bob Lemon run the operation today. Twenty years ago, when Lemon Creek was a fruit farm only, their father started experimenting with the French hybrid and vinifera grapes. As demand for premium wine grapes grew, the Lemons decided to propagate and plant 45 acres in wine grapes. One winter they cut and heeled in 80,000 four-budded sticks of vine.

In 1981, after years of falling fruit prices, many other southwest Michigan fruit farmers also replaced their

Tabor Hill Winery
& Restaurant   ★

185 Mt. Tabor Road. From I-94 and Chicago/New Buffalo, take Exit 16 at Bridgman, go north about a mile to Lake St./Shawnee Road, turn east and follow signs. From 4-corners in downtown Berrien Springs, take Snow Rd. west about 4 miles to Mt. Tabor, turn south. (616) 422-1161. Tours free. June-Oct: daily 11:30-4:30. Off-season: Mon-Thurs by appt. only. See p. 43 for restaurant

Where the nearby Lemon Creek winery is pleasantly farmy and tastefully down-to-earth, Tabor Hill projects a sophisticated image for city people — upbeat, promotionally savvy, even slick. The tasting room is combined with the bar in the front of the new restaurant; you may have to be aggressive in asking for samples.

The restaurant and terrace have a vaguely California look with bleached wood and stone. The view — of vineyards, orchards, and the distant Lake Michigan dunes.— is stunning. These vineyards are on the west side of a long moraine, which keeps them above dangerous low-lying frost pockets in spring.

Tabor Hill's restaurant is so busy and bustling that the crowds can overwhelm one's visit on a busy day. You might call first, or plan a mid-afternoon tour. The experienced marketing staff gives weekday tours; weekends the guides are trained high school students.

As winery tours compare, this has some real plusses. You can walk through the vineyards. The crusher-destemmer is right outside, and at harvest time in late summer, you can hang around and watch lugs of grapes being dumped into the hopper, where they are spun in a centrifuge and emerge as juice. (The bees buzzing around it are far more interested in the juice than people.) Some fermenting tanks are outdoors, too, chilled for free by cold winter air.

Inside, the shiny new German and Italian bottling equipment has a capacity of 600 to 800 cases a day — quite a contrast to the hand bottle capper on a table at Lemon Creek. Tabor Hill has become the second-biggest winery in Michigan, with about half the output of St. Julian's.

Tabor Hill today reflects the investment of owner David Upton, whose father and uncle founded Whirlpool. Winemaker Rick Moersch also produces his own, limited-production wines (including chardonnay and the spicy German *scheurebe,* so far on an experimental basis). It's a far cry from the creative chaos of Tabor Hill's early days under wine visionary and pathfinder Len Olson. Brash and bold, Olson was convinced by intuition, not research and experience that Michigan could produce premium wines. When he founded Tabor Hill in 1972, he was the first in Michigan to take a gamble and plant chardonnay and riesling, two varieties of vinifera or "noble grapes" used in fine European wines. (Michigan winters, colder than Europe's, made them chancey.) Olson's Tabor Hill "was like a commune," recalls Michigan State wine professor Stan Howell. "A lot of people came there to live and work. It was an interesting time. His wines were so much better than any others being produced in Michigan." Upton rescued the financially shaky operation in the late 1970s. Huge oak wine barrels, hand-carved with scenes depicting events of each particular year at Tabor Hill, are a Len Olson legacy and a highlight of the tour.

Today's reorganized Tabor Hill covers all the winemaking categories, from pop wines like its $4.50 sangria to its Hartford Cream Sherry ($8.95), aged 10 years, and some estate-bottled vinifera wines like its $11.95 Chardonnay. But its mainstays have been middle-priced wines made from hardier French hybrid grapes, like its Berrien Ridge proprietary blend ($6.95, a fragrant, well-balanced, near-dry table wine) and its Vidal Demi-Sec ($6.29), a sweeter, easy-drinking, summer-picnic kind of wine considered by wine experts Tabor Hill's best value.

Tabor Hill hosts a **harvest festival** the weekend before Labor Day, with jazz, a food tent, and A competitive grape stomp.

Fernwood   ★★★

13988 Range Line Rd. between Berrien Springs and Buchanan. From Niles or Berrien Springs, take U.S. 31/33 to Walton Rd. turn west and follow the signs. From U.S. 12 and Buchanan, take Red Bud trail to Walton, turn east (right), cross the river and turn north onto Range Line and follow the signs. (616) 695-6491 or 683-8653. **Visitor center and gift shop:** *Mon-Sat 9-5, Sun 12-5.* **Grounds** *open to members sunrise to sunset. $2 adults, children 12 and younger free. Pick up a free trail map to plan your visit and see the highlights.*

Though Fernwood has grown into an impressive facility for nature and arts and crafts education, it is first and foremost a gardener's garden. It bears the very personal stamp of the late Kay Boydston, a longtime teacher in Niles. A serious self-taught horticulturist originally from Chicago, Boydston and her husband show that people of modest means can, with enough time and knowledge, create extraordinary gardens.

Fernwood's heart is a serene, sensuous small universe compressed into six acres of linked gardens she planted. She and her husband Walter discovered this ravine and brookside area. Elevations descend 125 feet from dry old fields down to the St. Joseph River, creating a range of microclimates, where soils vary from sand to clay to leaf mold, both wet and dry. She planted a **lilac garden** with lily pool; a **boxwood garden** with shady groundcovers; a **perennial garden**; a **fern trail** leading to a rustic bridge by a corkscrew falls; and an enchanting **rock garden**, where dwarf conifers, primroses, heathers, and many little flowers from mountains, meadows, and bogs of the world bloom in the pockets of tufa stone between April and May.

Boydston's gardens are a sensory delight, filled with the sounds of plashing water and birdsong and the smells of flowers, pines, and leaf mold in the air. She planted them around their simple, shingled cottage homes (one was oriented for summer, one for winter) as a series of picturesque small spaces like outdoor rooms. They are accented by arbors, bridges, benches, stone walls, and

pools that encourage visitors to stop
and contemplate a small area. Many
famous American gardens are patterned on aristocratic European prototypes, requiring expensive upkeep,
statuary, and garden structures.
Fernwood is more relaxed and natural; its purpose is to inspire home
gardeners in these climes. Any of the
walls and benches could be built by
an interested amateur — just as Walter Boydston built these. Bulbs poke
up through fall's leaves, and fallen
branches remain in place in wilder
areas.

Kay Boydston's habit was to
choose a plant type — ferns (her favorite) or Alpine flowers, for instance
— study it intensely, landscape with
it, and move on to another subject
years later. Many of her gardens are
impressive collections of a type, and
they do have instructive labels, but
her part of Fernwood wears its
learning lightly.

In 1964, the Boydstons turned
their home into a nature center and
garden open to the public. Financial
support came from Mary Plym, wife of
the owner of Kawneer, the Niles
storefront design firm responsible
for aluminum coverups of countless
ornate old downtown buildings
across America. Since then Fernwood has expanded into a much bigger facility — impressive, but without
the special magic of Kay Boydston's
gardens. It is only approached in effect by the Main Garden, planted in
1964 by a former director of Chicago's Morton Arboretum. His garden
showcases a fine viburnum collection and provide special winter twig
and bark interest, complemented in
summer by bedding plants.

There's much to draw repeat visitors to Fernwood: miles of **nature
trails** with excellent trail guides; a
splendid **tallgrass prairie** with
overlook platform (another trail
guide points out highlights of its
blooming season, from May through
August); an **arboretum** of 60 trees
recommended for city lots, now
coming into its own; and a **Japanese**

In April and May Kay Boydston's rock
garden is abloom with the little flowers of
mountains and bogs. Primroses, iris,
gentians, and wild tulips and daffodils are
planted among the dwarf conifers and
ferns. Fernwood's diverse gardens have
been planned for year-round interest.
Even in winter it's worth a visit.

garden, rose garden, an **All-Amer-
ica test garden** (where new flowers
are tested), and a **pioneer dooryard
garden**.

The new **Visitors' Center** has a
big tropical plant room (nice in winter), space for changing exhibits, horticulture classroom space, and a **gift
shop**, romantic in mood, with garden
books and a wide selection of note-
cards, gifts, and china with botanical
and bird motifs. A very reasonably
priced **tea room** (open Tues-Fri
11:30-2) looks out onto the interesting **herb and sensory garden**.

Fernwood offers a host of inexpensive and unusually wide-ranging
gardening, nature and crafts classes
and workshops for adults and children; ask for a catalog. Full-day,
week-long summer nature classes for
children and Japanese crafts classes
for adults could be highlights of a
summer vacation in the area.

Bear Cave

4085 Bear Cave Rd. 3 miles north of Buchanan. The cave and campground are just east of Red Bud Trail, which runs north-south between U.S. 31/33 2 miles west of Berrien Springs down to Buchanan and U.S. 12. (616) 695-3050. Open in season 9-5 daily at least. $2.50 for adults, $1 for children 12 and under.

Michigan's only natural cave is nestled in the exceedingly picturesque Bear Cave Campground on the broad and beautiful St. Joseph River. Some 50 steps lead down from the entrance in the camp store into a series of rooms in a tufa bed. This unusual kind of spongey limestone occurs at only three places in the U.S. Springs dripped down and created both the limestone formations and the stream which now flows through the cave.

A competent 20-minute audiotaped tour points out the geology of the cave's origins and various historical anecdotes and natural curiosities in the lumpy rock formations. It's interesting enough if you can match the overloud, confusing narrative with where you're supposed to be. Nearby Pottawatomi Indians are said to have used iron oxide from the cave to make face paint.

Concrete paths make walking easy, but with narrow spaces, drippy water, and an occasional bat, Bear Cave isn't for the claustrophobic or squeamish. It's not much of an adventure, either, compared with caves in the limestone region of Indiana, Kentucky, and Missouri, though it would certainly interest amateur geologists.

The cave exits onto a path that leads to a scenic fishing platform along the river, past beeches, ferns, and a lovely waterfall. **Bear Cave Campground** would be a splendid place to camp or picnic if only it didn't require purchasing a $6,000 membership in U.S. Vacation Resorts.

Pears Mill

Between Days and Oak St. just south of Front in downtown Buchanan. (616) 695-5525. Open weekends & holidays 1-5, Mem.. thru Labor Day, often earlier and later. No fee.

Gristmill enthusiasts have installed old gristmill machinery in this 1853 mill, and they operate it on summer weekends. It is quite thrilling to witness this once vital, ubiquitous process in ancient, timer-frame mills like this. The whole building shakes and rumbles as belts move which link the millstones and various sifters to the giant water-powered mill wheel— all to take advantage of an amount of energy that would seem almost trivial by today's standards.

The setting isn't exactly quaint — it's the middle of a parking lot behind the main business block of this interesting town, which has been economically devastated by the pullout of Clark Equipment's headquarters and manufacturing facility a few blocks away off Red Bud Trail.

Pears Mill (pronounced "Peers") operates with an old-fashioned wood waterwheel. (Michigan's other operating mills, at Frankenmuth, Crossroads Village near Flint, Scotts near Kalamazoo, and Bowens Mill near Hastings, have turbines, a late-19th-century introduction.) The interior of the old mill is being restored with scrupulous authenticity, and some of the guides are unusually knowledgeable.

Madron Lake Hills Winery

(616) 695-5660. 14387 Madron Lake Rd. 3 miles northwest of Buchanan. From U. S. 12 and the south, take Red Bud Trail north through Buchanan and turn west onto Miller Rd. about 2 miles from downtown. After 2.8 miles, turn south onto Madron Lake Rd. Look for the winery in 1/2 mile, just past a bend. From the north and I-94, take the Bridgman exit (16), go north

on Red Arrow Hwy. to Lake/Shawnee, east 8 miles to Burgoyne Rd., south on Burgoyne until it turns into Madron Lake Rd. (which is gravel). When you pass Miller Rd. look for the winery in 1/2 mile. (616) 695-5660.
Winery tours *Mem. Day through harvest in mid-October: weekdays 12-5, Sat 12-6, Sun by appt.*

What you see here is passionate, intensely serious viniculture and winemaking, without any trappings of tourism. There are no picturesque carvings or prettily landscaped terraces here. Winemaker Jim Eschner lives in a mobile home on the property. He and his partner, Franz-Bernard Lickteig, whose family has been in the wine business for 200 years, have sunk their money into excellent custom-grafted vine stock, a super-insulated winery, and the only overhead sprinkling system in Michigan, to protect the vines from early frost. (The site's only drawback is that it is in a frost-susceptible low pocket.) Their office/reception room has all the romance of a chemistry lab — which is what it also is.

At Madron Lake Hills, only vinifera grapes — classic European "noble" grapes — are grown: Riesling, Gewuerztraminer, Chardonnay, Pinot Noir, and 30 other varieties on a test basis. In 1988 the young winery's first production of Riesling and Gewuerztraminer (currently priced at $12 to $14 a bottle) won raves from leading Chicago wine people. Chicago writer/chef Michael Foley, the leading apostle of Midwest regional cuisine, was the first to spread the word about Madron Lake Hills and include both its current offerings on his wine list.

Eschner learned his winemaking lessons at nearby Tabor Hill. He was winemaker in 1974 and 1975, during its creative commune phase. There he learned his first rule: you can't get rich quick making premium wine. To make a super-premium wine, a winery needs the best grapes possible, suited specifically to its soil only through years of careful experimentation.

State-of-the-art technology won't make up for using grapes grown on contract by a supplier, Eschner feels. His vinifera grapes are too fussy to be profitable for regular contract grape-growers because they are less hardy, require more labor-intensive pruning, and more frequent fungicide applications.

Furthermore, low-wage hired help, traditionally paid by the bushel, can't be depended upon to select the very best grapes and distinguish the "noble rot" mildew from the putrid stuff. Madron Lake Hills gets friends and relatives to camp here and pick their grapes, in return for tasting wine and a fabulous meal cooked by the likes of Keith Fahmie of Les Auteurs in Royal Oak.

Eschner and Lickteig expect to invest 10 years of sweat equity in developing outstanding wines and the reputation to go with them. In aiming for the top of the market, they avoid the fad-prone middle market of $6- to $8-a-bottle wines.

Some wine critics say Madron Lake Hills' much-praised wine is likely to become Michigan's first competitor on the world market for premium wines. It's exciting to see the early stages of this pioneering effort to find the best vinifera grapes for this southwest Michigan soil. Madron Lake Hills currently has 20 acres in vines, of which 15 are in production.

To raise money and involve wine-lovers, the winery has started the **Madron Lake Hills Viticultural Society.** Membership ($25 a year) includes invitations to tastings of experimental wines and to Midwestern wine and food symposia, a newsletter, discounts, and a chance to help pick grapes at a festive harvest party in early October.

RESTAURANTS

Tabor Hill Restaurant ★

185 Mt. Tabor Rd. Exit 16 from I-94 in Bridgman. Take Lake (which becomes Shawnee) 5 miles east. (616) 422-1161. Lunch Wed-Sun 11:30-3. Dinner Wed-Sat 5:30-9. Lunches average $7.50, dinners $8.50. Full bar. MC & Visa.

See p. 38 for general description. Recommended choices are the mesquite grilled shrimp ($7.95 lunch, $12.95 dinner) and the raspberry chicken: chicken breast dipped in pecan bread crumbs and sautéed, served with light raspberry sauce ($6.95 lunch, $13.50 dinner).

Bill's Tap

8906 First at Lemon Creek, in the village of Baroda 5 milles northeast of Bridgman. Take exit 16 from I-94 toward St. Joseph. Right on Lemon Creek to First. (616) 422-1141. Lunch Tues-Fri 11-4:30. Dinner Tues-Sat, 4:30-11, Fri & Sat until 11:30. Lunches average $6, dinners $14. Full bar. Visa, MC.

Fried Canadian perch ($11.95 and $12.95) attracts diners from New Buffalo and St. Joe to this comfortable, dark pub. Dinner entrees includes soup, salad, and potato. Also popular are the deep-fried frog legs ($13.50). Each day the chef makes a special cheesecake ($2.50-$3). Lunch specials (meaty things like steak salad in a taco shell with blue cheese and broiled chicken steak) are mostly $4-5.

Apple Valley Deli

9067 U.S.31/33, 1 mile north of downtown Berrien Springs by Andrews University. (616) 471-3595. Mon-Fri 11-1:30, Mon-Fri. No alcohol or credit cards.

This vegetarian deli offers an unusual chance to sample some ingenious meat substitutes and judge for yourself whether they're worth the effort. Sam's deep-fried chicken ($1.99 for 4 pieces) is actually soya concocted to taste like chicken. The fettucine primavera ($1.99) is noodles, vegetables, and a cream sauce. There's a salad bar in addition to hot entrees. For more on health reforms of Adventists, see p. 32-33.

LODGINGS

Village Inn

(616) 471-1354
1223 St. Joseph Ave. (U.S. 31/33) a mile northwest of Berrien Springs by the Andrews University campus.
22 rooms on 2 floors. $35 single, $41 double.

Red Arrow Highway

For nostalgic fans of 1940s and 1950s roadside attractions, the Red Arrow Highway between St. Joseph and Stevensville to the north and to New Buffalo on the Indiana border is a great drive. As old U.S. 12, it was the main route from Chicago to Detroit. The name was changed to Red Arrow Highway following World War I to honor the army division in which many local men served.

Bypassed by I-94 in the 1950s, the four-lane road is still lined with a succession of aging motels, rock and antique shops, trim Cape Cod houses from the 1930s and 1940s, and jerry-built stands selling produce and pottery. The Snowflake Motel, the only motel Frank Lloyd Wright ever had a hand in, has a fascinating story of its own (pp. 46-47).

Roadhouses, tourist courts, and early drive-ins miraculously live on here, often refurbished as monuments to the childhoods of the war babies and aging baby boomers who vacationed here as kids. This trend is most pronounced towards New Buffalo, where a simple tourist court out of the movie "It Happened One Night" has been revamped into a surprisingly pleasant $70 a night bed and breakfast with Jacuzzis in every room. At the rate new galleries and such are transforming the holdovers from the early days of highway touring, the tacky charm of the Red Arrow Highway's south end should be savored soon, before it vanishes.

A long and colorful highway history

This road has been a major transportation artery since the 1870s, when area fruit farmers used it to haul produce to market. They had to use wide wagon tires to cope with its sandy surface until clay was found nearby to improve the surface. In 1912 it was macadamized (surfaced with stones in tar). The great Chicago-Detroit Auto Endurance Race was held about that time. A pit stop was in Stevensville, and the town's hotel was full. Stevensville's business district was bypassed in

Between Benton Harbor and Kalamazoo the Red Arrow Highway goes through Coloma, Hartford, Paw Paw and the heart of the Fruit Belt. It passes orchards, vineyards, some antique shops, some old towns that bear witness to hard times in agriculture, and some very old houses. The highway here is the old Territorial Road, going back to 1835. Most through traffic takes I-94, so the Red Arrow Highway makes for a pleasant drive, especially during blossom time in early May.

1928 when the road was relocated on top of the lake bluff (to avoid a dangerous curve), paved, and renamed U.S. 12.

The area's colorful history has been shaped by the highway and the wildly different subcultures from Chicago who all vacationed here. Two factions of the American Communist Party, which had been driven underground by the first Red Scare of the early 1920s, met secretly at a resort on a farm west of Bridgman in 1922. They pretended to be a singing society on vacation. The FBI infiltrated the meeting and broke it up. The communists were defended by H. S. Gray, the same Benton Harbor lawyer who had organized the development company that brought foundries to town in 1905. The case against them was eventually dismissed.

In 1929 a minor auto accident led to the investigating policeman's murder and the arrest of one Fred Dane. In his house in Stevensville on the Red Arrow Highway, a cache of weapons was discovered, including submachine guns used in the St. Valentine's Day Massacre in Chicago. Dane, a Stevensville newcomer seemingly so inept neighbors had to teach him how to shoot rabbits, turned out to be Chicago gangster Fred Burke, a probable hit man connected with Al Capone.

A tourist court with Southwestern panache

Glamor came to Stevensville in 1933, when Judge Harry Dewhirst, new leader of the House of David in Benton Harbor (p. 68), planned and opened the luxurious Grande Vista tourist court on the Red Arrow Highway, six miles south of St. Joseph. It had a Lake Michigan view, 28 deluxe units with kitchenettes, a cafe and a night club with a dance floor for 500. Most memorable was the changing illuminated fountain constructed of quartz crystals, various pieces of stalactites, petrified wood, aquamarine, and onyx. The AAA called it the finest tourist court in the Midwest.

House of David singers, dancers, and musicians shared the spotlight with local talent and celebrated performers of the big band era. The souvenir shop and museum displayed and sold mineral specimens, Navajo crafts, and artifacts from ancient New Mexico Indian cultures collected by Dewhirst. College classes came to see them.

A second Spanish-style motel was built across from the Grande Vista on the highway's east side. Ruined remnants of it can be seen today, along with a garage that was part of the original complex.

Where driving is a pleasure

This highway is rich with possibilities for people who like to stop and poke. You could spend all day driving the 30 miles from St. Joseph to New Buffalo. Period roadside architecture alternates with scenic

Grand Mere's wild dunelands, just off the tacky, touristy Red Arrow Highway, offer "an almost classic example of plant evolution and succession — from aquatic to terrestrial, from bare sand to climax forest — that began shortly after glaciers retreated from the state some 10,000 years ago," writes Tom Powers in his useful guide to Michigan parks. "Because the area is unusually protected, representatives from just about every phase of the process remain, and biologists, naturalists, and other scientists comb the park looking for often-rare species."

stretches: the dunes of Grand Mere and Warren Dunes state parks near Bridgman, and, farther south, woods that are full of sassafras's brilliant orange for outstanding fall color. Only during the 10 big summer weekends is the traffic unpleasant.

For some nice views of Lake Michigan and to see some attractive homes, take Lake Boulevard south from downtown St. Joseph. It turns into Lake Shore Drive, goes through suburban Shoreham (founded to keep out commercial development) and then hits a commercial strip with restaurants and motels where it meets I-94. About a mile and a quarter south of downtown St. Joseph, you can see a **Frank Lloyd Wright house** on a corner suburban lot overlooking the lake if you turn onto Sunnybank.

Just north of I-94 Glenlord Road leads to a pretty, cottage-y area along Lake Michigan whose low-key serenity has been recently intruded upon by some huge and ornate postmodern houses that overwhelm the area. Glenlord Road ends at public **Glenlord Beach**, with a fine view.

Frequent stretches of rural landscape south of I-94 reduce driver fatigue. For most of the small resort communities the Red Arrow Highway passes through, the highway comprises nearly the entire commercial area. Only Stevensville, Bridgman, and New Buffalo have real downtowns. The big summer homes along the lakeshore are less than half a mile west.

Note: Although this profile refers to the entire stretch of the Red Arrow Highway from St. Joseph to New Buffalo, the accompanying points of interest and restaurants only go as far south as Bridgman and Warren Dunes. See the New Buffalo chapter for Harbert, Lakeside, Union Pier, and New Buffalo.

POINTS OF INTEREST

Snow Flake Motel and Restaurant   ★★

3822 Red Arrow Hwy. (Lake Shore Dr.), 2 or so blocks north of Glenlord Rd. and about 4 miles south of downtown St. Joseph. Less than 1 mile north of I-94 exit 23 (Stevensville). (616) 429-3261. Single $30, double $35-40. Heated pool, free HBO. Bar/restaurant and cocktail lounge open 11 a.m.-1 a.m.

Staying or stopping to eat at the only motel designed by Frank Lloyd Wright gives you a unique opportunity to experience a distinctive space conceived of by the Master, and then, at the coffee shop or front desk, get an earful of complaints from the people who must operate and maintain a Wright creation.

The Snow Flake was commissioned by Sahag Sarkesian, an ebullient former Chicago rug merchant. In erecting a motel he could leave to his daughter, he insisted on "the best." Wright conceived the 56-room motel's star-shaped layout around a 2 1/2-acre court. A long reflecting pool and fountain lead to a hexagonal swimming pool with a custom-designed open steel dome and lots of hand-made geometric grillwork. The motel opened in 1962, three years after Wright's death. His associate, Wesley Peters, prepared the working drawings.

Each guest room has lots of characteristic Wright touches. Simple materials are played off dramatic spaces: cathedral ceilings and window-walls looking out on the courtyard, contrasted with low spaces for bathroom, entry, and dressing area —and hardly a right angle anywhere. Walls are painted concrete block or an early form of grooved plywood paneling. Ingenious built-in dresser-seats and a built-in desk are unusual amenities. The original 1950s-style metal chairs and tables, deemed "too cold" by recent owners, have been relegated to the terrace, but could be brought in for a more authentic Wrightian look.

While the serene guest rooms relate to the courtyard's natural beauty, the office, coffee shop, landmark pool dome, and vintage neon sign all key into the landscape of the commercial strip. The Snow Flake shows why Wright had so much influence on post-WWII roadside architecture in accentuating dramatic details you notice driving by at 35 mph.

You won't find the motel staff gushing over Wright's brilliant planning or detailing, however. "All his stuff is cosmetic," commented the desk manager. "As far as anything that makes the place run, the guy was a screwball from the word go! The roofs leak. The angled roof dumps snow into the parking lot ten feet away. In the restaurant, show me a pantry where you can store a can of soup. Climate control? You have heat or air conditioning — that's it! It's constant preventive maintenance."

The motel fell on hard times after a tragedy. Sarkisian, by all accounts a generous, optimistic man, became despondent after his daughter died in an auto accident. He lost interest in life and in maintaining his showplace motel.

Repairing the motel has challenged successive owners. Today velour bedspreads and occasional cobwebs are the kinds of things that keep the Snow Flake out of the Mobil guide. What's unique is the combination of inspiring if flawed architecture and friendly staff and patrons — the regular old-timers, truckers, and vacationers you meet in the coffee shop and bar, where high design meets Main Street America. Just don't count on a good night's sleep in a snowstorm, when wind whistles under the metal roof.

Grand Mere State Park ★

Between Stevensville and Lake Michigan, just north of the Cook Nuclear Plant. For information, contact Warren Dunes State Park, (616) 426-4013. Take I-94 exit 22 (Stevensville) and follow the signs onto Thornton Rd. (under the freeway to the west) and to the park. $18 state park sticker or $3.50/day. (616) 426-4013. **No camping or developed beach.**

The lakes, bogs, and dunes of Grand Mere are a prime example of the fascinating range of dune habitats, from desert-dry and barren to damp and fecund. The Michigan Nature Conservancy has donated this wild area to the state for use as a limited-development natural area. The park is one of only 12 National Natural Landmarks in Michigan.

Bogs, ponds, and other wetlands among the dunes prevented cottage development and left the area remarkably wild, though close to major population areas. It's wonderful for spring wildflowers and migrating birds. A new entrance road leads to a parking lot, picnic area, 2,200-foot handicapped-accessible **nature trail**, and four miles of **hiking and cross-country ski trails** circling a chain of small lakes, interdunal ponds, and cranberry and wintergreen bogs. Trails lead to Lake Michigan.

You could get disoriented and even lost here, although it's often within earshot of I-94. "Because of the checkerboard pattern of private

Looking for wintergreen berries. Illustration by Edward Shenton from *Dune Boy,* **naturalist Edwin Way Teale's boyhood memoirs. Available from Indiana University Press.**

and park property, the almost-total lack of signs, and the dense forest cover, rookie woodsmen can feel half lost and frustrated," warns Tom Powers in his guide to state parks. "But if you're a backwoods pro, dedicated birdwatcher, or experienced naturalist, you'll revel in the isolation and nearly undeveloped beauty." Since the park is new and more parcels of land are likely to be added, the trail system will likely be expanded. Call for current information.

Barb's Doll House

7451 Thornton Dr. near Grand Mere State Park. From I-94, take exit 22 (or go under the freeway near Stevensville if you're on the Red Arrow Hwy.) Go toward Lake Michigan, and turn left as soon as you pass under I-94. Go left on Thornton. At the curve you'll see signs for Barb's. (616) 465-3285. Open May 15-Nov. 15. Tues, Wed, Fri & Sat 10:30-4:30, otherwise by appt.

Barbara Hopkins loves dolls, especially the dolls of the Forties, Fifties, and Sixties that she and her daughter grew up with. They fill five rooms of a particle-board house her husband built just for her business. She has Storybook dolls, licensed

characters from Mickey and Minnie to Ronald McDonald, the Big Boy and Gerber Baby, Chrissie with grow-in hair, L'il Debbie, and lots of interesting ethnic dolls. These are not haughty, intimidating fashion plates, and the prices are generally affordable, except for special collectors' items. As Barb shows off her stock, she bubbles over with enthusiasm. "Here's Raggedy Ann and Andy, my very favorite doll!"

Cook Nuclear Plant/ Energy Information Center

On the Red Arrow Hwy. 3 miles north of Bridgman and I-94 exit 16. A traffic light is at the entrance. (616) 465-5901. Open 10-5 Tues.-Sun. year-round except for Dec. 15-Jan 15. Call for info on special weekend events. Free admission.

This nuclear plant, on the shore of Lake Michigan, is one of the largest in the country. It generates over 2 million kilowatts of electricity for users in southwest Michigan and northwest Indiana.

Next to its plant, the Indiana & Michigan Electric Company has built a tourist center that by a considerable margin is the fanciest and most expensive corporate tour facility in the state. The long paved road off the highway to the center was a huge investment in itself. The center next to the huge and somewhat ominous-looking Cook Nuclear Plant, might be mistaken for a plush, modern resort. The parking areas are tastefully landscaped, a fountain graces the entrance, and huge glass windows give the visitor inside striking views of Lake Michigan and of the adjacent plant. Visitors can also wander among multi-level terraces towards the lake, with expensive lighting, wrought-iron tables and chairs, and abundant, well-maintained shrubs and flowers.

Picnics are permitted, and there's a **snack bar** with hamburgers open on weekends.

Upstairs are an elaborate as-

sortment of fancy video games where visitors can learn about energy and how electricity is made. Every few minutes visitors are taken by a professional guide on a multi-stage presentation, one that takes them through three impressive auditoriums. In the first, the tour guide takes the stage to interact with a full-sized computer-driven robot, a presentation apparently geared for small children. Next the visitors file into a large circular amphitheater, where an elaborate model of the nuclear plant is explained. Finally, in a third and even larger auditorium, visitors see a wide-screen film about the Cook plant. One scene shows the churning area half a mile out in Lake Michigan where the plant gets its water to cool the steam which turns the giant turbines. A quarter of a mile out, the water is returned 3° F warmer.

Despite all the elaborate presentations, there is never a hint that nuclear power is controversial. It would have been more educational if the company had confronted head-on the serious issues involved.

Call for information on special **weekend events** and tours — exhibits of area artists, antiques, quilts,

From the picture window of the impressive visitor center at the Cook Nuclear Plant, you look down at the huge plant itself. Visitors aren't allowed inside, but elaborate displays and films show the plant's inner workings and scenes like the intake for the water-cooling system half a mile out in Lake Michigan.

flowers, woodcarvers, crafts, etc. — held from 10 or 11 to 5 on various weekends throughout the year.

The presence of this huge, private facility has given tiny Bridgman and its school district the strongest tax base in the state, the envy of any school administrator.

Weko Beach and Campground   ★

On Lake Michigan at the end of Lake St. just west of downtown Bridgman, about a mile north of I-94 exit 16. (616) 465-3406; call persistently. $4/day/car.

If the crowds and the vast scale of the state park at Warren Dunes are too much for you, this well-developed older park in an area of wooded dunes just west of Bridgman is an attractive option. There's a **boardwalk** (lighted at night) and **dune** stairway, a **concession** building with video games, children's **playground**, **picnic tables** with grills, and a large **campground**, partly shady, partly open. Camping fees are $14/night for modern sites, $10 for primitive sites. There's a $4 fee for the **boat launch** (small boats only).

Tabor Hill
Champagne Cellar

On the Red Arrow Hwy., just north of I-94 exit 16 in Bridgman. From I-94 exit 16, turn north onto Red Arrow Hwy. Tasting room is just ahead on the east side of the road. (616) 465-6566. Summer hours: 11-6 weekdays, 11-7 Sat, 12-7 Sun. Call for reduced winter hours; always open weekends.

This roadside sales room in an old block building doesn't look like much from the outside, but actually it is quite a pleasant place for tasting Tabor Hill's line of mostly medium-priced wines. (See p. 38 for more on Tabor Hill.) The atmosphere here may be more relaxed than at the Tabor Hill winery/tasting room/restaurant to the east, which can get crowded with large tour or lunch groups.

Visitors can see the champagne riddling racks in the basement, used in the traditional *methode champenoise.* Premium champagnes are aged for two years in the bottle. The riddling racks are huge eight-cornered, cube-shaped racks. They are turned daily from corner to corner to shake down the yeast so that it collects on the cork.

Warren Dunes State Park ★

On the Red Arrow Hwy. 3 miles south of Bridgman. From I-94, take Exit 16, follow the signs and go south. (616) 426-4013. Open all year. Gates open April 1-Sept. 30 from 8 a.m.-10 p.m. Otherwise, 8 a.m. til dusk. Restroom facilities closed Oct. 15-April 15. $3/car/day, or $15/year state parks sticker. Camping: 197 modern sites ($10/night) open all year. Half are

available on a first-come, first-served basis. Phone reservations recommended from mid-May through September.

Michigan's busiest park (in terms of revenue generated) features **spectacular views** of dunes and Lake Michigan, two and a half miles of fine sandy **beach** (the state's largest public beach), three immense bathhouse and parking areas, and hordes of people, mostly from Chicago. On a hot holiday there can be well over 20,000 people here, with 5,000 swimmers in the water. **Hang gliders** sail off the high dunes; a permit is required. Watching the sun set is another popular spectator activity. New improvements include an enlarged **concession area** with better food and a bigger camp store, and a new **picnic shelter** available to rent.

Though the park's developed part is quite intense from mid-June

The quiet beauty of winter in the dunes contrasts with dramatic ice formations in Lake Michigan. Warren Dunes State Park is open for winter camping and cross-country skiing, but the bathrooms are closed.

through mid-August, the northern two-thirds are completely undeveloped except for 6 miles of designated **hiking and skiing trails**, with two loops of 2.5 and 4 miles. You don't have to stay on the trails here, either.

It's not hard to get away from the crowds, even in a car. There's a beautiful, deeply shady, and relatively secluded **back-dune picnic area** with play equipment, grills, and restrooms. To find it, take the road that branches north just past the entrance station on the way to the beach. (The picnic area does fill up on weekends.) For the supremely fit and energetic, a much longer **foot trail** in the sand goes to the top of the **Great Warren Dune** and along the **undeveloped beach**, while a 1 1/2 mile segment climbs **Mt. Randall** between the campgrounds and the developed beach area. On a clear day you can see the Sears Tower and Hancock Building in Chicago.

The **197 campsites** are laid out for considerable privacy. Some back up to a wooded dune. Many are quite shady, though some are out in the open.

In the late 19th century most people considered sand dunes worthless if they considered them at all. Shifting sands and droughty conditions made them unsuitable for agriculture. Their only value was in providing sand for foundry molds and

---

Why dunelands fascinate scientists
The ecological systems observable in a walk through the Lake Michigan dunes range from extreme desert conditions to the constantly moist. Observing them in the late 19th century, University of Chicago botanists developed the laws of plant succession. Glenda Daniel's **Dune Country: A Guide for Hikers and Naturalists** is the classic for become acquainted with the natural history of the dunes. It's available for $8.95 at Brennen's Bookstore in New Buffalo and at area nature centers. Though it's based on the Indiana Dunes national lakeshore, it's just as relevant for Michigan's dunes.

---

building materials. But E. K. Warren, inventor of Warren Featherbone corset stays (see p. 22), was an ecologist way ahead of his time. He bought 250 acres of lakeshore dunes to preserve them for posterity. The Warren Foundation turned them over to the State of Michigan as the nucleus of Warren Dunes State Park, opened in 1938.

RESTAURANTS

Snow Flake Restaurant
See p. 46.

Tosi's Restaurant

4337 Ridge Rd. between St. Joseph and Stevensville. From the Red Arrow Hwy. just north of I-94, turn west onto Glenlord Rd., then south onto Ridge. (616) 429-3689. Closed Jan & Feb. Closed Sun. Open for dinner only through mid-April. Lunch 11:30-2:30, dinner Mon-Fri 5:30-10, Sat 5-10. Full bar. Visa, AmEx, Diners, MC.

An area institution for 50 years, Tosi's doesn't lie back on its laurels. The many Northern Italian dishes are complex, aromatic, memorable (and rich!), and the service is especially friendly and accommodating. As for atmosphere, you can have your pick, from the rustic informality of the old Sportsman's Bar and Cypress Room up front (it's not hard to imagine you're in the Italian Alps), to an enclosed patio of Florentine inspiration or the Venetian Room in gold, white, and mirrors. They were all concocted by founder Emil Tosi. His parents ran the tourist resort and cabins that used to be out back; his mother's cooking gained a reputation, and he quit his job at Chicago's Berghof to expand the resort dining room into a real restaurant. The décor and the many Italian specialties on the menu reflect his annual winter trips to Italy. Now longtime employees own the restaurant, but Tosi still consults.

Specialties (all wonderful) include malfatti (spinach rolls with mushrooms; $9.95´as a dinner, $4.95 as an appetizer), chicken breast sauteed with pancetta and rosemary with fettucine ($12.50), and barbecued babyback ribs ($14.95). There are also American-style char-grilled prime aged steaks, lamb chops, and prime rib ($14.95-$19.95), fish broiled or in butter sauces, and veal and steaks in wine sauces. Pasta and oyster antipasti are from $4 to $5.75, caesar salad $5.95 for two (all dressings are housemade). The staff doesn't mind if you order Chinese-style and share. Dinner prices include excellent minestrone, salad, and good bread.

Schuler's   ★

500 Red Arrow Hwy. just south of I-94 exit 23. (616) 429-3273. Mon-Fri: lunch 11-4, dinner 4-10. Fri-Sat until 11. Sun brunch 10:30-2, dinner 1-10. Full bar. All credit cards.

Win Schuler's grandson, also a fabled host who makes repeat customers feel like they're old friends, presides over this offshoot of the famous Marshall restaurant. It's been updated to suit the times, but still with an Old English, traditional tone. The specialty is prime rib, $16.85, with second cuts on the house. For lunch a prime rib special is $7.50. Dinners have ample accompaniments including Bar Scheeze, a Schuler's innovation, and bread sticks. Less traditional dinner entrees include Traverse Bay chicken ($13.45) — boneless breast of chicken stuffed with wild rice, dried tart Michigan cherries, and walnuts, served with peach cream sauce; and Lake Superior whitefish ($14.85) is over broiled with chardonnay and toasted pecans. For lunch chowder poured into a loaf plus salad is $6.45.

Grand Mere Inn

5800 Red Arrow Hwy. less than a mile south of I-94. From I-94 exit 222, take John Beers Rd. east, then turn south onto Red Arrow Hwy. (616) 429-3591.Tues-Fri 11-3 and 5-10. Sat 5-11. Closed Sun & Mon. Full bar. Visa, MC, Diners.

This very popular restaurant doesn't serve trendy dishes. It's very much a resort-area restaurant, relaxed and fun, the kind of place where golf-loving retired executives and their wives and young people will all feel comfortable. The menu offers a mix of traditional favorites like its specialty, slow-cooked barbecue pork ribs ($11.95/half slab), deep-fried perch ($9.95), or top-notch fresh seafood, plus some updated dishes like roast duckling with green peppercorn sauce ($11.95). Dinners include choice of two side dishes (homemade soup, a simple, crisp salad, coleslaw, or potato) along with an outstanding variety bread basket, herb butter, and liver paté. Homemade desserts are also a specialty. The Cranberry Bog bar, where you may have to wait for a table, offers a $4.50 burger, fried appetizers, and soup.

The lake view is marred by parked cars. Service in this bustling place is extremely competent, and the atmosphere is lively. Reservations are advised, and be prepared to wait.

Hyerdall's

9673 Red Arrow Hwy. just north of Shawnee Rd. at the center of Bridgman. (616) 465-5546. Just north of the light at Shawnee, on east side of highway. Tues-Sat 7 a.m.-9 p.m. Lunches average $5-6, dinners $8. No alcohol or credit cards.

This legendary restaurant, in operation since 1927, remains Everyman's diner despite its spiffed-up and expanded quarters. "Real food for real people" could be its motto. A terrific bread basket with homemade rolls and muffins comes with every dinner, and all dinner entrees are available at lunch, in addition to a sandwich menu. The broasted chicken dinner is also delicious, served with a light, fluffy biscuit, excellent mashed potatoes with good chicken gravy, and a tossed salad. Down-home specials such as meat loaf and sausage with kraut are $6-$7 with potato and salad. The day's offering of homemade pies ($1.25 a slice) includes two cream and two fruit pies using locally available fruit.

Olympus

9735 Red Arrow Highway at Lake, across from Weko Beach in Bridgman. (616) 465-5541. 6 a.m.-9:30 p.m. daily except Wed. No alcohol or credit cards.

A competent diner with early-morning hours, the Olympus also serves Greek specialties. It boasts of having the "best burgers in Bridgman." They grind their own meat here. Their big cheeseburger with french fries and cole slaw is $3.70. You also get a large amount of beer-steamed shrimp along with potatoes and a vegetable for $5.95. The specialty is sautéed fish (whitefish, orange roughy, cod, perch, walleye, scrod), which also come with potato and vegetable, are $6 to $7.

Golda's ★

Red Arrow Highway right by Warren Dunes State Park in Sawyer, 4 miles south of Bridgman. (616) 426-4114. 11-10 daily. No alcohol or credit cards.

Chicago style hot dogs are the main event at this restored wood drive-in. An arty retro flair is much in evidence; the founder is a former art student from Chicago. The basic dog is a Sinai kosher frank with mustard, pickle relish, hot pepper, tomatoes, cucumber, and onions ($2.30). The 1/3 lb. Original, on an Italian roll, is $4.45. Also popular is the 1/2 lb. double-patty Goldaburger ($3.75). They've got Ben & Jerry's ice cream

(super-premium and socially responsible), malts and other fountain treats, made the old-fashioned way, and picnic tables outside, for a refreshing break from highway driving.

> *See also: restaurant listings for nearby St. Joseph, New Buffalo and vicinity, and Berrien Springs. Bill's Tap in Baroda and the Tabor Hill restaurant are a few miles in from Lake Michigan east of Bridgman.*

LODGINGS

Lazy V Motel
(616) 465-3189.
9999 Red Arrow Hwy. south of Bridgman. 3 miles north of Warren Dunes State Park, 1 mile south of Weko Beach.
33 rooms on 1 and 2 floors. Newer rooms are larger, on one floor, have refrigerators, cost more. Phones. From May 15 thru September: $45 & $59. Off-season rates: $31 & $41. Well-run, pleasant older motel with large lawn, picnic area, basketball, horseshoes, small outdoor pool in rear.

Benton Harbor/ St. Joseph

Crossing the Blossomland Bridge over the wide St. Joseph River from St. Joseph to its "twin city" of Benton Harbor is an unforgettable and profoundly disturbing experience. St. Joe, as it's generally known, is a bustling, kempt, little town of 10,000. Perched on a hill west of the river, it has pleasant streets of turn-of-the-century homes, a pretty downtown of specialty shops in trim, turn-of-the-century buildings, and an imposing view of Lake Michigan from a fine old park on a high bluff.

Across the river is Benton Harbor. More prosperous than St. Joseph through the 1950s, it has recently won fame as one of the very most depressed cities in the entire country. 1980 census statistics showed Benton Harbor to have a higher percentage of people in poverty and a higher percentage of African-Americans (86.3%) than anyplace else in Michigan. Today roughly 70% of its 14,000 residents are on welfare. The *Chicago Sun-Times* has called it "the worst city in America." In 1988 the *Wall Street Journal* profiled it, along with East St. Louis, Illinois, and Camden, New Jersey, as "forgotten cities" much worse off than big-city ghettoes of New York, Chicago, Los Angeles, and Detroit because their tax base has vanished. So many out-of-town journalists have visited the local library to research the sensational story of Benton Harbor's fall that librarians have encased in plastic the national news clippings about the city's decline to protect against excessive wear.

Downtown Benton Harbor is finally beginning to revive. Driving along Benton Harbor's streets in 1988 at midday was an eerie experience. Almost the entire downtown was boarded up, including some impressive commercial buildings and 1920s office towers. There were few cars and no people, as if some mysterious epidemic had vanquished not just ordinary citizens but the indigent street people who populate skid rows. Benton Harbor had fallen so far that graffiti came to be viewed as a positive sign of caring.

Today things look better. Some office buildings are full, and there's even a functioning movie theater.

A dynamic small city's dramatic disintegration

It's hard to believe that up into the 1960s, Benton Harbor was a thriving, pleasant industrial city of about 20,000 with both well-paid blue-collar residents and a

Two helpful sources of area information by mail or in person:
St. Joseph Today
520 Pleasant at State (upstairs)
(616) 923-6739.
Mon-Fri 8:30-5
Southwest Michigan Tourism Council
2300 Pipestone just east of I-94 exit #29. (616) 9256301.
Mon-Sat 9-5.

substantial professional class. In 1960 blacks amounted to a 25% minority. Sedate St. Joseph on the lake enjoyed a resort-like ambiance which attracted wealthy retirees and out-of-towners. But Benton Harbor was Berrien County's shopping hub and dynamic workplace. Here money was made by turning ideas into well-known products: Whirlpool washers, Heathkit ham radios, V-M stereo sets, and Zenith TVs. Heavy industry like Superior Steel, Auto Specialties, and the Benton Harbor Malleable foundry provided good jobs for poorly educated black men from the South working their way up into the middle class.

In the memories of the Benton Harbor High School class of 1960, black and white, growing up here was almost paradise on earth: good schools, a nice mix of people, wonderful neighborhoods, parks, and beaches.

Benton Harbor, a scant half mile from Lake Michigan, was also a resort, with fancy hotels for Chicago vacationers, and trolleys to take them to Edgewater Beach (now Tiscornia Park), to Silver Beach, in St. Joseph, and to the amusement park just east of town run by the House of David sect. That picturesque park was one of Lake Michigan's biggest tourist attractions, with a zoo, train ride, theatricals and vaudeville shows, and exhibition baseball field.

A longstanding rivalry
between go-getters and gentlemen

Throughout Benton Harbor's history, residents of genteel St. Joe have felt superior to their upstart neighbor and its focus on commerce. In the late 19th century, they called Benton Harbor "Bungtown" from the name of its principal early industry, making wooden barrels for shipping fruit.

St. Joseph, established in 1831 as a shipping port, was much older, and it became more cultivated. Its pedigree went back to the great French explorer La Salle. In 1679 he had established Fort Miami at the mouth of the St. Joseph River, where the Whitcomb

An inner-city
success story
*Sherron Weeks had been a
longtime music promoter
when she moved to
Benton Harbor for a new
job that fell through. She
bought the theater for a
song and got local and
Dutch Reformed church
volunteers and funds to fix
it up as a safe haven for
kids. "It takes new blood
and holy boldness" to
make such projects work,
she says. "You have to
have a plan. It was divine
order that I got stuck here.
Hebrew 11:1 says, 'Faith
is the substance of things
hoped for, the evidence of
things not seen.'"*
*Call (616) 927-4044
for program information.
Admission is $3, movies
are screened for adoles-
cent consumption (not too
much sex or violence), and
the Friday teens are
trained to behave. Theater
tours available.*

Hotel now stands, right in downtown St. Joseph. Fort Miami had been one of the chain of trading-post forts founded by the French (Detroit was the most important) to give the French king a monopoly on the lucrative fur trade in the Upper Great Lakes.

Platted in 1831, St. Joseph was a busy lake port through the mid-1840s. It shipped wheat and flour from inland farms. At that time Benton Township, across the river, consisted of only a few pioneer farms and Eleazer Morton's tavern on the Territorial Road. But the new Michigan Central Railroad bypassed St. Joe for a more direct route to Chicago through Niles and New Buffalo. By 1849 competition from the railroad had caused St. Joe's shipping to decline.

Beginning in the 1850s, the area's aggressive business development took place in Benton Township, the future site of Benton Harbor. Out on Morton Hill on the Territorial Road, Ohio investors planted the Cincinnati Orchard, largest in the world. In 1860 three Benton Township men, Eleazer Morton, his son Henry, and Sterne Brunson, laid out the village of Brunson's Harbor. The name was changed to Benton Harbor in 1865 to honor Missouri Senator Thomas Hart Benton, a key backer of Michigan statehood.

Benton Harbor's site had a good deal of low, marshy land and enjoyed few natural advantages. But its early settlers were unusually enterprising. When St. Joseph leaders refused to help rebuild the bridge between the two settlements, Benton Harbor men decided to dig a canal so that Great Lakes ships could turn in the mouth of the broad St. Joseph River and

Chicagoans' summer holidays in Benton Harbor and St. Joseph were made convenient and fun by Graham and Morton's steamships. By the early 1900s, several ships made three trips a day. Attractions included St. Joseph's Silver Beach amusement park, the health waters and mineral baths at local hotels, trips up the St. Joseph River in a double-deck steamer, and excursions to Paw Paw Lake.

Benton Harbor's early developers were spurned by St. Joseph in trying to rebuild the bridge between the villages. So they dug their own canal and harbor connecting Benton Harbor to the mouth of the St. Joseph River and Lake Michigan. The canal and port facility was directly behind the central business block, and it brought a great deal of Chicago tourist traffic and fruit-related business to Benton Harbor. In the 1960s it was filled in and converted to parking. Today Benton Harbor's promotional handle is "Port of Opportunity," and plans are to reopen the canal and take advantage of Benton Harbor's excellent location for pleasure boating.

Lake Michigan — KLOCK PARK — Paw Paw River — turning basin — 1860 ship canal — Main St. — TISCORNIA PARK — SILVER BEACH — DOWNTOWN BENTON HARBOR — DOWNTOWN ST. JOSEPH — St. Joseph R. — St. Joseph River dock in Benton Harbor. They laid out the village with unusually wide streets, reflecting the scope of their aspirations. In 1863, the canal opened — just in time for Brunson's Harbor to profit from the Civil War by shipping grain, lumber, and fruit.

Key port of the Fruit Belt

The lack of a main railroad line delayed the development of heavy industry in Benton Harbor. But steamship traffic on the canal made up for deficient railroads by encouraging early tourism, fruit shipping, fruit packaging factories, and, in 1872, a fruit cannery. As Benton Harbor surpassed St. Joe, its older rival fought it at numerous points, instigated a border dispute, and, in 1891, refused the state legislature's recommendation that the towns merge. Nevertheless, the next year Benton Harbor supported St. Joseph in its successful effort to win the county seat from rural Berrien Springs, centrally located but without reliable rail connections.

Just after the turn of the century, Benton Harbor's growth was spurred by a large office supply firm and the arrival of a religious cult called the Israelite Tribe of the House of David. Its talented, tractable, unselfish members proved extremely successful in developing not only a famous amusement park and exhibition baseball teams, but in running the organization's farms, hotels, motels, nightclubs, and a cold-storage warehouse for fruit. Also, a development company induced a foundry and several other heavy industries to build factories in Benton Harbor.

How suburbanization and the Sixties caused Benton Harbor's abrupt fall

Many outsiders see Benton Harbor today and think they know the reason for its precipitous decline: that whites fled a growing black underclass. In fact, however, that's not the case. African-Americans seldom, if ever, *pushed* whites out of American urban neighborhoods. Rather, whites were lured by the suburbs with its new houses with nicer kitchens and bigger yards than Benton Harbor's frame housing stock from the early 1900s. Then, in classic trickle-down economics, people with less money moved into neighborhoods where lots of houses were for sale. Real estate agents reinforced fears of remaining whites and hastened the process, to their own profit. Zoning changed to multi-family, reflecting the soft market for single-family housing. Renters increased, and the percentage of homeowners decreased. Maintenance went down. Once-stable neighborhoods of homeowners became temporary way-stations.

In Benton Harbor, large numbers of black people had moved up from the rural South during World War II to work in local industries converted to war work. They

A remarkable historic event occurred at Silver Beach in St. Joseph in 1898. August Herring, who owned a St. Joseph sporting goods store, flew an airplane with a motor here. His 100-foot flight lasted 10 seconds. But his plane was considered more of a glider than an airplane, and the first powered flight was credited to the Wright brothers eight years later. A model of Herring's aircraft can be seen at the Twin Cities Airport on Territorial, just outside Benton Harbor.

Southwest Michigan's fruit belt developed when early farmers around Benton Harbor and St. Joseph noticed that their peach trees survived severe winters that killed off peach trees in other parts of Michigan. Demand for fruit in Chicago was so great and shipping from Benton Harbor so convenient that by the 1860s, productive orchards fetched $1,000 an acre.

were confined to certain areas: jerry-built rural housing in Benton Township and an old, once-German area
by the river, called the Flats. As whites in the 1950s vacated older working-class neighborhoods for the suburbs, banks and real estate agents started opening
them to blacks. So by 1960 what had been quite a seg-
regated city had a black population of 25%.

The buildup of racial tension

As more blacks moved into Benton Harbor from the
township, tensions gradually built up. The *Benton
Harbor Herald-Pallladium* (which joined the exodus
and moved across the river to St. Joe, dropping
"Benton Harbor" from its name), actually promoted
these tensions — some say, to sell more papers. Front-
page stories spotlighted common domestic disputes
and run-of-the-mill fights in the all-black Flats.

In the mid-1960s, a number of events coincided to
bring latent tensions to a head and provoke a virtual
evacuation of the city's middle class. The Twin Cities'
economy was quietly, gradually souring. Its consumer
electronics firms, Heath and V-M, were being upstaged
by the Japanese. Whirlpool, the area's major player,
was vulnerable to the vicissitudes of the building cycle,
like all appliance firms. It eventually moved some
3,000 manufacturing jobs from Benton Harbor to
Arkansas. High union wages were convincing many
Michigan firms to relocate. Foundries here and all over
Michigan seldom lasted through the 1970s.

Benton Harbor's unfortunate geography

Circumstances in Benton Harbor came together to leave
its central city far more vulnerable than others. First
there's the fact that the land area of Benton Harbor (and
St. Joe as well) is unusually small for cities of their size
(4.6 and 3.2 square miles, respectively). Michigan's pro-
township zoning laws make it hard for core cities to annex land for new development and an increased tax base.
With limited tax dollars the core cities must deal with aging housing and infrastructure and increasingly low-in-
come residents who need more services. Benton Harbor
and St. Joe were further constricted by water surrounding them.

Second, there's the unusual situation that two contigu-
ous cities are separated into two governmental units
with two separate tax bases. Logically, they should have
been combined into one city, but in 1891 St. Joseph successfully fought a state attempt to unify them under a
single city charter.

Benton Harbor is only half a city — the industrial half.
When it prospered, from 1890 through 1960 or so, it overshadowed St. Joe, the pleasant bedroom community to
its west. During the economic and social turmoil of the
1960s and 1970s, Benton Harbor would have been greatly
helped by a bigger tax base and a larger pool of concerned
and committed leaders. As it happened, it was easier for
most of the middle class to escape to St. Joe and suburban
Fairplain than learn to share power with the newly em-
powered underclass and solve the city's problems.

Michigan's generous welfare benefits doubtless drew
some jobless foundry workers, most of them black,
from nearby Chicago and Gary.

Growing nervousness among whites and pent-up
resentment among blacks set the stage for the
widespread pullout of whites (and soon for middle-
class blacks as well) during the social turmoil of the
mid-1960s. Disturbances after the Detroit riots and
Martin Luther King's assassination prompted further
white flight here and in many outstate Michigan cities.
After a black man shot a white police officer, downtown business fell off and many stores left. Picketing
by angry black groups also made it difficult to do
business in the city.

Pervasive mistrust destroyed a city

Between 1965 and 1975 blacks in the city of Benton
Harbor had gone from being a powerless minority with
no leadership experience to a controlling majority.
Benton Harbor's first black elected officials were in a
fishbowl, under minute scrutiny of the newspaper and
the big-business old guard, who found it difficult to
share power. The first black mayor, Charles Joseph, a
Republican and talented Whirlpool staffer, refused to
take orders from the establishment. He was investigated by a grand jury and driven out of office in 1976,
without being charged with anything. The prosecutor
admitted he began the probe out of mere "curiosity."

Conspiracy theories soon flourished among blacks
about plans of the white establishment to destroy the
black-run city. Many blacks didn't trust any leader
perceived to be backed by the white power structure,
which most people felt centered on Whirlpool. "Any
time a white made a statement about what's in the interests of the city, he'd be attacked by blacks," recalls a
black official. Competent candidates became hard to
find. Soon city government was run by very inexper-
ienced people. Mismanagment and nepotism — but not
necessarily corruption — were common.

City government deteriorated rapidly. Soon council
meetings were referred to as the "Monday-night fights."
Arguments sometimes came to blows. The city couldn't
collect its taxes or generate enough revenue to pay its
bills. Some homeowners didn't receive water bills for
years. At one time the entire police and fire departments were reduced to a skeleton crew and people
worried about whether the tap water was fit to drink.

Finally a turnaround

Today things are looking up for Benton Harbor. You
see cars parked downtown, and there are even two new
retail stores. (The old retailing, greatly diminished
after about 1970, completely collapsed after Penney's
and Sears left for The Orchards mall.) The principal
block of Main Street between Pipestone and Colfax

has been renovated. The seven-story Vincent Hotel, where Al Capone's gang liked to vacation, had been renovated to the tune of $3 million as a federal jobs center, then abandoned when the entire program was scrapped. Today it is back on the tax rolls as Vincent Place, occupied by the Twin Cities Chamber of Commerce and urban branches of two colleges. There are plans for renovating much remaining office space.

Long-neglected major streets have been repaved. The city government has a modest surplus and enjoys the confidence of the state, which had hassled it for years over repaying bailout loans. Picnic tables and grills are scattered throughout the long **park** that runs alongside the river and Riverview, starting at the foot of the Blossomland Bridge. The park continues to a new state **boat launch** and a private marina half a mile south. Not surprisingly, the waterfront here has become the spine for redevelopment, and several popular family restaurants are along here. Nearby, Heath/Zenith renovated a vacant K Mart for its headquarters.

The beautiful turn-of-the-century mansions out Pipestone are being restored, and a successful Chicago black family from Benton Harbor is rehabbing homes in the hospital area. Rumors and conspiracy theories have lost much of their virulence, thanks to regular meetings of community leaders and to the successful Neighborhood Information Sharing Program, the one successful legacy of Michigan State University's Benton Harbor Project.

Rebuilding the local economy?

Many of these achievements can be attributed to changes in local politics. After years of destructive disputes and pervasive mistrust, voters became totally disillusioned. Moderate voices of longtime residents and some ministers came to the fore. In 1987 voters elected a problem-solving, business-oriented white man as mayor. Bill Wolf, then 34, a quiet, unassuming West Point graduate with an M.B.A. from the University of Chicago, grew up in St. Joe.

When Wolf left the army, he found a nice house in a pleasant, upper-middle-class neighborhood of Benton Harbor. Land in Benton Harbor had become remarkably cheap, considering its good central location on water. He saw an opportunity to "grow with the city" and urged his brother to rebuild his big boat dealership in Benton Harbor after fire destroyed its St. Joseph location. Wolf was elected to city council and won broad support among moderates. He looked for economic solutions of present problems, rather than dissecting the tragic tangle of developments that started when he was in grade school and taking sides.

Wolf persuaded Steve Manning, a Harvard M.B.A., to become city manager and move into the city. (Most of the previous hired guns never really lived in Benton Harbor proper.) They have set about rebuilding the city's economic infrastructure with successful use of grants, state and local incentives, and judicious selling of tax-delinquent property the city has inherited.

In 1991, however, voters rejected Wolf and elected Emma Hall, a black nutritionist. Her platform stressed developing neighborhoods and emphasized her complete innocence of knowledge about city affairs. Wolf's pro-business push for fiscal stability was exploiting the city, some critics charged. They said it failed to create enough new jobs for black city residents. Manning was criticized and later fired for the way he dealt with layoffs of city employees.

A brick street and attractive landscaping and architecture, plus a lake view and many shops make downtown St. Joe special.

After four years of a positive cash flow in city government under Wolf and Manning, red ink is again flowing in Benton Harbor. The downtown looks better than it has in many years. But the city's direction is uncertain.

POINTS OF INTEREST

Downtown St. Joseph   ★

Centered on State between Ship and Elm. Parking lots along Lake Bluff Blvd. and Elm. Typical store hours: Mon-Sat 10-5:30, Fri until 9.

St. Joseph's downtown is one of Michigan's most attractive. Other places have more amazing buildings than these trim, mostly two-story brick storefronts from the early 20th century. And other Lake Michigan towns have more interesting and unusual shops and restaurants. But St. Joseph's total visual environment is almost unmatched, especially for people who like to get out and walk.

Just one block west of the main retail street is long **Lake Bluff Park**, looking out onto Lake Michigan and studded with a century's worth of interesting sculptures. You can stay downtown in the elegant, reasonably priced, all-suite **Boulevard Hotel** (with a great Lake Michigan view), walk over and swim at nearby **Silver Beach,** and walk to the **Curious Kids' Museum, Krasl Art Center,**

and an attractive historic district.

State Street, the main retail boulevard, is an old brick street that has been landscaped in an updated turn-of-the-century vein, with slow one-way traffic and angled parking. It has not only benches, trees, decorative lights, and planters but also sculptures and a popcorn wagon.

Nearly all the downtown stores are individually owned or part of small West Michigan chains. There's even a 92-year-old department store, **Rimes**, in a blank modernized building on State at Broad. St. Joe's shopping strength is in women's wear stores and gift, tabletop, and home accessory shops that are big on dolls and collectibles. They mostly cater to fairly conservative, well-to-do women who expect good service and get it here. **C & Company Clothiers** at 220 State (616-983-1300) stands out with its contemporary classic women's clothing. The Art Moderne space it occupies, the old quarters of the Gillespie Drug Store, is distinctive, too. Thestained glass window frieze is best viewed from inside.

Next door to it at 222 State at Pleasant is **Tootie & Dreamer's** (616-983-5228), a charming blend of earth-friendly cosmetics and toiletries with green, good-for-you gift and food items. Just around the corner at 521 Pleasant is **Elise Marie** (616-982-0550), a fresh blend of gifts, lots of interesting jewelry (from $1.50 rings to striking necklaces of charms for $30 and up), ethnic textiles, some clothing, and things like pairs of tranquility balls to roll and massage in your hand and Screaming Man cartoon T shirts ("Screaming Man responds to Regis and Kathie Lee). It's a refreshing dash of offbeat humor and exotica in staid St. Joe.

It's worth exploring other side streets off State between Lake and Main. At 611 Broad east of State, next to the perennially popular Wilbur's Ice Cream, **Gallery on the Alley** offers a colorful, upbeat melange of jewelry, contemporary handcrafts, and watercolor landscapes in a tiny space. Across the alley is a video & games arcade and Creative Teaching, a teachers' supply store.

Children are well served here, with the **Silver Balloon** (213 State; 616-983-6044), a large, attractive children's clothing store, and **The Toy Company** (505 Pleasant at State; 616-983-0600), the kind of toy store

that ignores advertised-on-TV toys in favor of colorful basics like Brio trains, dolls, blocks, puzzles, and appealingly educational toys. It has excellent selections of children's books and crafts. A new children's bookstore, **Once Upon a Time,** is at 515 Ship at State in the impressive 1912 People's State Bank Building with the distinctive domed tower.

Toward the lake at 509 Ship is another architectural landmark, the elegant neo-Tudor **Whitcomb Hotel,** now a retirement residence. It was built for resorters in 1927-28 on the very site of La Salle's 1679 fort. He built it as part of the French king's fur-trading empire. You are welcome to visit the parlor and see the mural of Pere Marquette and Louis Joliet's 1669 canoe journey down the St. Joseph River past the future site of St. Joseph.

Downtown St. Joseph has a picture-perfect small-town downtown look, a legendary ice cream parlor (Wilbur's, p. 74), and a top-notch old-fashioned variety store, complete with squeaky wood floor, in **G. C. Murphy** at 307 State.

State Street also has a good newsstand/bookstore (Majerek's), an antiques mall, and two gourmet shops. All that's missing is a movie theater — and a greater representation of brown faces. African-Americans are made to feel unwelcome in some stores, and unfortunately the feeling generalizes to the entire shopping district.

Curious Kids' Museum ★

415 Lake Blvd. between Broad and Elm. Parking next door even for buses and RVs. (616) 983-2543. Wed- Sat 10-5, Sun 12-5. Also open Tues. from June thru August. Closed 1st 2 weeks Sept. Adults $2.50, kids 3-18 $1.50.

A lot of time-tested favorites of hands-on museums are here: the giant bubble, the toaster-powered hot air balloon, a beehive, simple Body Works medical tests on yourself. And there's a lot of messing-around fun: bubble-blowing, face-painting, kaleidoscopes, a log cabin for make-believe pioneer living, trying out musical instruments. The mechanical section is a highlight, with a see-through washing machine and toilet. So is the handicap area, where kids can learn what it's like to go up a ramp in a wheelchair or wear leg braces.

The tone here is kid-centered and not irritatingly self-important. Changing **traveling exhibits** encourage repeat visits. The **gift shop** is geared to affordable, educational fun. This is a remarkably good museum, especially considering that it's a mostly volunteer effort, just opened in late 1989.

Krasl Art Center ★

707 Lake Blvd. between Park and Pearl, 3 blocks south of downtown St. Joseph. (616) 983-0271. Mon-Thurs & Sat 10-4, Fri 10-1, Sun 1-4. Free.

There's no permanent collection in this very attractive, well-run exhibit and classroom facility sponsored by the St. Joseph Art Association. So all the space in three large galleries is devoted to changing exhibits, occasionally from the Smithsonian. They are unusually diverse, accessible, and interesting to a wide variety of people. Artists range from high school students to well-known regional artists to Renoir and Leger. Samples from the 1993 schedule: "Flora and Fauna" sculptures by six artists; Chinese woodblock prints; the American Watercolor Society traveling exhibit; and one-person shows by various southwest Michigan artists.

The **gallery shop** is strong on jewelry, scarves, ceramics, and other gifts hand-crafted by area artists, as well as the usual cards and notebooks. The center sponsors a high-caliber juried **art fair** in mid July (usually the first weekend after July 4) in the extremely pleasant Lake Bluff Park across the street.

Lake Bluff Park/ Howard Bandshell ★

Begins at the foot of State St. overlooking the St. Joseph River and curves around to the west and south along Lake Blvd. 7 blocks to Park St.

For almost a century, civic groups from the D.A.R. to the American Legion and garden clubs have erected monuments along this blufftop park. There's the romantic "Maids of the Mist" fountain, a revolutionary war cannon, a bronze plaque commemorating La Salle. The monuments, combined with the view of Lake Michigan, make for a memorable walk. The most poignant monument, a bronze firefighter carrying a child, honors the 12 firemen who perished in an opera house fire. A **guide** to the monuments is available from St. Joseph Today, 520 Pleasant.

On the slope below Port Street between State and Lake is the **John Howard Bandshell**, the gift of the longtime conductor of the St. Joseph Municipal Band. (It's the only tax-supported band in Michigan.) The bandshell was designed not to block the audience's view of the lake; the musical sunsets are wonderful.

Opposite the Whitcomb Hotel on Ship at Lake, a stairway descends to the railroad station (now Zitta's cafe) and Silver Beach a few blocks away. Takeout sandwiches and salads for **lunch in the park** are conveniently available at **Clancy's Deli** on Pleasant, half a block from the park, or **Wilbur's Ice Cream & Sandwich Shop** at 609 Broad. **Mama Martorano's** (p. 74) is also a good option.

Free band concerts each Sunday and holiday begin the last Sunday in June and run through Labor Day. They're held at 3:30 and 7:30; the Upton Foundation provides **free wagon rides** drawn by Bennet's Belgians between 4 and 7 p.m. **Wednesday brown bag concerts** from noon to 1 run from the last week in June through August. Free **horse-drawn trolley rides** are Wednesdays 11:30-2:30.

The Board Walk at Silver Beach, St. Joseph, Mich.

Silver Beach County Park/ South Pier

Along Lake just south of the South Pier and St. Joseph River. Park in the lot at the foot of Broad St. 7 a.m.-10 p.m. No alcohol or pets. $3/car for nonresidents, $2 for Berrien County residents.

After the turn of the century, the Silver Beach amusement park that stood here developed into one of the premiere entertainment spots for Chicagoans (who arrived by lake steamers) and local people. The dance pavilion and and later the Shadowland Ballroom were glamorous places with big-name dance bands, visited by movie stars and celebrities. Moonlight strolls along the boardwalk, giant slides, penny arcades, picnic pavilions, and the beach itself were some of the numerous attractions. The park stayed in operation until 1971 and was torn down three years later.

Today Silver Beach is simply a beach, albeit quite a nice beach. Silver Beach Park has restrooms, changing rooms, and some picnic tables and grills. And it has access to the **South Pier**. The two piers at the

The Silver Beach boardwalk with its penny arcades and refreshment stands was already a big attraction in this postcard, circa 1910. Every year for decades new attractions were added to make it one of the leading amusement parks for Chicagoans, who arrived by steamer.

mouth of the St. Joseph River are each a thousand feet long, so they really take you out away from the land, with good views of the coast. Fishing from them can be excellent.

Sailboards can be rented at The Outpost surf shop (corner of Park and Lions' Park; 616-983-2010), and lessons made by appointment. **Zitta's,** in the old Pere Marquette train station between the beach and the stairway up the bluff to downtown, is a good place for a sandwich, ice cream, beer, or a meal (p. 74).

> **Fishing is big**
> in St. Joseph and Benton Harbor. Charter boats go out in the lake and up the St. Joseph River. Perch, coho, lake trout, and steelhead can be caught from the long piers. For more information, contact the Southwest Michigan Tourist Council, 2300 Pipestone, Benton Harbor, MI 49002. (616) 925-6301.

A few blocks farther south along Lake Michigan is **Lions' Park**, with a big picnic pavilion and **children's playground.** Swimming is not allowed here.

The cottages by Silver Beach have been used as humble year-round residences for years. Today locals are stunned to see them selling for as much as $100,000 and up, only to be torn down for elaborate new beach houses.

Tiscornia Park/ North Pier and Light   ★

At the north pier where the St. Joseph River enters Lake Michigan. From downtown St. Joseph, follow Main St./ U. S. 33 across the river, get off at the first exit and go west. From Main St. in Benton Harbor, take Water/North Shore north 1/2 mile to Klock, go west across freeway, turn left onto Ridgeway. Park is off of Ridgeway (the shore drive) at its end. $3/car, $2 for St. Joseph residents.

In the 1890s quite a resort colony clustered around the channel and lighthouse here. Now St. Joseph's

Pier fishing off North Pier.

most impressive beachfront homes are here on this spit of land, isolated by the highway and by the Paw Paw River and rail yards, which separate the area from Benton Harbor.

The big old resort hotels with their 400-foot verandas are long gone, but the 1911 Edgewater Club Annex survives with few changes at 375 Ridgeway. The three-story Romanesque light-saving station and the commandant's Shingle Style house between the pier and the marina date from 1893.

The park consists of about a quarter mile of sandy **Lake Michigan beach** with restrooms. The thousand-foot north **pier**, a popular spot for fishing, is unusual in having **two lighthouses**: an outer light, to mark the harbor, and an inner light, as an additional navigational aid. A separate part of the park west of Ridgeway wraps around the municipal **marina** on the St. Joseph River. It has **picnic tables**.

Jean Klock Park

1 mile north of Tiscornia Park along Lake Michigan, west of Lakeshore Dr./U.S. 31. See directions for Tiscornia Park, but once you get west of U.S. 33, follow the signs to Klock Park and stay to the right (north). Lifeguard on duty 1-9 p.m. Weekday fee $2/car. Weekends: $4. $1 and $2 for city residents.

Once this large park was the the pride of Benton Harbor. It is Benton Harbor's only Lake Michigan access, with almost half a mile of Lake Michigan beach. Along with the city, it fell on hard times. But a grant has not only put the buildings, playgrounds, and parking area in order again but added **hiking trails** through the dunes behind and a **lookout platform**

Today there are **picnic tables** and **grills**, a **basketball court**, **playground**, concession, bath house, and pavilion.

Rocky Gap County Park ★

Tricky to get to, though it's only 1/4 mile north of Klock Park via the beach. From U.S. 33 about 1 1/2 miles north of the St. Joseph river, take Golf Dr. north, then west on Rocky Gap to the park. From downtown Benton Harbor, go north on Water and North Shore 1 mile to Higman Park. Turn left. As soon as you pass under the highway, go right onto Rocky Gap.

Looking out onto Lake Michigan from a scenic perch on this aptly named rocky shore, the view looks more like New England than what you'd expect to see in southwest Michigan. The wild, natural setting and big beech trees across the road make you forget you're quite close to an attractive subdivision of custom homes in suburban Benton Harbor that also enjoy the panoramic lake view. There is a small, unattended **beach** for swimming and sunbathing (you climb down the steep slope to reach it). The roadside overlook has ample benches for sitting.

Benton Harbor Public Library/ House of David Room

213 E. Wall, 1 block south of Main and 1 block east of Pipestone. (616) 926-6139. Mon-Wed 9-8, Thurs & Fri 9-6, Sat 9-5.

The surroundings are an urban wasteland of empty spaces and big, impersonal buildings from the urban renewal era. But a visit to this library — modern, friendly, and seemingly unaffected by the decline of the city it serves — smashes the stereotype of Benton Harbor as uniformly down and out. It also brings home the role of libraries as refuges of order, learning, entertainment, and advancement, available to all even under difficult circumstances. A gifted director kept this library going with just a few payless paydays during the city's worst years.

Players on a House of David exhibition baseball team, in a photo from the Benton Harbor Public Library. The team started as recreation for the colony's boys. (Children were born before members converted; after, members vowed to be celibate.) They proved outstanding. Teams developed a fast-paced, showy style and caught the ball behind their backs. Non-members, including retired pitching great Grover Cleveland Alexander, played on their teams.

The chief attraction here for many visitors is the **House of David Room**. Librarian Florence Rachuig has meticulously preserved and organized all available documents, photographs, publications, clippings, and such related to that fascinating Benton Harbor religious cult and its amusement park (p. 68). She provides interested visitors with a brief printed history and brings out upon request documents selected from the contents list. She has a clear-headed, sophisticated, yet sympathetic view of these talented, gullible people.

The best introduction to the House of David is *And There Was War in Heaven*, an unpublished manuscript kept here. Neatly hand-printed and copiously illustrated, it is by the House of David's youngest member, Ron Taylor. He's under 40, grandchild of a member and himself a convert. A book is forthcoming by a St. Joseph High School history teacher who briefly lived at the House as part of his research.

Wolf's Marine

250 W. Main between downtown Benton Harbor and the St. Joseph River. (616) 926-1068. Mon-Fri 9-6, Sat 9-5.

You don't have to be a boater to find a lot of useful, fun, inexpensive stuff at this cavernous place which claims to be the largest marine accessory store in the Midwest. We saw several styles of rubber shoes for $2.99 a pair, 99¢ sunglasses, Sea Trac rubber boots on special for $12.99, and great functional clothes from slickers to warm-up suits. Shoes, including Top-Siders, are discounted at least 20% off. Then there are seashells, netting, nautical-inspired brass doodads, little shelves and brackets designed for boat interiors — not to mention fishing poles, inflatable boats, inner tubes.

In accessories, Wolf's carries many varieties of things most stores only have one or two of, and it makes a point to stock hard-to-find parts and supplies for repairing boats. "If you find a lower price advertised anywhere else, we will try to match or beat that price!!!" Wolf's promises. Other specialties at Wolf's are **windsurfing** (lessons are available through the store) and **divers' supplies**. Many kinds of smaller boats (up to 25 feet) are sold here.

After Wolf's St. Joseph location burned, owner Warren Wolf was urged to move to Benton Harbor by his brother Bill, who had a boat brokerage and repair business here. The businesses combined until Bill got into local politics and his brother bought him out. Now Bill Wolf works here part-time in addition to being mayor of Benton Harbor.

Josephine Morton Memorial Home

501 Territorial Rd. at Fourth, 1/2 mile east of downtown Benton Harbor. (616) 925-7011. Open April through October, Sun 2-4, Thurs 1-4; guided

tours by appointment. Free; donation appreciated.

This home, built in 1849, housed four generations of the Morton family — key figures in Benton Harbor history. The builders, Eleazer Morton and his son, Henry, were principal backers of the canal which gave Benton Harbor critical steamship access to Lake Michigan. They built their house here on the **Territorial Road**, on what became known as Morton's Hill. During Michigan's main pioneering years in the 1830s, this rude Detroit-to-Chicago federal highway was the main route of western settlement and an important stagecoach line. On its completion in 1835, it took five days to get from Detroit to Chicago by coach and steamship.

The Mortons were the first settlers in Benton Township. Their earlier cabin and this house also served as inns and taverns, way stations for travelers, including Indians, passing through the area.

Henry's son, James Stanley Morton, started the Graham & Morton Steamship line that spurred the area's substantial resort development. He remodeled the house substantially in 1912. With its two-story columns and portico, it resembles a grand Southern mansion more than the simple Greek Revival house and inn it once was.

By the Depression Great Lakes steamers were in decline and Morton was virtually bankrupt. He gave the house to the local Federation of Women's Clubs in 1936; members maintain it to this day as a sort of historical museum.

As historical homes go, the Morton Home is not all that remarkable. Major alterations have removed walls, and few family furnishings remain. There is a case of small antique boxes, various historical artifacts, a good deal of 19th-century clothing, and nine **period rooms,** plus a spinning area and a bathroom dating from 1912.

This neighborhood is Benton Harbor's oldest, and some of the most decrepit streets and houses are just around here down the hill. If you go east up Territorial and turn north on to Nowlen, you'll soon come to the **Morton Hill Cemetery** where the city's early founders and promoters are buried.

Historic mansions on Pipestone

From downtown, drive southwest on Pipestone to Britain.

Up the hill from the downtown lowlands, past the city's finest churches, is Benton Harbor's turn-of-the-century show street where successful businesspeople displayed their wealth. There's quite a range of styles, from Queen Anne to Arts and Crafts to Classic Revival in the grand manner, complete with big columns. The most spectacular, near the intersection of Pipestone with Britain, are being renovated. The days are over when Benton Harbor's most beautiful houses could be picked up for next to nothing. These, it's said, would fetch over $100,000, even though the neighborhood east of them is still in bad shape.

To see the choicest part of Benton Harbor, go west on Britain, turn south onto Colfax, and pass the high school and Empire Avenue. Off Colfax to the west (your left) is an extremely pleasant, well maintained area of brick colonials, Cape Cods, and ranches. Beyond it, the winding roads of large houses on large lots are outside the city limits, close to the Berrien Hills Country Club next to the St. Joseph River at Napier. On

Miami, the winding street closest to the river, there's a hard-to-see **Frank Lloyd Wright house** near Western Avenue.

House of David/ City of David   ★★

Along and off Britain Ave.,1/4 mile east of Fair (M-139). From downtown Benton Harbor, take Colfax or Pipestone south to Fair, turn left (east). From I-94, take Napier Ave. (exit 30) west to Pipestone, go northwest (right), turn north onto Fair in 1 mile, then right onto Britain. No trespassing onto private property; only use public roads.

If you ever visited the House of David amusement park and zoo here in the 1950s, rode the miniature train or drove the kiddie cars, it's an eerie sight to see the decaying state of those once-fanciful grounds. The large and ornate communal residences of the members of this religious sect are along the north side of Britain Avenue. Diamond House, at the end of a long drive on the south side of the street, housed their leader, "King Benjamin" Purnell and his retinue. Today these look like late-Victorian exuberance grown shabby.

If you turn south onto the side street of Eastman and into the overgrown amusement part, you feel like you've stumbled upon the remnants of a vanished civilization. There are beehives, broken greenhouses, tourist cabins, and orchards that produced the jams and honey and apple butter once sold here. At the back of the drive is a picturesquely rustic log structure with a long veranda. Behind it was the beer hall (the teetotaling cult wasn't averse to selling alcohol to non-members) and the band stand where musicals and vaudeville shows were held. The rusting tracks of the railroad cross a wild gully. Everywhere are pretty rock walls, terraced gardens, and the kind of cement planters that were popular garden ornaments in the 1920s.

The House of David were followers

of a Pentecostal cult founded in 18th-century England by Joanna South-cutt. She prophesied that they would have seven angelic messengers, as in the Book of Revelations, and the seventh would gather all the chosen people together to prepare for the millennium. They styled themselves after the lost tribe of Israelites, let their hair and beards grow in imitation of Jesus, and vowed to live communally without private property and abstain from sex, tobacco, alcohol, and meat.

The Israelites arrived in Benton Harbor in 1903 after the charismatic Benjamin Purnell, who claimed to have had a vision that he was the seventh messenger, located this piece of property (it had been the resort of Eastman Springs) for the anticipated "in-gathering" of the tribe. He left to gather the far-flung cult, returned in 1905 with 85 Australian followers, and went about developing the amusement park.

Purnell proved an astute businessman and showman (he was already a spellbinding preacher), and a politic leader. The House of David

A flair for the picturesque marked most House of David projects, from the memorable miniature railroad and the sparkling cement blocks in the House of David Hotel downtown to this miniature house. Rock walls and planters like these remain on the overgrown property.

was well accepted by local Benton Harbor people as a law-abiding, well-organized, and competent asset to the community. Indeed, the House of David park soon became a tourist magnet, followed by a successful nightclub and motel in Stevensville (p. 45), the House of David Hotel (now the Landmark Inn) in Benton Harbor, and a big cold storage warehouse that still stands off Riverview downtown.

Israelite missionaries generally spread their message in a low-key way and didn't actively proselytize the general public. But they sought out and cultivated especially talented people whose skills they needed — carpenters and musicians, bookkeepers and lawyers. That practice helps account for the unusual quality of all their many-sided operations, not just their song-and-dance acts and famous baseball teams, but their picturesque style of building and landscaping. "They're just the kind of people you'd expect to come to an earthly utopia," says Florence Rachuig, House of David authority whose grandparents joined. "They were simplistic, gentle, trusting people."

Their reputation was sullied by a sensational investigation in 1923. It was based on the reports of adolescent House of David girls that Purnell had sexually abused them under the guise of initiation rites. After years in hiding, he was discovered and brought to trial but soon died.

His widow, Queen Mary, fought ex-judge Harry Dewhirst over control of the community and its assets. She split off to form the City of David, which consisted of the property east of Eastman Avenue and south of Britain. The City of David didn't cater to the public, except for its vegetarian restaurant, but derived most of its income from farms and other ordinary businesses, just as the House of David had before the amusement park became so profitable. Queen Mary is buried in a small mausoleum behind the quaint kiosk, just west of today's Treasure Chest resale shop.

Many outsiders are fascinated by this strange story, have fond memories of the place, and would like to preserve some remnants of it, but the surviving House of David and City of David members have rejected all such proposals and are in the process of demolishing most structures except for the main buildings along Britain Avenue. The bandstand, beer garden, and refreshment and souvenir stands are already gone.

Illustrated lectures
about the House of David are given frequently in many Michigan cities by librarian Florence Rachuig, who maintains archives on the cult at the Benton Harbor Public Library (p.66). She goes way beyond the colorful, sensational facts of the colony to delve into the psychology of group behavior. Call the Benton Harbor Public Library (616- 926-6139) for upcoming dates.

House of David Arts

Behind Jerusalem House on Britain Ave. in the House of David complex. Take drive between Jerusalem and Shiloh houses. (616) 925-1891. Mon-Fri 8-12 and 1-5, Sat 8-12.

The sign on Britain Avenue is weathered, but the once-bustling frame shop is still open, staffed by a delightful Scottish woman who came to the House of David with her parents in the 1940s. She reportedly does a fine job of framing pictures, and she loves to talk about life in the old days at the House of David. Picture postcards and other House of David publications are sold here, as is honey produced at the commune.

Benton Harbor Fruit Market ★

1891 Territorial Rd. east of Crystal and just west of Euclid in Benton Twp. about 2 1/2 miles from downtown Benton Harbor. From I-94 and Kalamazoo, take exit 33, go north on Crystal, east on Territorial From I-94 and Chicago/New Buffalo, take exit 30, go west on Napier to Crystal, north to Territorial, then east. (616) 925-0681. Market open May 1 (with melons from south Fla.) through Oct. 31, daily and Sun 8-3., except Sat, when it closes at noon.

This big, busy 24-acre wholesale produce market in the capital of Michigan's fruit belt is the largest cash-to-grower market in the world. Hundreds of southwest Michigan farmers bring their fresh-picked produce here to deliver or sell to representatives of supermarkets and farm stands from all over the eastern United States.

The market isn't set up for outsiders. There are lots of trucks and hi-los moving around, so watch out, stay out of the way, and don't bring small children. Visitors are welcome to witness the activity. To buy anything, you have to get a $5 buyer's permit from the market.

You can join farmers and long-distance truckers having coffee and donuts or ham and eggs and Reuben sandwiches in the surprisingly good **Chuck Wagon** restaurant (open 7 a.m. until 1, later when busy).

You can also pick up some great **free handouts** in the market office, just inside the entrance to your left. Excellent free pamphlets on how to select, store, and prepare many kinds of fruits and vegetables clear up confusion on varieties of produce and include good recipes. Wonderfully **colorful posters** and **calendars** present Michigan fruits, vegetables, and farm settings in the best tradition of vivid, voluptuous orange-crate art.

Next door to the office, **Midwest Fruit Package** (616-927-3371) is geared to growers' needs. Here you can buy single wood **baskets and crates**.

The most interesting area to watch is under the big shed in the center rear. Here growers of produce that hasn't been pre-sold on contract negotiate and sell the produce on their pickups and one-ton trucks to day buyers from farm stands, independent grocers, and small chains. They come around 8 a.m. and line up, six trucks abreast, in the long east entryway before being admitted, 18 at a time, to the trading shed about 9 a.m. A U.S. Department of Agriculture reporter takes the prices from bidding there. These very prices establish wholesale price guidelines for

Wood, baskets and crates for picking and shipping produce can be bought in small quantities at Midwest Fruit Package next to the market office.

Benton Harbor's big fruit market goes back to the 1870s, when farmers' wagons lined up for a mile to load onto the fruit boats at the canal west of Main St. downtown. Steamers transported the fruit to wholesale commission houses in Chicago and Milwaukee. People from cities learned they could buy fruit in quantity direct from the farmers waiting in line. The market today is in its 5th location.

the entire state. Behind that shed are the direct-sales stalls where bigger growers rent space to sell their produce.

Only 7% of market transactions are of the direct, cash-to-grower variety that takes place in the two big sheds. The rest are deliveries on pre-sold produce. Commission houses representing firms like Meijer's, Publix (a big Florida grocer), and the Spartan grocers' co-operative have little trailer-like office cubes on long loading docks. Growers deliver produce to these commission brokers mostly in the afternoon. The brokers used to be Italian, but now they're mostly Dutch, known in the business for their negotiating and marketing savvy. The growers are largely German-Americans, descendents of fruit farmers over a century ago.

Michigan produce is the first true "vine ripe" produce to come on the national market, according to market master Marty Bass. Most other produce is picked green. Michigan commercial practice — with tomatoes, for instance — is to pick at the "breaker," when the tomato is flesh-colored. (Truly ripe produce would be overripe by the time it gets to the supermarket.) The biggest-volume produce that passes through this market are blueberries, strawberries, cantaloupe, sweet and Indian corn, cucumbers, peaches, peppers, tomatoes, and summer squash.

Scott's Produce

In front of the Benton Harbor Fruit Market (see above). (616) 926-8565. Open April 1-Oct. 31. Mon-Sat 8 a.m.-6 p.m.

This new wholesale-retail market takes advantage of its location adjacent to the fruit market to buy fresh produce from local farmers in season and, in the off-season, from the wholesalers who truck in produce to the fruit market from the South. Prices are lower than supermarkets, and the produce is fresher. Many things are available by the bushel or in large bags. Semi-tropical fruits like pineapples, citrus, and kiwi are also on hand at good prices. Specials change weekly.

Sarett Nature Center ★★★

2300 Benton Center Rd. in Benton Township. (616) 927-4832. Northeast of Benton Harbor/St. Joseph on the Paw Paw River, 1 mile n. of the Red Arrow Hwy. From I-94, take I-196 north (toward South Haven), but get off in one mile at the Red Arrow Hwy. exit, go east to Benton Center Rd., then north. From St. Joseph and downtown Benton Harbor, take Main or Territorial 2 miles east to Crystal, north (left) on Crystal to Red Arrow Hwy. **Interpretive center hours:** *Tues-Fri 9-5, Sat 10-5, Sun 1-5. Trails and parking lot open dawn to dusk.*

Sarett (it's pronounced Sa-RETT) consists of 350 acres of prime natural habitats along the Paw Paw River, northeast of Benton Harbor and its rural suburb of Benton Heights.

Here upland meadows and forests overlook lowland marshes and swamp forests going down to the riverbank. Some five miles of **trails** include a good deal of boardwalk for good viewing of wetland habitats. The trails are planned as a series of short loops, so you could plan hikes from 1/2 to 2 1/2 hours. **Cross-country skiers** are welcome in winter. Trails are not handicapped-accessible be-

Shorebirds like the virginia rail remain north in winter if there is open water, like the bayous of the Paw Paw River at Sarett.

cause of occasional stairways, but they are otherwise easy. Highway noise is occasionally distracting.

What's really special about Sarrett are the many benches and elevated towers, strategically located in different habitats. They are comfortable places for birdwatchers to sit and stay still and quiet enough to observe wildlife without disturbing it. Excellent trail booklets are available at all hours at the trailhead by the parking lot. They are keyed to views you can often enjoy while sitting. You

Towers and treehouses like this let birdwatchers look down on the bird life attracted by the wetlands of the Paw Paw River's floodplain. Here you may see the unusual prothonotary warbler, which nests only in hollow trees close to water. Owls, who also nest in dead trees in the marsh, can be heard evenings.

could even buy a nature book at the top-notch gift shop and read it comfortably as you sit by an alder thicket, pond, or tamarack bog. A tree house lets you observe from a tree canopy; a bench overlooks a dogwood thicket.

In spring and fall the river floods, attracting many migratory waterfowl. A diverse sedge meadow produces a fine fall wildflower display. Dead trees, created by rising water levels in swamp forests, have created plenty of tree holes for wood ducks, owls, woodpeckers, and the uncommon prothonotary warbler. **Cross-country ski trails** are marked for winter.

Sarett's **gift shop** is among the very best for nature publications, notecards, bird feeders, seed, and the like. The adjoining meeting/observation room has some well-done displays of mounted birds, seeds, and antlers. A naturalist is usually on hand to answer questions. The center sponsors a busy schedule of **talks**, **nature walks**, demonstrations, outings, and adults' and children's summer **classes**.

Sarett was founded by Whirlpool heiress Elizabeth Upton Vawter in 1964 and named after poet-naturalist Lew Sarett, a Northwestern speech professor and her husband's lifelong friend from their high school days in Benton Harbor. It is owned by the Michigan Audubon Society.

A splendid introduction to bird watching in Michigan is a free pamphlet from the Michigan Audubon Society detailing 15 prime sites. Look for it at Michigan Visitor Information Centers on major interstates going into Michigan, or send a self-addressed, stamped envelope with 45¢ postage to: Michigan Audubon Society, 6011 W. St. Joseph #403, Lansing, MI 48917. Their book shop carries other natural history books on Michigan.

Good Old Times Antiques

3076 Napier Rd. 2 miles east of I-94 exit 30 (Napier). (616) 925-8422. Sat 11-5, Sun 1-5, otherwise by chance or *appt.*

This large, high-quality, general-line store is warmly recommended by respected people in the business. Clocks are a specialty.

Antique Exchange

4823 Territorial in Millburg, about 5 miles west of downtown Benton Harbor. From I-94 take Watervliet exit 41, go south on M-140 4 miles, then 4 miles west on Territorial. Or take Exit 30 (Napier), go east 2 miles, north on Benton Center 3 miles, east 2 miles to Millburg. (616) 944-1987. Fri 1-5, Sat & Sun 11-5, by chance Tues and Wed (check at the strip shop next door).

"Quality antiques at affordable prices" is what this large, owner-operated, general-line shop advertises. There's quite a bit of furniture, especially Victorian and primitives.

Kountry Kubbard Antiques

4828 Territorial, across the street from the Antique Exchange. (616) 944-5227. Fri-Sun 12-5, except closed Fri Jan-April.

Furniture, primitives, and glass are specialties at this shop. On a drive along the 1835 Territorial Road, one of Michigan's first highways, you pass a lot of very old houses. In Keeler, some 10 miles east, you can have lunch or dinner at the cheery Keeler Keg, then go north and get on I-94 at Hartford.

Bay Antiques ★

5907 Mountain Rd. outside Coloma. From I-94, take Exit 39 (Coloma), turn south (left) in 1/8 mile turn on Mountain Rd. (616) 468-3221. April-Sept: open daily incl. Sun 12-5, Fri & Sat until 7. Oct-March: Wed-Sun 12-5.

A minute from the freeway, this outstanding big shop is a regular stop for antique-lovers who travel a lot on I-94. In addition to a general line and rough and refined furniture, specialties include architectural artifacts and leaded glass, bisque dolls, and oriental rugs.

The Herb Barn

1955 Greenley Ave., east of I-94. From I-94 Exit 30, head east on Napier, then turn immediately south onto Greeley. It's behind a farmhouse in about 1/4 mile; east side of road. (616) 927-2044. Mon-Fri 10-5, Sat 10-4, Sun 12-4.

Just a minute off the freeway, you can enter the slow-paced, sensuous world of aromatic plants. Nancy Johns makes the elaborate dried herb wreaths and flower arrangements that have become such a big part of the country look, but she also does more with teas, pot herbs, relaxing teasbath preparations, and medicinal herbs than many comparable small gardens.

Most impressively, she propagates and sells a hundred varieties of herbs. (Annuals are $1.75 for a 4" pot, perennials are $2.) The full selection is available from May to September, with about three dozen of the commonest plants available year-round. Nancy is happy to advise novices how to plan many kinds of herb gardens (for potpourri, tea, and kitchen use), how to incorporate herbs into landscaping, and how to plant, propagate, and harvest them.

RESTAURANTS

Wilbur's Ice Cream

609 Broad at Main in downtown St. Joe. (616) 983-5065. Mon-Sat 7 a.m.-10 p.m., Sun 1-10. No alcohol or credit cards.

Founded in 1930, Wilbur's has achieved institutional status as a survival of the old-fashioned soda and sandwich shoppe genre. Egg salad ($1.85) and chicken salad ($2.70) sandwiches are popular. Ice

cream is homemade two to three times a week, as are the waffle cones. A single dip sugar cones are $1.15, with waffel cone $1.48. Favorite flavors are butter pecan, chocolate turtle, and fresh fruit. Be sure to try the fresh red raspberry when in season.

Mama Martorano's   ★★

422 State, 1 store down from Elm in downtown St. Joseph. (616) 982-0387. Mon-Sat 11:30-11, Sun 4-10. No alcohol or credit cards.

Mostaccioli ($4.25 with salad and bread) is a favorite at this simple, self-serve Italian restaurant and carryout, along with pizza ($7.75 for a 14-inch pizza, $1 for each addition item; expect a 25-minute wait). But Mama's home cooking also shines in dishes like Chicken Vesuvius ($5.50), baked in butter, lemon, and garlic with a wine sauce, roast potato, salad, and bread. The dining room is pleasant, perfumed with garlic and tomato sauce, and decorated with amateur art for sale. You could order first and stroll around downtown St. Joe.

Zitta's at the Depot

410 Vine, St. Joseph. Take Port St. (the street that parallels the St. Joseph River just north of downtown and down the bluff a little) west to Vine at the foot of the bluff. (616) 983-6800. Mon-Fri 11- midnight, Sat & Sun 8 a.m.-midnight. Full bar. No credit cards.

The Zitta family have been cooking their hamburgers on the same grill since 1951. Now they have renovated St. Joe's 1914 train station at the foot of the bluff, between downtown (accessible by a stairway that leads to the Whitcomb and Ship Street) and Silver Beach. The décor is spare and sophisticated, but kids will like this place for the big variety of sundaes, malts ($2.75), and fountain treats. The good $1.75 hamburger is the single most popular item, along with the hot beef sandwich and southern-recipe barbecue pork sandwich (both $4.50). The interesting salads are another big draw — pasta crab salad ($5.95), or the Bombay chicken salad ($5.95), which combines chicken with slivered almonds, raisins, pineapple, with a Dijon mustard and curry dressing. Fresh vegetable stir-fries without meat ($5.50-$6.95) are a healthy option. Open for weekend breakfast.

Boulevard Hotel

521 Lake Blvd. at Pearl in downtown St. Joseph. (616) 983-6600. Breakfast Mon-Fri 6-10:30, lunch Mon-Fri 11:30-2:30, dinner Tues-Sat 5:30-10. Full bar. MC & Visa.

Sitting on a high bluff overlooking Lake Michigan, this restaurant enjoys one of the finest views along the coast. Decor is traditional, and the food, though not the equal to Tosi's (p. 51), enjoys a good local reputation. The sautée veal with shiitake mushroom sauce served over angel hair pasta pancakes ($13.95) is a house specialty. Also recommended is the salmon baked in parchment ($13.95). For lunch the favorite is the chicken stir-fry ($5.95). A dinnertime bar menu is available Monday through Saturday.

Caffe Tosi

617 Pleasant between State and Lake in downtown St. Joseph. (616) 983-DELI. My into Oct: open daily 7:30 a.m.-9 p.m. Off-season: closed Sun. No alcohol. V, MC.

New for summer '93: a casual cafe from Tosi's, the venerable Italian restaurant south of St. Joe (p. 51). Features a lighter, considerably cheaper sampling from Tosi's menu in a much more casual setting with the sunny atmosphere of a traditional Italian cafe. Croissants, muffins, and an egg casserole for breakfast; light pasta and chicken dishes plus soups, salads, cold pastas, and sandwiches throughout the day. Cappucino. espresso, and desserts. Expect excellent food and service based on Tosi's high standards.

LODGINGS

The Chestnut House
(616) 983-7413
1911 Lakeshore Dr., 10 blocks south of downtown St. Joseph

5 rooms, each with bath, on the 1st and 2nd floor. From April 15 to Oct. 15: $85-$110. Off-season $60-$85. 2 rooms have whirlpools. Ample brick Craftsman-style home with beautifully landscaped yard, deck, and small outdoor swimming pool. Guests may use cozy living room with fireplace, glassed-in front porch looking out across road to Lake Michigan. Dramatic decor with many antiques. Full breakfast, substantial hors d'oeuvres.

The Boulevard
(616) 983-6600.
521 Lake Blvd. on the bluff in downtown St. Joseph.

90 suites on six floors, all with two rooms, kitchenette with refrigerator, color TV, microwave. Mem.-Labor Day $70 (downtown view), $90 (lake view). Winter rates about $20 less. Call for weekend, romance, and golf packages. Continental breakfast included. Dining, cocktails, breakfast on the premises. Large lobby with lake view. Traditional decor in mauve and teal, lots of brass. Excellent location across from park, walking distance to Silver Beach.

St. Joseph Holiday Inn
(616) 983-7341.
100 Main (U.S. 33) in downtown St. Joseph, overlooking the Blossomand Bridge and St. Joseph River.
156 rooms on 6 floors. $66 for standard double, more for king rooms and concierge floor. Call for winter rates, golf, and winter weekend packages. Restaurant and lounge. with dancing. Some rooms with river view. Goodsized indoor pool, sauna, steam bath, and whirlpool.

Ramada Inn .
(616) 927-2421.
798 Ferguson Rd. 3 miles south of downtown Benton Harbor. From I-94, take exit 28 (M-139) north a 1/4 mile to Ferguson, turn left.
117 rooms on 2 floors. $49/single, $54 double, poolside $10 more. Completely remodeled. Restaurant, lounge, good-size pool, hot tub. Highway interchange location at one end of the busy commercial strip on M-139, but walking distance to a park overlooking the St. Joseph River.

Red Roof Inn
(616) 927-2484.
1630 Mall Dr. at The Orchards Mall on Pipestone at Napier outside Benton Harbor. From I-94 exit 29, north on Pipestone less than half a mile.
109 rooms on 2 floors. May-Oct. single $33, double $41. HBO. On the service drive to the area's leading regional mall.

South Cliff Inn
Bed and Breakfast
1900 Lakeshore Dr. in St. Joseph, about 10 blocks south of downtown. On the bluff overlooking Lake Michigan.
6 rooms with private baths. May 15-Oct. 31: $55-$90. Winter rates: $40-$60. Traditional decor. Sunroom and living room with TV. Two decks overlooking the lake. Small beach down the bluff and across the train tracks. Continental breakfast. Beautiful location in attractive neighborhood within walking distance to downtown.

---

*See also: **Snow Flake Motel** in Red Arrow Highway chapter.*

South Haven

T his growing Michigan resort town swells to over 20,000 inhabitants during the summer, then becomes a sleepy small city of 6,000 the rest of the year. South Haven's long and colorful resort history goes back to the 1880s. Pleasant countryside hotels and wide, sandy beaches extending north and south of the mouth of the Black River attracted hoards of tourists from Chicago, 80 miles away by boat. For a $1 round trip, as many as 5,000 vacationers at a time boarded giant steamers for the short voyage. South Haven's capacious harbor, formed by the Black River's wide, protected banks, provided plenty of docking room for the huge passenger steamers.

By early in the century, South Haven had become a popular vacation spot for Chicago Jews, and many of the hotels catered exclusively to them. Vaudeville performers and Yiddish stars made regular stops here at "the Catskills of the Midwest."

The town was a bustling place to visit. Beyond the beaches were an amusement park, big dance halls, a casino, and lots more. Visitors could even take smaller steamers up river a few miles to visit yet more resorts. Many South Haven resorts were simple places in the country, where guests from the city enjoyed just walking out in the meadows and orchards to enjoy the cool, fresh air and talk and talk.

South Haven, like most West Michigan ports, had originally been a lumber town. It was settled in the 1850s. Millions of logs were floated down the Black River to the city's lumber mills, and South Haven shipped millions of board feet a year to other Great Lakes ports. Business boomed after the great Chicago fire of 1871. But as the lumber gave out, commercial fishing and fruit farming, along with tourism, became the city's major sources of revenue.

The fall and rise of tourism

The tourist trade peaked the 1920s. Hurt badly by the demise of the big lake steamers, it had declined greatly by the early 1940s. By the 1960s interstates, cheap air fares, and air-conditioning had nearly finished it off, to the point that South Haven leaders regarded tourism as an inconsequential part of the local economy. South Haven's low point as a tourist destination was probably in the late 1960s and early 1970s, when alewives invaded the Great Lakes from the Atlantic via the St. Lawrence Seaway. The little fish thrived in Lake Michigan. The soaring alewife

Expensive condos
Although some South Haven condominiums can be bought for under $100,000, most cost a lot more. The exclusive Beach Club complex on North Shore Drive contains only six units. They cost $275,000 to $325,000 per condo. The 12-unit Water's Edge condos go for $250,000 and up, and the 30-unit Bent Tree condos can cost as much as $400,000.

The Eastland disaster
One of the big steamers which ferried Chicagoans to South Haven was the 5,500-passenger Eastland. Starting in 1903, it sailed the 80-mile distance at over 20 miles an hour. But one day in 1915, it capsized in the Chicago harbor, drowning 838, the greatest loss of life ever on the Great Lakes. After the disaster, passenger traffic on the lakes plummeted for years.

population was followed by giant die-offs. Dead fish washed up on the beaches, making them virtually unusable. The alewife problem was ultimately solved by the introduction of coho and chinook salmon, which preyed on the smaller fish. The giant salmon simultaneously spurred a tremendous increase in sport fishing, a great boon to this and other Michigan towns.

Now tourism is back, but on a smaller scale. Where big dance halls and resort hotels once stood, there now are condominium developments, restaurants, and shops. The building of some 250 waterfront condos since the 1970s has greatly fueled South Haven's revival. These second homes cost as much as $400,000. Today Kalamazoo, not Chicago, supplies most of the

South Haven in this 1880 bird's-eye view was already a busy fruit-shipping port of 2,000. Orchards ringed the city (visible in the upper-left corner. The Pomological Society had a hall for exhibiting fruit (numbered 8 in the left mid-foreground).

visitors and condo owners. Also important has been the massive expansion in marinas.

Today South Haven is clearly perking up. A lively new arts center has become the focus for fresh blood and energy. The attractive transient marina and South Pier riverwalk is finished. Retailing in Old Harbor Village, a pseudo-quaint riverfront complex, failed to thrive, but each season brings a new, generally improved round of tourist businesses to downtown. In a town with a small year-round population, survival is dicey. 1993's promising picks include a Mexican cafe, Mexican gift shop, and coffee and tea store on Phoenix and a deli behind Venezia restaurant on Kalamazoo. The city's biggest draw is **North Beach.** On hot summer days it is a colorful beehive of youth-

But tourism had not yet taken hold. By the early 1900s, Lake Ave. (foreground along the lake) was lined with hotels and inns. Many of them survive, several as bed-and-breakfasts.

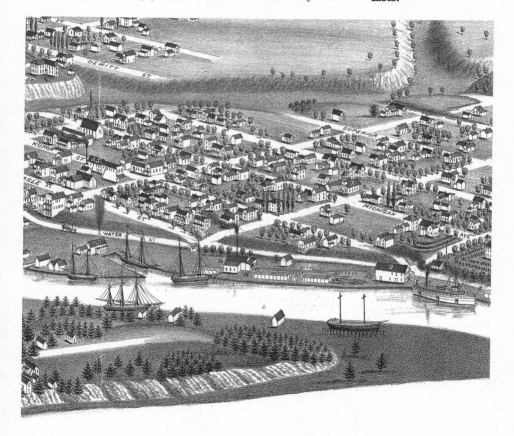

ful activity. In addition to swimming and sunbathing, there are lively volleyball games, surf sailing, and jet skiing.

The peach bust and the blueberry boom

South Haven was once famous for its peach crop. At the turn of the century, 144,000 acres were planted in peach orchards, more than all the other Michigan fruit crops combined. So abundant were the harvests that a mile-long line of peach-filled horse-drawn wagons would be waiting to load big steamers, which took the fruit to Chicago processing plants.

A devastating freeze in 1919 killed most of the peach trees, and another freeze in the 1920s led to the conversion of many of the orchards to apples. Then early, cold-resistant Haven peaches were developed here, which revolutionized the peach industry in general but failed to halt the local decline of peach-growing. California growers have come to dominate the field. When the Chicago peach processors folded in the 1950s, peach acreage plummeted to just about 8,000 acres, where it remains today.

By comparison, blueberry plantations have become a boom crop. Stanley Johnston also facilitated their emergence when he domesticated a wild high-bush variety. Unlike most other fruits, blueberries like what had been considered junk land: low, relatively chilly swamp-prone areas with dark, acidic, sandy soil. The South Haven area happens to have a lot of this land, and this region has emerged as the world's leading blueberry producer. Michigan's 15,000 acres planted in blueberries can yield three tons an acre. At the going wholesale rate of 50¢ a pound, blueberries are Michigan's best-paying legal crop. The blueberry farmers with plantations within ten or twelve miles of Lake Michigan are especially blessed. The lake effect tends to depress temperatures 3° to 4° F. in the spring, safely slowing early blossoms until danger of warmings followed by frosts are past. The lake elevates temperatures the same amount in the fall, extending the growing season. Traditionally, migrant pickers have been used to harvest the crop, but $100,000 mechanical berry pickers increasingly do the job.

Manufacturing decline

South Haven is becoming more and more dependent on tourism, and the manufacturing sector has steadily declined in recent decades. National Motors, makers of truck engine blocks, shut down in the early 1980s. Century-old Everett Piano occupied the town's largest building, an almost 350,000-square-foot factory on Indiana. Everett was famous for its sturdily built upright pianos used in school classrooms. Yamaha bought Everett in the early 1980s but shut it down in

In the 1930s, Haven peaches revolutionized the peach-growing industry. Peaches had been yellow, late-picked fruits used mostly for canning. Then Stanley Johnston, at Michigan State's South Haven experiment station, developed Haven peaches with an eye-pleasing reddish color. They can be picked much earlier, and they produce over a longer period, so eating fresh peaches has become much more popular. Red Haven is currently the most prevalent freestone variety in the world.

The resort bustle of South Haven in the 1920s was captured in the unusually interesting work of Appleyard Photography, still active in South Haven today. Old Appleyard photos are available as postcards and books at the Maritime Museum and Macdonald's drugstore on Phoenix.

1987, idling several hundred workers. The huge building is now used as a business incubator, housing several local firms. Bohn, maker of aluminum pistons used by the Big Three Detroit carmakers, is South Haven's largest employer, with 400 workers. Many South Haven residents also work in the big Palisades Nuclear Plant south of town, which employs 800.

POINTS OF INTEREST

North Beach ★

Take Dyckman west over the drawbridge to North Shore, left (south) 1/3 mile to Avery. Right to beach parking lot. No charge for parking or use of beach. 7 a.m.- 10 p.m. No alcohol.

North is one of Lake Michigan's premiere teenage and college student beaches. Summer days you will usually find it packed with kids. Volleyball games are big here, as are jet skis and windsurfing. There's a concession stand and restrooms. On summer weekends in good weather, plan to arrive early, by around 9 o'clock, to get a parking place.

To the north is another, more sedate city beach at the foot of Dyckman, separated by some private property. Parking is limited. You can actually legally travel from one beach to the other if you walk through the water, which is state-owned.

Black River boardwalks

Along the river's north side.

A 600-foot boardwalk along the Black River begins at the Maritime Museum and extends to the city marina. From it you can see the town's harbor, which today is busy with pleasure boats. Freighters haven't appeared regularly since the 1970s.

Another, shorter boardwalk extends along the river from Lake Michigan and the north pier at Lake Shore Drive to the foot of North Shore Drive.

Wind surfing on North Beach
You can rent wind surfing gear at North Shore Aqua Sports, on 114 Dyckman two blocks east of the beach. $40 for a full day; $25 for 1/2 day. Three hours of lessons (highly recommended for beginners) are $40, gear included.

Michigan Maritime Museum

On Dyckman just west of the Black River drawbridge.(616) 637-8078. May thru Sept: Tues-Sun 10-5. Oct thru April: Wed-Sat 10-4. $2.50 adults, $1.50 ages 5-12.

This small, growing museum provides a historical overview of all the people who built and used boats on the Great Lakes, from prehistory to today. The harborfront setting on the turning basin makes this a pleasant place to sit and stroll down to the marina.

Good explanatory signs accompany the exhibits. Old Great Lakes maps show what a primitive notion explorer Louis Joliet had of the region in 1673 and how quickly cartographers were able to accurately map the Lakes — by the 1680s. Indian dugout and birchbark canoes are displayed. A wonderfully detailed model of the S.S. City of South Haven (1903-1918) evokes the colorful era when thousands of Chicago tourists flooded the little town daily. The gallery for rotating exhibits features Michigan Coast Guard history (1993) and recreational boating in Michigan (1994). A new exhibit building opening in August, 1993 has a permanent Coast Guard display with three vintage craft: a 36-foot motor lifeboat and two 26-foot surfboats, with and without motors.

The **museum shop** carries a good selection of books, tapes, and teaching materials about Great Lakes maritime activities, as well as jewelry, gifts, and model boat-building kits. A **research library** with publications, journals, maps, and photographs, is open to the public by appointment.

Downtown

On Phoenix from Broadway (Business I-196) to Kalamazoo near Lake Michigan. In summer many stores stay open to 7 and on Sunday afternoon. Extra parking in lot on Huron south of Phoenix and off Broadway/ Bus.196.

Compared with many West Michigan lakeshore resort communities, South Haven feels like a real town, with more than a hint of small-town atmosphere from the 1940s and 1950s. Local businesspeople gather for a morning coffee klatsch at the soda fountain at **Macdonald's Drug Store** on Phoenix. Rich, locally made Sherman's ice cream is used in its fountain treats. The **Michigan Theater** at 210 Center has a terrific Art Deco marquee and three screens showing almost-first-run movies daily for $3, or for $1.50 if you buy a book of 15 tickets. Call (616) 637-1662 for program information. There's usually one movie for children,

The **Golden Brown Bakery** at 421 Phoenix opens at 6 daily except Sunday and offers a full bakery line, including a dense, satisfying six-grain bread and blueberry muffins and coffee cakes using fresh-frozen South Haven berries.

The most interesting shop in town is **Lighthouse Row Gallery** (616-637-2782), both for the variety of works shown by 40 Michigan artists and for its unusual multi-level layout radiating around a realistic-looking artificial tree. Media include jewelry, clay, wood, fiber, glass, sculpture, prints, and watercolors. Special invitational shows are mounted monthly. Open daily to 6, June-August & Dec. Open 5 days/week (closed Tues & Wed) May, Sept & Oct. Open weekends (Sat 10-6, Sun 12-4) in off-off-season.

The lively **South Haven Center for the Arts** occupies a splendid space in the former Carnegie Library at 602 Phoenix just east of Broadway. (616-637-1041. Open Mon-Fri 10-3 and also Sat & Sun 1-4 if an exhibit is up.) Summer '93 shows include area landscapes and handmade paper.

South Beach

Along Lake Michigan south of the Black River between Michigan Ave. and South Haven St. Free parking.

Fishing in Lake Michigan from the long pier near South Beach offers good views of the shore and good perch fishing.

Compared to North Beach, South Beach is more of the town beach, less crowded, with fewer teens from Kalamazoo and more families. It extends for five blocks along Jay Monroe Boulevard, with stairs going down to the beach. Parking is along the boulevard or in a lot below.

Across Monroe Boulevard from the south end of the beach is **Kids' Corner,** an innovative playground designed by kids in the southeast corner of Monroe Park on the corner of South Haven and St. Joseph streets.

South Pier & Light, Boardwalk

Boardwalk begins past the western end of Phoenix & Water St. Limited parking is at bottom of hill near pier.

With its catwalk to get to the lighthouse during storms, the south pier and light tower are a South Haven landmark. Visitors are welcome to walk out to the end, a popular fishing spot (see box). But don't walk out there during a stormy day. It's not all that rare for someone to be swept off the pier and drowned.

The distinctive red, conical lighthouse at the end of the pier is 36 feet high. Sheathed in steel plate, it was built in 1903. A new boardwalk now leads from the pyramidal-roofed office of the new, 36-slip transient marina to the pier.

Sherman's Dairy Bar

Corner of Phoenix & I-196, just west of South Haven. Summer hours: daily 11-11. (616) 637-8251.

Sherman's, housed next to its ice cream plant on the outskirts of town, is a popular local attraction. Its niche is between most standard ice creams and the super-rich premium ice creams. It also makes a frozen yogurt. One specialty is the $1.45 ice cream bar: 1/2 pint of ice cream on a stick, coated with chocolate and peanuts. Chocolate and peanut-covered frozen bananas are $1.10. Single cones, available in 40 flavors, are 96¢.

Dr. Liberty Hyde Bailey Birthsite Museum

*903 Bailey St. (M-43) just west of city limits. (616) 637-3251. **Mem. Day through Labor Day:** Tues & Fri 2-4:30. Other times by appointment. Donation appreciated.*

Legendary botanist Liberty Hyde Bailey grew up in this modest Greek Revival house. He graduated from Michigan Agricultural College (now Michigan State) in 1882, taught there for four years, and went on to become a famous professor of botany and horticulture at Cornell, dean of its agriculture college, influential editor,

---

Fishing on the pier

The last 100 feet of South Haven's south pier is an interesting place to fish. The 15- to 18-foot-deep water has perch, steelhead, browns, bluegill, and lake trout. Rent a casting rod for 50¢ an hour ($4 a day) at Fisherman Wharf, just left of the drawbridge next to the Maritime Museum. They've also got all sorts of bait, from minnows and wigglers for perch to spawn bags for lake trout. Daily fishing licenses are $5.25.

and chairman of Theodore Roosevelt's important Commission of Country Life. Prodigiously energetic, he became a nationally known leader in improving the quality of rural life and agricultural education at the same time as he edited encyclopaedias and wrote 63 books in many fields (on rural sociology, religion, poetry, and philosophy, in addition to horticultural references still in print today).

The home has some Bailey family artifacts, furniture, and books, but it also functions as a local historical museum, with assorted collections of rocks, arrowheads, tools, knives, medicine bottles, and old household furnishings.

DeGrandchamps Blueberry Plantation

Three miles south of South Haven on Blue Star Highway. One mile north of Van Buren State Park. July through mid-Sept. Daily 8-6.

One of the growing number of blueberry plantations in the region, DeGrandchamps has 100 acres in blueberries. In half an hour you can fill a gallon container with 6 pounds of blueberries at 75¢ a pound. You are also welcome to watch the commercial operations here as they process and pack the berries.

Throughout July you can also pick raspberries ($1.25/lb.). In August the blackberries come in, also $1.25/lb.

Van Buren State Park

On Ruggles Rd. 3 miles southwest of South Haven. Take the Blue Star Hwy. out of South Haven (all major north-south streets run into it) to Ruggles Rd. From U. S. 31/I-196, take Exit 13 and follow the signs. (616) 637-2788. $3/day/vehicle, or $15 annual state parks sticker. Camping: $9/night.

Between South Haven and Benton Harbor, driving on the Blue Star Highway and U. S. 31/I-196, you see high, rugged dunes covered with trees

to the west. The lakeshore here looks wilder and much less touristically developed than that north of South Haven. Van Buren State Park is one of the very few public access points to this stretch of shoreline. The park has a beautiful, sandy **beach**, set against a background of wooded dunes, with the usual bathhouse and concession.

But the 350-acre park is a disappointment for fishermen (there's no fishing), boaters (no boat launch), and nature lovers. There are no hiking or cross-country skiing trails or scenic drives with attractive picnic spots. (To ski, you can make your own trail.) Climbing the fragile dunes isn't allowed, and there are no dune overlooks with stairs. The 220 **modern campsites** east of the dunes, though large, are treeless and not buffered with shrubs for privacy or a natural look. They fill up on quickly on weekends; reservations are recommended. Campsites at Covert Township Park three miles south are much more attractive, beneath a canopy of big trees.

Covert Township Park

80559 32nd Ave. just west of the Blue Star Hwy. on Lake Michigan. 3 miles south of Van Buren State Park. (616) 764-1421. $2/car/day. Camping: $12/night, open April through September. Campers can stay up to a month.

The sandy **beach** here is backed by high dunes, with the **camping area** beneath big trees behind them. The 68 modern sites are separated from each other by posts and ropes, but the 12 primitive sites for tents (no electricity or water) have considerable privacy. For summer weekends, reserve in advance 1-2 weeks, though space is sometimes available on short notice. All campers can use hot showers, and there's a **camp store** with supplies, coffee, and video games. There are no boat launches or marked trails, though **cross-country skiers** use the beach.

Kal-Haven Trail
State Park ★★

38 mile path between South Haven and Kalamazoo. South Haven trailhead: on the Blue Star Hwy. at the Black River just northeast of South Haven. Kalamazoo trailhead: in Orion Twp. 3/4 mile west of U.S.-131 on 10th St. between G and H Ave. Call (616) 637-2788 for an illustrated map/ brochure. Trail fee: $2/day individual, $5/family; annual pass $10/$25. Register at trailheads or access points.

This splendid 38-mile trail over a stretch of former Penn Central railroad bed is a wonderful place for a bicycle trip. Hikers and horseback riders are also welcome. It begins by the Black River just north of South Haven and ends up just west of Kalamazoo, passing through a string of small towns which developed with the arrival of the railroad in the 19th century— Lacota, Grand Junction, Bloomingdale, Gobles, Kendall, and Alamo.

The flat trail on this old railroad right-of-way passes through varied terrain and many wildlife habitats. It starts with the flat fields, blueberry farms, and lakes just east of South Haven and ends at the hilly Kalamazoo River valley. The extensive blueberry-growing region is a delight when the berries are ripe in July. Wetlands (great for bird-watching) are common between Grand Junction and Gobles. **Lake Eleven** east of Grand Junction has a public access fishing site. **Grandpa's Animal Farm** (also

known as the Beehive Farm) is a quaint visitor attraction along the route just east of Gobles. In early May, dogwood are in bloom along the trail between Gobles and Kendall.The trail passes the village of Mentha, where an enormous barn and other buildings attest to the scope of the A. M. Todd spearmint-growing and distilling operation from the turn of the century.

Call (616) 637-2788 during business hours or write Van Buren State Park, 23960 Ruggles Rd., South Haven MI 49090 for a helpful, illustrated map/brochure with information about restaurants, food stores, bed and breakfasts, and other points of interest. Bicycle rentals ($16/day) are available at Healy True Value Hardware in Gobles on the trail. (616-628-2584). The cinder surface of the old rail bed is well drained and fairly good, except for a few spots where a person on a 10-speed with narrow tires might have to get off and push the bicycle. There are about 10 restrooms along the trail, which also goes right through three towns.

RESTAURANTS

Clementine's Saloon

418 Phoenix between Center and Kalamazoo in downtown South Haven. (616) 637-4755. Mon-Sat 11-11, Sun 12-11. Full bar. No credit cards; out-of-town checks OK.

South Haven's most popular year-round restaurant has a Gold Rush theme. It manages to pack a lot of activity into a relatively small space in an old building with beat-up wood floors. Clemtine's is not just for tourists; large portions and $5 specials on sandwiches and homemade soup draw downtown business folks and families. Soup is a good deal at $1.95 a bowl with a small bread loaf. So is the tasty wet burrito ($6.95), enough to feed two. Babyback BBQ ribs ($9.95 for a full slab) heads a dinner menu that also includes salads ($4.25-$6.95) and beer-steamed shrimp. Burgers ($4.25-$5.25) include fries and slaw or a crock of soup. The management recommends homemade onion rings served on a peg: $1.75 for 12 inches.

The Idler

515 Williams just west of the draw-bridge and overlooking the harbor. Next to Old Harbor Village shopping complex. (616) 637-8435. Open daily and Sundays April through Oct. Lunch 11-3, dinner 5-10, until 11 Fri & Sat. Full bar. Visa, MC, AmEx.

A small Mississippi riverboat, built in 1897 and refurbished as a personal partyboat in 1920 by actor Vincent Price's father, is now a restaurant. Nobody raves about the food lately, but it's a good-time place with a nice view of the harbor, and the setting is unique in Michigan. Having drinks at the open-air upper-deck bar would be pleasant. The burger and the Maui Wowee sandwich (a chicken-pine-apple-cheese and ham affair) are $5.95. Downstairs at the Magnolia Grille the mood is still casual, and the fresh seafood ($12-$14), prime rib ($12.95), and blackened prime rib with BBQ shrimp are popular dinner choices. Lighter pasta and steak salads are under $10.

Jensen's Fishery

On Dyckman at the harbor in South Haven, just over the drawbridge to your left. (616) 637-2008. Mon-Thurs 10-7, Fri & Sat 10-9, Sun 11-9. Take-out beer & wine.

Jensen's is a basic, functional fish market with tile interior walls, where you can buy fresh or cooked fish. Most business is takeout, but there are about 15 seats at three large tables overlooking the river and another 15 on a screened-in deck.

Jensen's is best known for shrimp: smoked, fried, or fresh, $12.30 a pound

cooked. Lake perch is $9 a pound, and whitefish is $6.25 a pound.

Dinners come with fries, cole slaw and roll. The shrimp dinner is $6.29, the barbecue baby-back pork rib dinner is $7.50, and the barbecue chicken dinner (1/2 chicken) is $3.95. You can also get subs and sandwiches.

Three Pelicans   ★

At the southern end of North Shore Drive. (616) 637-5123. Lunch Mon-Sat 11:30-2:30, dinner Mon-Thurs 4:30-10, Fri & Sat 4:30-11, Sun 4:30-9. Full bar. Visa, MC, AmEx.

Overlooking the Black River, the Three Pelicans (formerly Ruppert's) is the new incarnation of a large and strategically located restaurant which has changed hands and names several times. Service is good, and the food can be excellent. Quite popular is the honey-Dijon glazed salmon ($13), char-grilled with a thin glaze and served with baked potato and vegetable of the day. Also good is the Santa Fe Smothered Prime Rib ($13 large, $11 medium cut), topped with bell peppers and onions and bar-be-cue sauce. Turkey, chicken, shrimp, fish, and ribs are smoked on the premises. A full slab of the ribs is $13. For lunch, the smoked turkey makes the big, tasty Pelican Pub Club ($6) a popular choice.

The quiet main-level dining room looks out over the harbor, busy with pleasure boats. The lively lower-level bar is a destination of choice for college students.

North Beach Inn

51 North Shore Dr. From downtown South Haven, take Dyckman to North Shore, turn left, go almost to end of street. (616) 637-8943. Open April through November, possibly week-ends in December. Breakfast & lunch 7:30-1:30 daily; dinner Wed-Sat 5:30-8. No alcohol. MC and Visa.

This big Victorian house overlooking Lake Michigan and the river is your best bet for a delicious breakfast. (The inn is also a bed and breakfast.) You can choose from strawberry waffles ($4.95), blueberry pancakes ($4.25), homemade corned beef hash ($4.95), oatmeal pancakes ($4.25), and skillet potatoes ($4.95). For lunch there are a variety of sandwiches, of which the most popular may be the Chicken George ($5.50): breast of chicken with spinch, mushrooms, bacon, pineapple, and melted swiss cheese. For the evening dinners there are specials like chicken roasted in garlic and wine ($9) and spinach lasagna ($7.50).

Sea Wolf   ★★

Blue Star Hwy. 2 1/2 miles north of downtown South Haven, 2 blocks north of North Shore Drive. From I-196/U.S. 31, it's 2 blocks north of Exit 22. (616) 637-2007. Open Mother's Day into October (call for Oct. hours). Every day 5:30-9:30. Full bar. Visa, MC.

This is one of the very best fine dining restaurants in western Michigan. Reflecting the facility's past history as Weinstein's Resort, meals are complete, including matzoh ball soup, liver paté, rolls, salad, vegetables, and wonderful desserts based on local fruits in season, from strawberry shortcakes to apple pie in fall. (For less money, you can request a simpler meal.) Fresh fish is dependably excellent. Whitefish ($13) comes broiled, fried, almondine, piccata, veronique, bernaise, or tropical. Lake perch, deep fried or pan fried, is $13.25. Walleye — broiled, pan friend, or blackened — is $14. The live Maine lobster is usually $17-$18, depending on the market. Also popular are chicken Milanaise ($13) and veal Oscar ($16).

Sundays from 10:30-2, there is a feast of a brunch ($8.95), with fresh shrimp, 30 kinds of salads, eggs Benedict, cheese blintzes, honey-baked ham, prime rib, and desserts.

LODGINGS

The Colonial
(616) 637-2887.
532 Dyckman by the bridge in downtown South Haven.
24 rooms on 4 floors. Half have good views of the river. October through April: all rooms $50. May-September: $75 weekdays, Fri & Sat $85-$175. No movie channels. Full kitchens, jacuzzis. This 1890s former coffee warehouse is a local landmark.

Old Harbor Inn
(616) 637-8480.
515 Williams at the drawbridge in downtown South Haven, overlooking the river.
31 rooms on 2 floors in 4 separate buildings. Rates vary depending on river or streetside room, jacuzzi or hot tub in room. Spring & fall $60-$170, summer $75-$175, winter $50-$170. Midweek $89 special: riverside room, including $10 restaurant ticket to Clementine's and 2 movie tickets. No movie channels. Small heated pool and sauna.

Sun 'n' Sand Motel
(616) 637-2007.
Blue Star Hwy., 2 1/2 miles north of downtown South Haven. From I-196/ U.S. 31, it's 2 blocks north of Exit 22.
30 units. Open May through Sept. $35. Double rooms (no air-conditioning) in 2-story main building; newer air-conditioned double rooms in separate motel-like unit $45. $5 for each additional person. Cool quiet, rural location within a mile of Lake Michigan; orchard view across the road. Pets and kids welcome. Lap-sized swimming pool with solar cover. No cable or movie channels. The former Weinstein farm-resort goes back to the 1920s and retains the 1950s look of a past renovation. Simple, clean, tasteful accommodations at a very reasonable price. The Sea Wolf restaurant, South Haven's

best, is attached and run by owners
Jim and Susan Wolf. (He's the grandson of the resort's founder.) Golf
courses nearby; fishermen and boat
trailers welcome.

The Last Resort
(616) 637-8943.
*86 North Shore Dr. just south of
Dyckman. Open mid-April through
October, for weekends only except
daily June-August.*
Bed and breakfast with 15 rooms, all
but one with views of harbor or lake.
$48 for small rooms, $60 for large
ones, $150 for penthouse suites with
bath, kitchenette, fabulous view. 5th
day free. Air-conditioned. Shared
baths , sinks in rooms. At the center
of the beach/resort/restaurant area,
walking distance to downtown. North
Beach access 1/2 block away.
Delightful big deck, large breakfast
and living areas, small TV room.
Continental breakfast. Civil War
Captain Barney Dyckman built this
as South Haven's first resort inn in
1883; artists Wayne and Mary
Babcock restored it beautifully 100
years later. Tasteful, fresh decor.
Their jewelry and print-making studios and showroom are on the
premises.

Yelton Manor
(616) 637-5220.
*140 North Shore Dr., just south of
Dyckman.*
Bed and breakfast with 11 rooms
with baths from $85-$100, many with
lake views, $125 for very large rooms
with jacuzzis. Same location as The
Last Resort (above). Don't be put off
by the overdone landscaping or
"Chalet de la Mere" sign, which refers
to the original name of this rambling
Victorian house, built in 1873 as a
rooming house. People rave about
Yelton Manor not for its elegance (the
decor is actually country Victorian
with lots of new oak reproductions),
but because innkeeper Joyce Yelton
loves to cook and take care of people.
Starting at 5:30 she's up making bis-
cuits, home fries, egg casserole, fruit

cup, and coffee cake for breakfast.
She stocks the separate guest
kitchen with cookies, drinks, and a
homemade bedtime snack. Plus,
there's hore d'oeuvres at 5:30 — almost a meal. The huge, three-story
house has seven common areas, big
and small, for conversation, games,
and reading. Renovating this old ark
has been a retirement project for
successful Kalamazoo contractor
Jay Yelton.

A Country Place
(616) 637-5523.
*North Shore Dr. north of Base Line
Rd. about 1 1/2 miles from downtown
South Haven.*
5 rooms with baths, two share
shower. $50-$60 double occupancy,
weekday singles are $40. 10% off for 5
or more days. Quiet country setting.
Greek Revival farmhouse remodeled
with two common rooms open to
views of woods. Guests share owners'
living room. Tasteful country decor.
Full breakfast. Less than 1 block to
neighborhood beach. Three cottages
(1 on the grounds, 2 on Lake
Michigan) rent for $400-$600/week,
daily in spring and fall ($60-$85).

Lake Bluff Motel
*76648 11th Ave., overlooking Lake
Michigan less than 2 miles south of
downtown South Haven. 11th is a
short street between 76th St. (a major
street intersecting with the Blue Star
Hwy.) and the lake. (616) 637-8531.*
Rooms in 3 single-story buildings
vary in finish (cement block, ordinary
dark paneling), decor, and price. May
through Sept: $51 for a double bed,
$56 for a queen, $65 for two doubles.
Off-season: $35, $39, $47. Some
rooms with kitchenettes.
Outstanding, quiet setting on Lake
Michigan (but no beach access),
rooms face big lawn and lake, shade
trees. Decent-sized pool, wading
pool, sauna, video game room with
pool table. Picnic tables, outdoor
grilles. Uneven, but with great potential.

Pier Cove

outh of Saugatuck along Lake Michigan, it's quite a surprise to drive along Lakeshore Road (70th Street) south of M-89 and come upon numerous Greek Revival houses scattered among the beech-maple woods, in what otherwise looks like a typical leafy resort area of cottages and woodsy ranch houses favored by nature-loving retirees.

A roadside historical marker overlooking the lake explains the mystery. The Greek Revival houses are from the days when Pier Cove was a busy little lumber-shipping port, from the early 1850s until the lumber ran out after the Civil War. A long pier was built in a natural cove that gives the area its name. The histori-cal marker overlooks the pier's site. Wagons carried lumber out onto the pier to waiting lumber schooners. The adjacent village once had a sawmill, store, church, tavern, and furniture factory. Now only houses are left.

After the timber ran out, fruit from nearby Fennville's fertile orchards was shipped from the pier, but after 1871 the railroad took over most of that busi-ness. By the turn of the century, Pier Cove had acquired its present character, that of a vacation retreat hidden away in the woods. When a great storm destroyed the pier, there was no reason to replace it. The Porches (p. 90), an 1896 summer home that's now a moderately priced bed and breakfast, enables visitors to enjoy Pier Cove's quiet charms, convenient to Saugatuck but re-moved from its fun-loving bustle.

Pier Cove was briefly the busiest port between St. Joseph and Muskegon, when lumber and tanbark was shipped from its pier. After the sawmill moved to Fennville, shipping declined, then briefly flourished during the peach boom until the freeze of 1899 finished it off.

The shady, moist woods behind dunes and in the Pier Cove Creek ravine are a perfect environment for spectacular spring displays of wildflow-ers like the trillium here. The Gillette Visitors' Center south of Muskegon holds its Trillium Festival each Mother's Day.

POINTS OF INTEREST

LODGINGS

West Side Park

On Lakeshore Dr. (70th St.) 1 1/2 miles south of M-89 on Lake Michigan. From I-196, take M-89 west from Exit 34. About 9 miles west of Fennville and 6 miles south of Saugatuck.

Lake Michigan beachfront — 630 feet of it — is the big attraction of this simple, 11-acre Allegan County park, tucked between cottages and a trailer park. A stairway goes down a dune to the beach. Above, back from the road, there are picnic tables with grills, restrooms, a ball diamond, and a play area with a popular giant slide.

Wavecrest Nursery ★

2509 Lakeshore Dr., about half a mile north of the western terminus of M-89. From I-194, take M-89 west from Exit 34. About 9 miles west of Fennville and 6 miles south of Saugatuck. (616) 543-4175. Open mid-March through Dec. Mon-Sat 8-5, Sun & holidays 12-5.

Rare and unusual woody plants are the specialty of this highly picturesque nursery. Many varieties of azaleas, rhododendrons, viburnum, and many other shrubs and trees — over 900 varieties in all — are set out in beautiful display gardens, complete with rockery, ponds, and benches. Broadleaf evergreens are a specialty: mountain laurel, holly, inkberry, boxwood, euonymous, and pyracantha. Here you can get an idea of how to use plants in landscaped settings, rather than choosing among plants lined up on a nursery lot.

These plants have been grown here, so they are adapted to Michigan conditions. Wavecrest's specialty is a grafted weeping larch. There's a big selection of hostas, too, and a garden store with birdhouses, feeders, and statuary (mostly in the traditional, romantic Italian vein.

The Porches

(616) 543-4162
2297 70th St. (Lakeshore Dr.), 1/2 mile south of M-89.
Bed and breakfast with 5 rooms, each with bath. Season: May 1-Nov. 1. $55/night weekdays, $64 weekends. No smoking, no pets. Children over 12. Continental breakfast. Grills.

Built as a summer home by the owner's grandfather, the Porches has a genuine, old-fashioned cottage atmosphere: relaxed, roomy, unpretentious, full of bric à brac from many decades, with an evolving mix of cottage furniture: wicker, Mission, rustic, and moderne. All guest rooms open onto huge wrap-around porches, upstairs and down, that overlook Lake Michigan. Two rooms have lake views. Private beach access is across the street. The common area with fireplace has lots of old books and navigational charts. A sunken side garden overlooks a ravine, connecting with hiking trails through 70 acres owned by the Pier Cove Ravine Trust.

Saugatuck

T his small resort community of 1,100 enjoys one of the most pleasing settings along Lake Michigan. Nestled along the Kalamazoo River on a half-mile-long plain between hills and dunes to both east and west, it is a colorful village. bustling with boaters and tourists in summer. Because Saugatuck was largely bypassed by railroads and late-19th-century commerce, it has the quaint look of preindustrial New England, complete with a lovely old village green (p. 99) and small-scale clapboard buildings, frequently white, often embellished with Victorian gingerbread trim. Interesting pathways lead to tucked-away shops, patios, and balconies set back from the sidewalk activity. Small public gardens and parks are delightful. Bed-and-breakfast inns abound, ranging from super-elegant to country relaxed.

Long a popular resort, Saugatuck has some of the most interesting shops and galleries along Michigan's west coast. The community has been invigorated by gays and other talented urban refugees even as Saugatuck's reputation as an art colony diminishes. In marked contrast to Holland, its staid neighbor 10 miles to the north, Saugatuck has a long reputation as a more freewheeling, fun-loving place where some people stay up late dancing and drinking and Sunday is just another day for strolling and shopping.

Saugatuck is one of the most purely touristic communities in Michigan, and local shopkeepers are acutely aware that the lion's share of their business comes on 14 summer weekends. Actually, most shops stay open much longer. Even in winter most are open Saturdays and Sundays at least. Neighboring lakeside towns have picked up in tourist trade in recent years, perhaps at the expense of Saugatuck, which declined in

Saugatuck's unusual site on a bend of the Kalamazoo River near its mouth is shown in this view from Mt. Baldhead circa 1910. In the foreground is the wooded back side of Mt. Baldhead, dotted with cottages reached by the ferry. Across the river on Water St. are the since removed roller rink (center) and the Big Pavilion (far right, at the point). Above them is the town of Douglas, linked to Saugatuck by a bridge across the wide river (center rear). Among the trees on the steep hill to the left can be seen two Saugatuck churches and a school.

tourist traffic the last three years of the 1980s. Now more assertive marketing by the local visitors' bureau is seeking to reverse that decline by promoting Saugatuck's upscale bed and breakfasts and increasing its cultural attractions.

Mt. Baldhead and the Oval Beach

The downtown sits right across the Kalamazoo River from Mount Baldhead, at 262 feet one of the lakeshore's highest dunes. On top of this striking landmark rests a big, exotic-looking white ball — a highly conspicuous memento of the Cold War. It is a radar antenna installed in 1957, part of the DEW line stretching across northern America to warn of Soviet attacks from the north. Dismantled years ago and given to the city, it now holds a ship-to-shore antenna.

Mount Baldhead was used in ceremonies by Indians before they were shoved aside by white settlers. It was bought by the city in 1884 for $275 and has been used as a park ever since. Two years later the city built an elaborate pavilion at its eastern base; a more modest facility is there now.

The park became a big attraction around the turn of the century. The city had already installed a **chain ferry** at the end of Mary Street across the 150-yard span of the Kalamazoo. The ferry saved visitors the long alternate route around Kalamazoo Lake to the south. A chain ferry was revived in 1965 and remains a popular attraction today. Equally popular is climbing the **stairway to the top of Mount Baldhead**, where you can get a splendid view of the city and lake.

Turn-of-the-century visitors also used the chain ferry to get to the public beach on Lake Michigan located next to the old mouth of the Kalamazoo River. More commonly, however, bathers took one of several small steam launches down the river to the beach. That service quickly became obsolete when, in 1936, Lincoln Road was extended and the newly created Oval Beach was accessible by auto from Douglas.

The village under the sand

The very mouth of the Kalamazoo River, two miles downstream from the center of Saugatuck, was once the site of Singapore. In the mid-19th century Singapore was more prosperous and populous than its older neighbor. Saugatuck had been founded in the 1830s, well before most Lake Michigan towns, but remained tiny for decades. Singapore, more accessible to Great Lakes shipping, boomed and died with the brief but robust Michigan timber industry. Here the white pine logs which had been floated down the Kalamazoo River were sawn and shipped by boat. This pine, some of the earliest cut in Michigan, gave out by the Civil War. By 1870 the village, which once had numerous homes and commercial buildings, was abandoned.

Saugatuck's most exotic company is Broward Marine, overlooking Lake Michigan just north of the Kalamazoo River. Here Floridian Frank Denison bought the 1920 mansion built by David Cook, the wealthy Chicago publisher of religious literature. In 1978 he began building fancy yachts here. Now some 92 people make about four yachts a year, costing from $3 million to $5 million each and ranging from 77 to 121 feet in length. Made for the ocean, all of them end up in places like Florida and the Bahamas. A larger Broward Marine facility is in Florida.

Saugatuck was named Kalamazoo by town founder William Butler in 1830. Its third postmaster started using its old Indian name, Saugatuck — Pottawatomie for "river's mouth."

Saugatuck's "standing
as 'the brightest spot
on the Great Lakes'
dates from 1909, when
a group of California
investors built the Big
Pavilion (left), the
largest dance hall in
the Middle West,"
according to the
fascinating and
authoritative Allegan
County history, *River
and Lake*, by Joe
Armstrong and John
Pahl. Interurbans and
steamers disgorged
crowds of visitors at
the Big Pavilion's
doors. In May, 1960,
flames consumed the
glamorous landmark
within an hour.

Before long the shifting sands had covered the entire
town. Legend has it that the last sight of Singapore was
in 1890, when a couple of youths set fire to the top of a
gable peeking up through the sand.

The present canal linking the Kalamazoo River with
Lake Michigan cuts right through the extinct village.
Originally the Kalamazoo emptied into the lake farther
south, but since the new 1906 canal, that short stretch
has filled in on both ends, creating a lake.

Effects of a poor harbor

For various reasons, Saugatuck never became a big
city like other ports on Lake Michigan's east coast. Big
steamers couldn't easily make it up the treacherously
sinuous Kalamazoo River to Saugatuck's docks until
1906 when a new route was cut to the lake. Boat passenger service to the little village ceased almost entirely after the 1915 Eastland steamship disaster in
which 812 vacationers were drowned in Chicago.
Tourism was also hurt by the local banning of alcohol
sales in 1907, which lasted until Prohibition was lifted
in 1933.

Many pies and a few big yachts

The town's poor 19th-century harbor and failure to
attract a major railroad line doomed its industrial development. Today its chief employer, Rich Products on
Culver, makes frozen fruit pies sold to restaurants and
bakeries across the country. Working at its peak in the
late summer, Rich employs about 120, who can turn out
99,000 pies a day. For years this was the Lloyd J. Harris
Pie Company, which bought the old 1915 Co-operative
Fruit Association warehouse in 1954. Rich Products, a
Buffalo, N.Y. company best known for its non-dairy
whipped cream and coffee lightener, took over operations in 1982.

Bigger than Rich's is the Haworth office furniture
plant on Washington Road in adjacent Douglas. The
300-employee plant makes parts that go into
Haworth's office systems made in Holland.

$1 cab service
*Dial-a-ride service is
available anywhere
within the township,
including Saugatuck
and Douglas. Call 857-
1418 and allow 30
minutes for the van to
arrive. Service June-
August is 7:30-7 week-
days, 9-10:30 Sat., 9-4
Sun. Sept-May closed
Sundays.*

Parking
*is surprisingly ample
if you're willing to
walk a few blocks. If
weekend on-street
parking downtown is
tight, try the high
school up the hill on
Francis at Elizabeth,
two blocks east of
Butler, or the Rich
Products lot on Culver
east of Butler.*

Early 20th-century art colony

Ox-Bow, a summer school of art connected with the Chicago Institute of Art, still operates in Saugatuck's picturesque Old Harbor area at the remote tip of the peninsula across the river from downtown. The school was originated by Chicago artist Frederick Fursman back in 1910. He acquired the old Riverside Hotel, which had lost its clientele after the new 1906 harbor diverted tourist traffic to the north. Known as a school for serious students of art, Ox-Bow enjoys an uncommonly serene and picturesque setting. The 1940 WPA guide to Michigan pointed to an even more exotic setting nearby: "A prominent art colony has been established on the river bank. The group of tumble-down shacks and cabins, in which the artists live with Bohemian informality, is said to have been a 'hobo jungle' before they took it over." Today the town's most visible artistic presence are the unusually interesting art galleries downtown (see Downtown shopping, pp. 95-98).

Peterson's many projects

Few people have had a greater effect on the community over the past two decades than have the Peterson family from Gary, Indiana. Arriving in the 1960s, they built an authentic grist mill on Moore's Creek (now a private home), revived the chain ferry, and built the 300-slip Tower Marina on Kalamazoo Lake.

But the most audacious move of all occurred in 1965 when Rolland Peterson learned that the giant coal-burning steamer Keewatin was being retired by the Canadian Pacific Railroad. Peterson bought the majestic 346-foot-long ship, and in 1967 it was slowly towed up the Kalamazoo River. However, it ran aground right under Mt. Baldhead and remained in the middle of the river for months until the water rose enough for it to dock in Kalamazoo Lake. Today it is a visitors' sight (p. 101). Peterson also acquired the 71-foot steam tug Peter Reiss and in 1977 bought the City of Douglas for tourist excursions on the lake.

The twin cities

Saugatuck is by far better known, but adjacent Douglas is almost as big, with a population of 1,000. Back in 1890, both communities also had similar populations (900 for Saugatuck; 700 for Douglas), and both were heavily involved in the fruit-growing business. Today Douglas has virtually no shops geared to visitors. Its neighborhood of homes along Lake Michigan is appealingly serene and shady. Many residents of both communities marvel that the two little towns haven't united to save money on things like police protection. Instead, they have maintained a rather testy relationship, jealously guarding an autonomy that appears to observers more harmful than helpful.

Exploring side street and rear courtyards is part of the charm of Saugatuck. Don't miss the **courtyards** behind **134 Butler** (formerly Joyce Petter's) and alongside **The Butler Pantry**, the alleyway across Butler from the Town Common, and **Spare Parts**, a new shop on Griffith across from Toulouse restaurant. Much-praised lunches are served on the deck and porch of the **Maplewood Hotel** (p. 104). Outdoor patios at the **Loaf and Mug** on Culver and **Good Goods** on Mason are nice places to have refreshments and watch the passing scene.

Arts events — $5 art lessons and ballroom dancing in Wicks Park, chamber music concerts, and art exhibits — dominate the events calendar. Call (616) 857-5801 to get one.

Escape from the crowds and high prices and eat in the quaint village of Douglas at the quaint **Douglas Dinette** (closes at 2 p.m.) or **Auction House**, both on Center St. (Douglas's stately old schoolhouse and nicest historic buildings are up the hill on Center.) Or go to the Super Valu supermarket on the Blue Star Highway south of Center for picnic fixings to enjoy at the lakefront park at the foot of Center.

Although condominiums have sprouted up on both sides of Kalamazoo Lake, the area looks like it hasn't changed much for decades. Saugatuck decided in 1985 to ban further building of multifamily dwellings. That patently illegal move has nonetheless stopped such developments and effectively preserved the town's quaint look.

Saugatuck is one of the state's jewels, a town blessed with a combination of natural and man-made beauty. Too small to handle large crowds gracefully, it can strike a dissonant note when jammed with tourists on summer weekends. On less crowded mid-week days and in the off-season, it is a relaxed and pleasant place.

Visitor information is available at the Saugatuck/Douglas Conv. & Visitors' Bureau in the lower level of Citizens Bank on Mason at Butler, across from the drugstore, or on weekends at the kiosk on Culver at Butler, across from the Town Hall. Call (616) 857-5801; write Box 28, Saugatuck, MI 49453.

POINTS OF INTEREST

Downtown Saugatuck shops and galleries ★★

Most stores (except for seasonal T-shirt and resortwear shops) are open year-round. Many close on Tuesdays and Wednesdays after Christmas; others open only on weekends. A few close altogether for a two months or so. Call to confirm for mid-week winter trips.

Water Street along the river was once Saugatuck's main street. Now Butler, one street over, firmly holds that title, though shops are scattered all along Water and the other waterfront streets. There are a number of small antique shops along Holland (part of the Blue Star Highway) north of town before you get to U. S. 31/I-196.

Starting from Butler's northern end, here are some highlights :

das bauhaus

546 Butler. (616) 857-2495. Weekends 10-6.

Adjoining a residence, this small shop features "20th-century objects of high design," including Mission, Art Deco, and 1950s Moderne — choice and expensive. Period jewelry is also a specialty.

High Banks Wildlife Gallery

447 Butler. (616) 857-2963. Open year-round, Wed-Sun 11-5.

Bob VerPlank specializes in lim-ited-edition wildlife, nautical, and western prints, costing $200 to $1,500. Artists include Bateman, Engle, McCarthy, Wysocki, and Marris.

Wilkins Hardware

439 Butler. (616) 857-7501. Summer hours: Mon-Sat 8:30-5:30, Sun 11-2.

This beautifully maintained hardware store has been in operation since 1864. After a fire, it was rebuilt in 1904. An old hand-operated elevator goes down to the basement, where once ships' boilers were built. Owners Ron and Bonnie Wilkins live upstairs.

On nice weekends you'll often see husbands lounging on Butler Street benches, feet stretched out, while their wives browse in shops and galleries.

Water Street Galleries

403 Water. (616) 857-8485. Daily 10-5:30. Closed Tues. from Sept. through April .

Water Street carries fine contemporary art by artists from throughout the U.S. There are paintings by William Aiken of San Francisco, prints by Tony Saladino of Texas, bronze sculpture by Jean Jacques Porret of Chicago, and glass by Craig Campbell of Minnesota.

Polka Gallery

731 Water. (616) 857-2430. Year-round, daily 10-9.

Genial, European-trained oil painter John Polka has been a Saugatuck fixture since 1964. In his studio/gallery you can see him at work on his own dreamily romantic, impressionist paintings of flowers, landscapes, and figures ($100 to $5,000). Many scenes are local.

Cain Gallery

322 Butler. (616) 857-4353. Open June until Thanksgiving. June 1 through Labor Day: 11-5 daily. Thereafter, weekends until Thanksgiving.

This, the summer home of a gallery in suburban Oak Park, Illinois, is now in its 18th year. It shows paintings and prints, jewelry, sculpture, and art glass by living artists. Representative art includes contemporary impressionist landscapes, sea studies, and figure studies by William Tacke, formerly of Grand Rapids; bronzes by Kalamazoo sculptors Karla and Wiliam Tye (hers are bizarre, highly textured mythological figures, his are ballerinas and tall female nudes); and tall clay monoliths of almost-abstract female nudes with imaginative surface decorations.

Singapore Bank Bookstore

317 Butler (2nd floor). (616) 857-3785. May through Dec: Sun-Thurs 10-6. Fri & Sat 10-8. Winter: may close Tues-Thurs. Call to confirm.

Saugatuck's biggest bookstore is located in the old Singapore Bank, saved from entombment by dune sands when it was moved.

Simple old clapboard buildings, like the one housing East of the Sun gift shop, combine with attractive landscape touches to give Saugatuck a quaint, well-bred New England look.

East of the Sun

252 Butler. (616) 857-2640. Mon-Sat 10-5:30, Sun 11-5. Closed Tues-Thurs in Feb. & March.

Because this large gift shop has several talented buyers, the selection is interestingly varied. There are a number of rooms (including some upstairs) to mosey through, with lamps, home accessories, whimsical gifts, garden accessories, prints, and lots more. One room is devoted exclusively to Christmas ornaments.

The Design Shop

133 Main at Bustler, behind the village green. (616) 857-3225. Summer hours: Mon-Sat 10-5, Sun 12-5. Otherwise closed Tues & Wed, except for Jan. (weekends only) and Feb & March (closed).

Tucked away down a path from Butler Street by the park, this interior design studio also carries a relaxed mix of interesting accessories: antique prints (botanicals and birds), afghans, colorful handpainted Italian pitchers, afghans, unusual baskets, and posters from the Metropolitan Museum of Art. The little building used to be the town doctor's dispensary and infirmary; his office adjoined it on Butler, where the attractive **Poster Shop** is.

Saugatuck Drugs

210 Butler at Mason. (616) 857-2300,

Built in 1913 as the old Parrish Drug Store, this vast store is something of a hub for the town. It includes a **soda fountain, video arcade,** gift shop, and lots more, On the exterior wall facing Mason, a map of the vicinity gives a good overview of local points of interest and of the Kalamazoo River's confusing twists around Saugatuck.

Hoopdee Scootee

133 Mason. (616) 857-4141. Open April 15-Halloween. June-Aug: Mon-Sat 10-9, Sun 11-6. April, May & Sept: Mon-Fri 10-5:30, Sat 10-6, Sun 11-5:30.

This outrageous and amusing shop does a booming business in unisex clothing, Art Deco reproductions, T shirts, sculpture, and adult cards. Custom designed neon sells for $150 to $400. The decor is also fresh and inventive. The checkout counter is made out of the front of a 1 1/2 ton truck. A car door shields the dressing room.

Open Door Bookstore

403 Water St. (616) 857-4565. Mem. to Labor Day: open daily 11-5. Otherwise open Wed-Sun 11-5. Call to confirm Jan-March.

A little bit of many relaxing things, reflecting owner Ron Elmore's outlook on life. The books are strong on metaphysics and relationships, also regional, boating, American Indians, and children's. Cassettes and CDs of all forms of unusual piano music, from classical to jazz and New Age, have become a mail-order specialty; you can request to hear them. "They call me the music physician — I prescribe," Elmore jokes. Jewelry, wearable, art, and materials for massage and aroma therapy are on hand. Visitors are welcome to sit and examine the collection of "story stones" —

mixes of calcite and hematite in suggestive patterns found in beachside banks.

Good Goods

106 Mason at Water. (616) 857-1557. Mid-June-Labor Day: open daily 10-10. Jan-March: open Fri-Mon 10-6. Otherwise open 10-6 daily.

"Global art and artifacts" from traditional ethnic craftspeople and American artists. Everything from $5 Chinese papercuttings to fine contemporary gold and silver jewelry to wearable art and handblown glass perfume bottles. Many interesting textiles: caps with a Laplander look ($20-$30), elegantly draped ikat coats ($650), chenille scarves ($20-$30). African stringed instruments and drums ($5-$200), pottery flutes and ocarinas. New in 1993: an outdoor cafe with cappucino and espresso.

2nd Home

146 Butler. (616) 857-2353. May-October 10-6 daily (to 10 from Mem. to Labor Day). Call for winter hours.

Simple things with a highly refined sense of style — that's the idea behind this more distinctive new flower shop and accessories store. The fabulous cut flowers in French galvanized watering cans look like they're arranged for a photo shoot. (More plants are in the charming rear courtyard.) Things like rough cocoa mats ($35 for 4' by 6') contrast with the subtle iridescent effects of seashells. An experienced designer's touch is everywhere. The owner specializes in selling store display design work here and in Europe; the manager is a horticulturist and floral designer. Ask to see their quarterly newsletter.

Joyce Petter Gallery

New location in Douglas on the Blue Star Highway in the River Guild Gallery center just south of the bridge to Saugatuck. (616) 857-7861. Mon-Sat 10-5:30, Sun 12-5:30. Closed Jan & Feb. Call to confirm winter hours.

This interesting gallery showcases 50 high-caliber American painters, printmakers, sculptors, glassmakers, and ceramicists in an intriguing series of spaces fashioned in and around a small old hotel building. Special shows in the front galleries leave plenty of space for a wide sampling of their work. Painter Fran Larsen (formerly of South Haven, now of Santa Fe) has become a nationally popular success with her strong contemporary watercolors and acrylics, shown here since the gallery opened in 1973. One of San Francisco-based Etsuko Sakimura's gorgeous ceramic kimonos, richly glazed and embellished with scraps of antique kimonos and bits of poetry, was recently presented to the empress of Japan. Minnesotan Larry Welo's multicolor engravings are evocative appreciations of simple city houses and yards.

Look for Joyce Petter to personalize the new building with odd bits of architectural artifacts, the way the gallery's old home at 134 Butler evolved into such a charming place. Prices range from $85 or so for some small, framed prints to $7,000, with average sales of $200 to $400 for prints, $400 or $500 for ceramics (all nonfunctional and fairly large), and $1,000 and up for paintings.

Button Galleries
955 Center in Douglas, one block east of Lake Michigan. Turn west from Blue Star Hwy. onto center at the light, proceed toward lake. (616) 857-2175, Usually open daily 11-5 between mid-May and mid-Oct. Call first.

Button is one of the finest galleries in the state. The site alone is so attractive, it's worth the drive to Douglas's leafy area of summer homes along Lake Michigan. Owner Arthur Fredericks features paintings and prints by contemporary artists and 19th- and early 20th-century artists

from England and the U.S. You'll find works by batik artist John Soulliere, sculptor William Ludwig, seascape oil painter Charles Vickery, and figurative painter David Rich. Visitors can walk through the two-acre garden filled with rhododendrons and azaleas.

Coral Gables
220 Water. (616) 857-2162. Closed November through March. Open 5 days/week in April, 6 days in May, daily in summer. Call for details.

Overlooking the Kalamazoo River in downtown Saugatuck, this outgrowth of the old Saugatuck Hotel is a vast, rambling dancehall/restaurant complex, reminiscent of the big old nightspots up and down the coast that attracted thousands of partyers. The hottest action is at the **Crow Bar**, a rock 'n' roll dancehall with live band. Friday and Saturday nights from 8 to 2, it packs in a young crowd of hundreds. In the **Rathskeller** below, a trio entertains a more sedate and slightly smaller crowd of dancers. The **El Forno** dining room has the best view of the water; it serves lunch and dinner. **The Bootlegger** bar features shrimp and oysters. **The Galley**, a breakfast place open from 7 a.m. to about 2 p.m., also overlooks the water.

Wicks Park and boardwalk★
The park is on Water at Main. The boardwalk extends from the chain ferry on Water at Mary all the way past Butler to the foot of Griffith.

This peaceful park offers some lovely views over the river and across to the old cottage colony clustered around Mount Baldhead. **Riverside benches,** away from the summer crowds in downtown Saugatuck, make this a nice spot for a takeout picnic. Frequent daytime **art lessons** and evenings of **romantic dancing** or **concerts** take place around the **gazebo.** (See the events calendar at the visitors' kiosk, p. 000.)

The cinderblock public restroom

has been painted to resemble a huge outdoor copy of Georges Seurat's shimmering Pointellist masterpieces, surely a tour de force of remedial decorating.

The boardwalk extends north to the chain ferry and south to the marina, which is an intense knot of boating activity on weekends. It's much more restful in the park.

Town common   ★

On three corners of Butler at Main.

Town founder William Gay Butler, a Connecticut Yankee from Hartford, deeded these three corners as common public space. Today they continue to have a small-scale New England charm. The temple-like facade of the Christian Science church is an attractive backdrop for the delightful little garden in the southwest park. A bronze statue of a girl with a puppet commemorates Saugatuck summer resident Burr Tillstrom, creator of 1950s TV puppets "Kukla, Fran and Ollie," who died in 1985.

Across Main Street from it is a pleasant children's playground. **Tennis courts**, a **basketball court**, and another gaily painted **restroom** building are on the other side of Butler.

Queen of Saugatuck   ★

716 Water near Spear next to Gleason's Party Store, on the Kalamazoo River. (616) 857-4261.
Mem. Day to Labor Day: *trips at 1 & 3 daily, more frequently in July and Aug.* **May & Sept:** *weekends only. $5.50 adults, $3 children.*

Forget the hype they put out about this being an "authentic sternwheel paddleboat." The fake twin steamboat smokestacks and the rear paddlewheel connected to a modern metal boat aren't what make this a nifty 1 1/2 hour trip. It's the interestingly varied scenery, particularly the opportunity to go out on Lake Michigan when the waves aren't too high, and see the coastline from a distance. A bonus are the informative guides, who provide passengers with colorful commentary on what they see.

Passengers learn how the Kalamazoo Lake was created by the erosion over the centuries of the Kalamazoo River, how the little flags on charter fishing boats indicate the number of fish caught on the last outing, how the Lake Michigan shoreline has eroded 300 feet over the past 88 years, how the soft-sounding foghorn at the end of the channel going into Lake Michigan sounds much louder in a fog, and how the big lake is about 375 feet deep off Saugatuck, compared with 625 feet at its deepest point off Traverse City.

At Douglas Point, just south of the inlet, the terrain changes dramatically. To the north of the point, the shore and lake bottom is sandy, while to the south a glacial deposit has left a clay shore and gravel bottom. Passengers also see the vivid contrast of the dirty brown water from the Kalamazoo River, extending well out in bright blue Lake Michigan. The sharp "mud line" between the two is a good place to fish.

Your best bet is to take this pleasant voyage when it isn't too windy and the boat can safely make it out into Lake Michigan. The earlier in the day you take it, the more likely you'll find calm water. You can buy food and drinks, beer, and wine, on board.

Saugatuck Chain Ferry

Runs from Mary and Water in downtown Saugatuck to Ferry St, across the Kalamazoo River. 9-9, Memorial Day through Labor Day. Adults $1; children 50¢ one way. Available on demand.

This historic ferry crossing isn't all that interesting a ride, but it gets you to the other side without an automobile, avoiding parking hassles.

The crossing does have an interesting history. A chain ferry, operated by a hand crank aboard the vessel, has been operating here since 1838. Not, mind you, the frilly mock-Victorian white ferry used today by tourist

but much larger barges which provided a real service in saving someone with horse and wagon a five- to six-hour trip around Kalamazoo Lake to get to the other side of the river.

Mount Baldhead ★★

Park St. across the Kalamazoo River from downtown. Reach on foot by the chain ferry or arrive by car through Douglas.

Named for its once-bare crown before trees were planted on top, this 262-foot dune is the tallest in the region. It provides a superb view of Saugatuck, Lake Kalamazoo, and Douglas. There are no roads to the summit, so ascending it takes a rather arduous walk of 282 steps from the east or an even more difficult walk up a sand path from the Lake Michigan beach.

Pleasant picnic

For a delightful car-free picnic, you can pick up tasty sandwiches at Butler's Pantry Deli at 121 Butler. (They also have excellent wines as well as pop.) Take the chain ferry across the river and head north along Park St. to the foot of Mt. Baldhead. You can picnic either on the top or on the deck overlooking the river.

The old 40-foot observation tower atop Mt. Baldhead attracted visitors from hundreds of miles away around the turn of the century. It was torn down during World War I. Currently a deck overlooking Saugatuck greets tourists who climb the big dune.

The wooden stairway begins at the park across the street from the river, a few hundred yards north of the ferry landing. The stair entrance can be easy to miss; it's just to the right of the park restrooms.

On top you'll find the old 1957 radar dome, now used to house a marine ship-to-shore radio antenna.

From the top there are two interesting **trails,** one to the north and one to the south. They lead to scenic views of the lake and forested surroundings.

Oval Beach

Just west of Mt. Baldhead. Take Blue Star Highway to Douglas, west on Center, north on Park, and west on Lincoln. (616) 857-1121. $3 per car weekdays, $5 weekends.

This popular city-owned beach is just south of the original outlet of the Kalamazoo River. The mouth filled in naturally when the 1906 outlet to the north was dug.

The city provides an unusually complete facility here which includes restrooms, changing rooms, snack stand (chili is $2 a bowl), a game arcade, a big parking lot, and a place to buy beach paraphernalia. You can rent **giant tubes** for $1 an hour and also chairs and cabanas.

Just above the beach, signs point to some quite nice **walks up on the dunes**. The one which heads north along the ridge is especially recommended for its view over the lake.

Ox-Bow

Take Blue Star Highway to Center (at the light) in Douglas, west to Park, Park north to Ox-Bow. (312) 899-5130.

A 75-year-old summer art school, Ox-Bow occupies a picturesque area which was once on the bank of the Kalamazoo River. The 1906 channel to Lake Michigan left this part of the river stranded, forming an elongated lake. The 19th-century riverbank hotel forms the center of the rustic art school today.

The school, linked with the famed Art Institute of Chicago, claims it occupies 110 acres of land, although it actually owns only six acres. The surrounding land has been willed to the city with provision for its use by the school (as well as anyone else who cares to walk through it) as long as the hotel remains a nonprofit art school. But Ox-Bow over the years has insulated itself from the village of Saugatuck, not welcoming visitors and creating some degree of friction, which more recently it has attempted to bridge with its frequent **$5 public art lessons** in Wicks Park (p. 94).

Courses here included painting, papermaking, glassblowing, fiber, sculpture, and lithography. Those accepted to study pay $400 for 6-day workshops and $1,060 for 15-day workshops.

S.S. Keewatin ship museum ★★

In Harbour Village, on south bank of Kalamazoo Lake in Douglas. Take Blue Star Hwy. to Union in Douglas, north to Harbour Village. (616) 857-2107. Guided tours every half-hour 10-4:30 daily, Mem. Day to Labor Day. $3 adults, children 6-12 $1.50.

The 336-foot *Keewatin* , permanently moored here, is a rare vestige of the wonderful era of steamship travel on the Great Lakes. At the turn of the century, you could catch any of dozens of passenger boats and sail cheaply and in splendor for days on end. The *Keewatin*, in service until 1965, was one of the last of those big boats. Its route was from eastern Lake Huron to Thunder Bay on western Lake Superior, a six-day round trip. In 1908 it cost $30, including meals.

Now the *Keewatin* is a nautical museum. The tour of the old boat, by an admirably knowledgeable guide, gives a thorough look at it. You see the ornately carved mahogany interiors of the Scottish-built vessel, the compact

The glories of steamship travel on the Great Lakes survive in the S. S. Keewatin, a Canadian Pacific Railroad steamer than cruised lakes Huron and Superior. Permanently moored between Saugatuck and Douglas, it's now a remarkable museum.

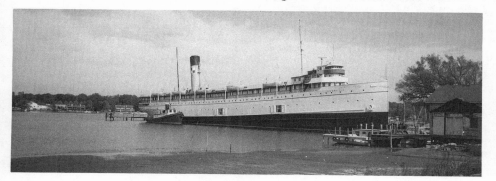

staterooms, the forward lounge for female passengers only, and the Edwardian dining room. The spartan galley had Chinese chefs. (The original French cooks drank too much.) In the bridge is the Marconi radar unit, still working, the first Great Lakes radar ever installed. On top is the great 50-foot funnel. Powered by coal, the boat's 3,300 horsepower engine took 150 tons of coal a week.

The *Keewatin* is the biggest boat ever to enter Saugatuck's harbor, and it only barely made it. It was hung up for months below Mount Baldhead on its way to Kalamazoo Lake.

Alongside the *Keewatin* is the last of the coal-powered Great Lakes steam tugs, the 1913 *Reiss*.

Saugatuck Dune Rides

Blue Star Highway, 1/2 miles west of I-196 on exit 41, 1 mile northeast of Saugatuck. (616) 857-2253. Open May 1 through October. Through September Mon-Sat 10-6, Sun 12-6. In July & Aug. open until 8. In October weekends only. $7.50 adults; $4.50 children ten and under.

Tearing through the fragile dune ecology in a converted 3/4 ton Dodge pickup, this 35-minute ride emphasizes amusement, not nature appreciation. Roaring up and down steep slopes, the driver is likely to suddenly

Occasional pine stumps, relics of Saugatuck logging a century ago, can still be seen in the dunes north of Saugatuck. In different places, the dunes support wild dune schooner rides and one of Michigan's most peaceful Great Lakes state parks, ideal not just for swimming but for cross-country skiing and even sledding — for the daring.

shout things like, "No brakes! We've lost the brakes!" Even without the histrionics, the journey is rather harrowing. The 16-seat open-air vehicles have no rollbars. However, in nine years under the current operators, there have been no accidents.

There are some nice views and amusing moments. The ride is a trip back to when there were lower ecological sensibilities and fears of crippling lawsuits, allowing a more freewheeling climate for amusement entrepreneurs.

Saugatuck Dunes State Park ★★

3 1/2 miles north of Saugatuck. Take Blue Star Highway to 64th St., go north 1 1/2 miles to 138th Ave., west 1 mile to park. (616) 399-9390. 8 a.m.-10 p.m. daily. $3/car/day, $15 annual state park sticker. No camping.

Protected from hoards of beachgoers by its remote location, Saugatuck Dunes is one of the more beautiful yet uncrowded nature spots in western Michigan. The 1,100 acres include over two miles of Lake Michigan **beach** and 14 miles of **hiking trails.** The parking lot is a mile from the beach, and the sandy, hilly path makes it seem even longer. In addition to paths through wild, pristine dune country, you can find wonderful dune-top views of the lake.

RESTAURANTS

Marro's Pizza ★

147 Water (across from the Coral Gables). (616) 857-4248. Open last weekend in April through last weekend in Oct. Mon-Thur 5-midnight, Fri 5-1, Sat & Sun noon-1 a.m. No deliveries.

This thin-crust pizza emporium is one of the most popular pizza joints in western Michigan. Most popular of all is the sausage, pepperoni, and mushroom pizza: $12.75 large, $9.75 medium, $6.75 small.

Plenty of the 18 items to choose from will suit a vegetarian, including broccoli, spinach, zucchini, garlic, and pineapple.

Restaurant Toulouse ★

248 Culver at Griffith in downtown Saugatuck. (616) 857-1561. Open daily from May thru color season: 11:30-10 p.m., to 11 Fri & Sat. Major credit cards. Full bar.

From the owners of Chequers, a much larger and just as popular place with a cool, French provincial air. Entrees include cassoulet (white beans and sausage, $10.50); boulliabaisse ($15.50), duck confit ($13.50), and beef tournedos ($17.50), all served with house salad, chef's side, and good bread. You can also dine elegantly on soup, pates or terrines, and salad with desserts.

Chequers

220 Culver (1/2 block east of Butler). Mon-Thurs 11:30-9, Fri-Sat 11:30-10, Sun noon-9 . Stays open one hour later in the summer.

Some people rave about this comfortable English-style pub with its convivial atmosphere, fish and chips, many imported beers and pub-style menu. Especially recommended is the shepherd's pie, $6.95. Space is limited, so come early at mealtime or expect to wait in line.

Cafe Sir Douglas ★

333 Blue Star Highway, Douglas. (616) 857-1401. May-Labor Day: Sun-Mon, & Wed-Thur 5-10, Fri & Sat 5-11. Closed Tues. April, Sept, Oct: open Fri-Sun only.

Decorated with stylish Art Deco trappings with a large and popular dining area, many believe the Cafe Sir Douglas is the best restaurant in the vicinity. There are usually five chef's specialties an evening, ranging from $8 to $17. The emphasis is on seafood, plus Black Angus beef. The black bean soup is a standby.

Clearbrook Restaurant & Golf Course ★

135th Ave. Take 196 to Blue Star Highway, Exit 41, west to 65th, south 1 block. (616) 857-1766. Open mid-May to mid-Sept. Lunch 11-3, dinner 6-9:30 daily. Reservations recommended. Visa, MC. Full bar.

This exceptionally pleasant restaurant overlooks an attractive championship golf course on the outskirts of Saugatuck. Clearbrook is especially well known for its sautéed fresh walleye ($15). Also popular are the housemade desserts ($3) including creme caramel and Clearbrook sacher torte.

> **Clearbrook Golf Course**
> Greens fees for this championship course are $22. It's heavily booked summers, so call (616) 857-1766 for reservations.

LODGINGS

Ship 'n Shore Motel
(616) 857-2194.
528 Water on the river downtown.
40 units, all but four overlooking the Kalamazoo River. 2 rooms have balconies, 4 have wet bars. Open April to mid-Oct. Double $110, $89 before Mem. Day & after Labor Day. Basic cable; no movie channels. Heated pool and jacuzzi.

This is the only in-town lodging overlooking the river. It's a great location. There's a large veranda, lots of landscaping.

Maplewood Hotel
(616) 857-2788.
428 Butler at Main in downtown Saugatuck.
Bed and breakfast with 13 rooms, all with bath. May-Oct.: $75 (double bed)-$105 (king), $10 more on weekends. Nov.-April $59-$89, $10 more on weekends. Greek Revival resort hotel from the 1860s, fully renovated. Traditional mahogany furniture; formal, plush effect in mauve and green. Continental breakfast. Some suites with double jacuzzi and fireplace. Large common areas, sunporch, delightful side porch overlooking park. Lap-pool on small deck in back. One block past Butler St.'s dense retail blocks; expect some noise from restaurant-goers, etc. The inn's Rolls Royce will pick up guests at the Holland train station.

Wickwood Inn
(616) 857-1097.
510 Butler at Mary, 2 blocks from Saugatuck's retail district.
Bed and breakfast with 11 rooms, all with bath, some on first floor. May through Dec.: $90-127. Jan. through April: $70-$105. Sophisticated, cheerful decor with family and area antiques, Laura Ashley papers and fabrics. Big living room, sunken garden-game room, library-bar. Screened gazebo. Continental breakfast, hors d'oeuvres at teatime. Perhaps the very nicest bed and breakfast in a town with many fine ones.

Kemah Guest House
(616) 857-2919.
633 Pleasant, 3 blocks from downtown Saugatuck but up a hill in a quieter residential area.
Bed and breakfast with 6 rooms with shared baths. May through Oct.: $75-$95 Nov.-April: $65-$85. 10% off weekdays and for seniors. Circa 1900 mansion, remodeled in the 1920s with many German custom touches with an Art Deco flavor (stained glass windows, carved beams and landscape scenes, stone and tile fireplaces). Large parlor with baby grand, solarium, enclosed sun porch, dining room with bay, beamed Rathskeller and game room. 2-acre hilltop site with a cave, quiet spots with view of river. A memorable setting, Saugatuck's most distinctive and romantic.

Twin Gables Country Inn
(616) 857-4346.
900 Lake St. overlooking Kalamazoo Lake and a 10-minute walk from downtown Saugatuck.
Bed and breakfast with 14 rooms with private baths. May to mid-Sept: $49-$59 weekdays, $69-$89 weekends. Nov.- April: $44-$54 weekdays, $58-$68 weekends. Oct. weekends are summer rates, weekdays are winter. Low-key country decor (no ducks) and a more casual feel than many Saugatuck B & B's. 1865 building used as a hotel since 1900, has the expected large dining and common areas and long front porch with rockers. Guest rooms have sitting areas. Indoor hot tub. Heated outdoor pool. On main street between Saugatuck and Douglas; rear rooms would be quieter.

Rosemont Inn

(616) 857-2637
83 Lakeshore Dr. in Douglas
Bed and breakfast with 14 rooms
with bath, 9 with gas fireplaces. May-
Oct. $85. Nov.-April: $50-$70 depend-
ing on time of week, length of stay,
fireplace or not. On the quiet, super-
shady shore drive of Douglas, with
other historic summer houses. Nice
walks. Douglas Beach across the
street and down. Must drive for meals.
Main section (6 guest rooms) is a
Queen Anne house with large parlor,
added contemporary garden room
overlooking attractively landscaped
outdoor swimming pool. 8 rooms in
new addition. Attractive but rather
spare decor with antique reproductions.

Lake Shore Motel

(616) 857-7121.
*2885 Lake Shore Dr. 3 miles from
downtown Saugatuck. Located south
of Douglas. West from Blue Star Hwy.
on 130th to Lake Michigan, left on
Lake Shore Dr.*
30 rooms, some with refrigerators.
Mid-June through August: double
$75-$89. Spring and fall: double $60-
80. Continental breakfast included in
summer and spring and on fall weekends. Large heated pool, no cable. 2-
mile nature trail. Sandy private beach
with swimming in Lake Michigan (one
of the state's few motels to have its
own beach). Deck on bluff overlooking
lake. Views of lake from all rooms and
pool.

Timberline Motel

(616) 857-2147
*3353 Blue Star Highway, between ex-
its 36 & 41 I-196.*
28 rooms on 1 floor. May-Sept 10:

single $45-$55, double $45-$75. Sept
11 through April: single $40-$45,
double $$40-$65. Heated pool, play-
ground. Unusually clean, well-main-
tained family-run motel.

Goshorn Lake Resort

(616) 857-4808.
*Just off Blue Star Hwy. north of
Saugatuck and west of the dune rides.
Follow signs.*
12 rustic wood cabins with kitchens,
screened porches. Open May through
Oct. Cabins rent by the day in May,
June, Sept. and Oct. ($55 sleeps 2-4,
$65 sleeps 4-6), by the week in July
and August ($275, $325). Bring own
sheets, towels, toaster, coffeemaker,
etc., or rent linens for $4/bed. This
outstanding budget vacation choice
includes an adjacent 400-foot sandy
beach and dock on spring-fed
Goshorn Lake. Nice lawn, spacious,
well-kept grounds, beautiful view
across road to dunes. Fish for bass,
pike, panfish. Boat and bike rentals,
shuffleboard, swings, horseshoes,
grills. Quiet setting. A hodge-podge of
old furniture from Mission to 1950s.

---

*See also: lodgings in Fennville
(which is quieter and somewhat
cheaper than downtown Saug-
atuck, but about 6 miles from
Lake Michigan) and Pier Cove.*
*Saugatuck styles itself the bed
and breakfast capital of the
Midwest, with over a dozen in the
area. For a complete listing and a
description of six Great Escape
B & B theme weekend packages
(Murder Mystery, Elizabethan
Christmas, Oktoberfest, and
others), contact the chamber of
commerce, (616) 857-5801; write
Box 28, Saugatuck, MI 49453.*

Blue Star Highway

T his old highway, often designated as A-2 on maps, was once the major north-south route along Lake Michigan's east coast. Now the four-lane U.S.-31 has made the Blue Star an interesting backwater. The stretch between its northernmost point just south of Holland to the Sea Wolf restaurant just above South Haven, a distance of about 25 miles, presents a curious medley of offbeat businesses, from a highway era before franchises and fancy signage.

Starting from the north, you get on the Blue Star from U.S.-31 just south of Holland. To your right is a big, modern **Prince** manufacturing facility. Founded in 1965, the Holland-based firm has quickly become a major maker of diecast parts and other parts for autos such as lighted vanity visors, arm and head rests, and map lights. To your left is the Tulip City Airport.

Many of the signs along the Blue Star are homemade, such as Rob's Body Repair on your left. Down the road a bit is a fading wooden sign:

Blue Star Hyway

Used Furniture - Antiques

Buy - Sell - Trade

Housed in a classic old chicken coop, the shop also has a smaller, neatly printed sign by the front door:

NOT RESPONSIBLE FOR ACCIDENTS

Inside you'll find Russ Bomers. Russ has had the place for 20 years. Before that he worked for 40 years at a pipe manufacturer in Holland. He says he opens up "when the spirit moves me" but generally stays open from 10 to 3:30 six days a week. His shop is well stocked with a wide variety of old things. While we were there he was urging a customer to buy a motor-driven belt hip slenderizer for just $10. "You already look better," he told her after she tried it out.

Down the road from Russ is **Blue Star Meat**. Big intriguing-looking black objects are lined up out front, each of them on two wheels like a small trailer. "Them's pig roasters," a young man named Scott explains as he slices bacon from a big carcass. They rent for $35 if you buy the pig from Blue Star Meat — $1.15 a pound, with your average roasting pig ranging from 70 to 120 pounds.

Scott also explained the presence of a startling-looking head of a deer lying on the concrete floor of the adjoining garage. The deer had been hit by a car, and

A leisurely drive down
the Blue Star Highway
from Holland to
South Haven is a trip
back in time to a
folksy, improvised,
loosely opportunistic
brand of roadside
tourism. The Paradise
Blueberry Garden
Farm south of
Douglas is one of
many blueberry farms
along the road.

he had processed the meat for the driver, a service performed for $30. During deer season, Blue Star Meat
gets so much business it shuts down all other operations to concentrate on processing deer for hunters. In
1988 it handled 550 deer.

Farther south on the Blue Star, a big Fiftyish sign
proclaims **Bush's Motel**. Behind it, standing starkly
in a big field, was a brick row of rooms. This is now
Hilda's Studio Apartments, and Hilda explains that
she charges $70 a month for visitors and won't take
anyone for less time because "it causes a lot of work."

Down the road form Hilda's is a commercial recreation spot called **Blue Star Playland**. (616-857-1044).
Here you can drive go-karts or bumper boats, play
miniature golf, or hit balls in a batting cage or a driving
range. South of this are the rather sad remnants of an
old drive-in movie theater. The big screen is gone, but
its substructure remains, as do the hundreds of posts
which held the car speakers. They now stick up out of a
weedy field.

On the east side of the highway farther south is a
surprisingly inviting-looking motel called the
Shangrai-La. Ensconced in a cool-looking glade of
tall trees, it sits next to the crowded Shangrai-La
Mobile Home Park.

A little past Shangrai La on the same side of the
road, 1/2 mile east of I-196 Exit 41, a sign announces **The Ark Gallery** (616-857-4210), the first of a
growing number of artists' studios on the Blue Star
Highway from Saugatuck to South Haven. Marcia

*This narrative starts
at Holland and moves
south*
*toward Saugatuck and
South Haven. If you're
traveling north from South
Haven on the Blue Star
Highway, start at the end.*

Perry, sculptor, poet, philosopher, is gradually renovating this odd, flat-roofed building originally erected as part of a futuristic plan to service would-be atomic-powered trucks coming off the interstate. Perry is fascinated by trees and the rooted, earth-loving, elemental approach to life they represent, as in Yggdrassil, the tree of life in Scandinavian mythology that binds earth, heaven, and hell together. Visitors are welcome to stop by The Ark between 10 a.m. and 9 p.m. Perry sometimes shows work by other artists (trees and myths are typical themes), and she gives occasional **workshops** on "Tree Zen: Creating with Wood." Group tours by appointment.

As you approach Saugatuck and Douglas, houses along the old highway are often occupied by antique dealers. From a distance you can see the eroded dunes of the Dune Schooner amusement ride company and the white radar tower on Mount Baldhead. Crossing into Douglas over Lake Kalamazoo, you see the splendid view of the old steamer, the S.S. Keewatin.

South of Douglas are several blueberry farms. By far the funkiest is **Paradise Blueberry Garden Farm** on the east side of the road. In a yard cluttered with strange ornaments and statues is a farm wagon from which the produce is sold.

Just before you pass through the little burg of Ganges, you can see, several hundred yards to the east, the **Vivekananda Monastery** in an old converted farm whose barn is now a temple. Here monks rise at four o'clock each morning to meditate, following the Indian Vedanta religious tradition. Members located here because they liked the name Ganges, given to the farm for unknown reasons in 1847 in honor of India's holy river. Visitors are welcome either to join in meditations or chanting, or to tour the facilities and visit the small museum and bookshop (616-543-4114.).

Below Ganges on the Blue Star Highway is the slightly larger village of **Glenn**. Once it was home to a number of peach and apple farmers who started their orchards after 1870. Later it became a bustling tourist area with several small hotels on the lake. Glenn used to be famous for its annual Pancake Festival, which the 1940 Michigan W.P.A. Guide called "a burlesque of the many fruit and flower festivals that have become so popular in Michigan." It began after the winter of 1937, when over 200 motorists were stranded in the village by a blizzard and were fed pancakes by the locals when other food ran out.

If you head east half a block on 114th Avenue in Glenn, you'll find the quaint old **Gerstner's Hardware & Variety Store** still filled with a robust assortment of merchandise. Georgia Gerstner bought the place in 1945 after a quick visit from Chicago. The beautiful flower garden in back was the deciding factor. She and her husband, Ed, have been tending store ever since.

South of Glenn, the pleasantly ramshackle

Marcia Perry's creations in wood range from big, earthy treetrunk figures to switchplates to massive carved-out seats like a surprisingly comfortable rocker. She works instinctively. "The trees talk to me. I translate so other people can see what they say," she says without a hint of pretentious mysticism. Don't miss a trip to her studio, where figures are emerging from chunks of tree trunks and piles of branches, acquired from tree crews and fruit farmers.

It's all at The Ark, on the Blue Star Highway just east of I-96. (616) 857-4210.

Radseck Farms sells honey, vegetables, and fruit. A sign tells visitors to leave the money for purchases in a jar. A half mile south of Radseck Farms, look for the **Vesuvius** sign and banners, also on the east side of the road at 1173. Here glassblowers Kathy and Jerry Catania have opened a gallery in their 1860 stone farmhouse, open weekends from noon to 5, by appointment other times. (616-227-3970). The gallery features their own work and changing invitational shows of emerging and mid-career Midwestern artists, planned around themes like "In the Garden of Earthly Delights," which features birdhouses, garden sculpture, and such. Why "Vesuvius"? "We like to feature hot work on the cutting edge," says Kathy. The Catanias became acquainted with the area when they started the glass-blowing program at Saugatuck's Oxbow summer art school.

For a delightful eight-mile detour, turn east onto 109th Street (it's a mile south of the Glenn Shores Golf Course), then in four miles go south on 64th. The second house to the right is home to **Foxglove Studios and Farm** (616-236-6150), a memorable small cosmos at the century-old farmhouse of Barb, Al, and Kyla Bare. It's open from May through October Friday through Sunday 12-5, otherwise by appointment. For years the Bares have been developing the farm's gardens and its menagerie of goats and sheep. The old place now yields cut flowers, everlastings and dried herbs for Barb's wreaths and garlands, herbs for teas, wool for her hand-woven pillows, rugs, shawls, and purses, and applewood branches for Al's twig furniture. Visitors may purchase all these products and buy perennials, herbs, and bedding plants raised in the greenhouse.

South on the Blue Star Highway from 109th St., **Sunset Junction Antiques** bursts at the seams with a bewildering hodgepodge of items. A little sign on the door proclaims the proprietors to be "Certified Junk Dealers." The gravel road just north of the shop takes you due west a hundred feet or so to Blue Star Glass Company and gives a surprising panoramic view of Lake Michigan. Two miles south, just three miles north of South Haven, you reach **Blue Star Pottery** (616-637-5787), the working studio of Mark Williams, tucked away in an old field gradually returning to woods. He makes reasonably priced functional stoneware in a variety of glazes, all lead-free — some earthy and flat, some colorful and lustrous in cobalt, greens, and lavenders. Mugs are $8 and $10, soup tureens $55. Hours are Friday and Saturday 1-5 from May to October, otherwise by appointment.

Don't drive too fast on the Blue Star Highway! Take the time to spot and enjoy old farmhouses, general stores, orchards, produce stands, and the like.

Fennville

Just 12 miles southeast of Holland and six miles from Saugatuck and Lake Michigan, Fennville is a very different place. Compared with the increasingly frenetic places on the coast nearby, it's a low-key small town, with a population of about a thousand. The local economy has been based on fruit-growing and related activities ever since lumber ran out in the 1870s. Sanocide, the biggest maker of orchard sprays in the Great Lakes region, was started here in 1910 and stayed until a buyout in 1950. A big cannery founded by fruit growers from here and nearby Coloma has been the main employer since 1920.

Farm markets and orchards

In the past two decades, when it's become almost impossible to make a reliable living growing fruit and selling it wholesale, more and more growers have been selling fruit direct to customers. As a result, the area has developed a low-key kind of tourism that takes advantage of Fennville's proximity to the Allegan Forest, Lake Michigan, Holland, and Saugatuck. Much of the tourism is related to fruit. **Crane's Pie Pantry** and the **Fenn Valley Winery** make products from the fruit they grow and have become visitor attractions in their own right.

It's a scenic drive past apple and cherry and pear orchards as you drive along M-40 from Holland and M-89 from near Saugatuck. The area is dotted with opportunities to buy and pick fresh fruit, or purchase plants. Numerous bed and breakfasts are in the area — quieter, more Middle American, and less expensive than those in Saugatuck, but still a short drive to Lake Michigan beaches. Fennville's promoters have sensibly chosen to play up its unpretentious, "everybody's home town" aspects in promotions like October's big Goose Festival.

Today the sprawling cannery, now Michigan Fruit Canners, also makes Thank You brand puddings and pie fillings. It is far and away the biggest employer in a town whose residents are largely retirees clustered around Higgins Lake or commuters to Holland or Allegan, home of the big Perrigo generic drug manufacturers. Now that Holland real estate prices are escalating, some people who have been transferred there are moving into and renovating Fennville's fine old homes on West Main and elsewhere.

Fennville's Annual Goose Festival is held the third Sat. and Sun. of October, when the goose migration at the nearby Allegan State Game Area is at its peak. It features a parade with the Scottville Clown Band; country, Dixieland, and big band music; the Goose Ball; an arts and crafts fair with a good deal of wildlife art; carnival rides, a 10K run, and games and contests including goose-calling and goose-hunting. For festival or general visitor information, contact the chamber of commerce, Box 484, Fennville, MI 49408; (616) 561-2720.

Allegan County visitor information, exceptionally helpful and well organized, makes it easy to find interesting things off the beaten track. For pamphlets and maps on events (including the popular monthly *Allegan Antiques Market*), farm and garden markets, skiing, snowmobiling, and parks, write *Allegan Co. Tourist Council,* Box 338, Allegan, MI 49001 or call or stop by the office at 300 Water in delightful downtown Allegan. (616) 673-2479, open 10-2 weekdays, or leave a message.

But Fennville's most distinctive residents are the Mexican-Americans who first came here as migrant pickers. Many have now found work at Michigan Fruit Canners and at area farms. Their social hub is **Su Casa**, a fascinating Mexican general store with a sizable (and very good) restaurant in back (p. 115). Just down the street but in a totally separate world is the **Blue Goose Cafe**, where retirees and farmers in feed caps eat broasted chicken.

POINTS OF INTEREST

Allegan State Game Area

Headquarters is at 4590 118th Ave. at 46th St., 2 miles southwest of the Allegan Dam, 8 miles southeast of Fennville via M-89 and 46th St. (616) 673-2430. State Park sticker required for entry: $3/day, $15/year.

This famous stopover spot for thousands of migrating geese and other waterfowl consists of nearly 45,000 acres of woodlands, marsh, lakes, and fields between Allegan and Fennville. It is Michigan's largest managed hunting area, financed in large part by hunters' fees. Though the facilities aren't as intensively developed as they would be in a state

Canada geese, endangered in the 1930s, have been coming to Todd's Fennville Farm ever since. Migrants start to arrive in mid-September and peak around the first of November — a spectacular sight, easily viewable from Carson and 118th Ave. 25,000 have been counted at once.

Geese enjoy the Peppermint King's Fennville legacy

Today the Allegan State Game Area attracts thousands of ducks and geese with its diked wetlands and huge food supply. At this wildlife management facility on 118th Ave. south of Hutchins Lake and southwest of Fennville, corn and other grains are raised, most of which is fed to the large visiting bird population.

Few visitors realize that the headquarters buildings here are the remains of a showplace company town built here by the Todd Mint Company of Kalamazoo around 1900. The town stood on a 1,640-acre mint farm called Campania. A. M. Todd, a chemist from Nottawa in St. Joseph County, developed a method for distilling peppermint oil by steam that produced unusually pure oil. By the 1890s his firm had become the world's largest dealer in essential oils. Soon he started growing mint at two huge farms,

Campania and, in northeast Van Buren County, Mentha. Campania had amenities like a good small library and lots of geraniums. It consisted of eight houses, a workers' rooming house, a school, a tin shop for making cans for peppermint oil, and the Todd family's vacation home. Most of the homes were built of Sears and Roebuck's pre-cut kits. leftover mint hay was fed to cattle shipped in from Todd's 7,000-acre Newaygo County ranch. A mammoth barn, reputedly Michigan's largest, housed the cattle. (It now houses antique autos at the Gilmore Car Museum at Hickory Corners north of Kalamazoo.)

In the 1920s disease infected most Michigan mint and remained in the soil. Todd switched to growing vegetables on contract with supermarkets. In the late 1930s he turned the farm into a wildlife refuge. The Michigan Conservation Dept. purchased it in 1950.

park, its varied habitats have much to offer hunters, fishermen, bird-watchers, cross-country skiers, campers, swimmers, hikers, and canoeists. There are even designated areas for horseback riding and dog-sledding. Wild blueberries, straw-berries, blackberries, morels, and cranberries occur in the area, and they can be legally picked.

Unscrupulous real estate devel-opers in the 1910s and 1920s had subdivided this logged-over land and sold it as starter farms to people without much money who were eager to trade Chicago for rural life. During the hard times of the 1930s, mailmen dreaded finding mailboxes full of old mail and the occupants starved to death. The state Conservation Department acquired land like this for demonstration projects in refor-estation.

Eighteen miles of **hiking trails** highlight the most scenic areas — streams and marshes, lakes and forests, full of dogwood and redbuds in spring. The lack of many big trees testifies to the poor soil and repeated forest fires that led to the state buy-ing up large amounts of this marginal land during the Depression. The sec-ond-growth woods of the Allegan State Forest are mostly oak with pockets of pine and aspen. They have a scrubby look like much of northern Michigan. Trailers and extremely modest homes are on private prop-erty parcels within the game area.

Other parts of the game area today include former crop acreage now managed as grain fields or diked marshes to attract waterfowl. Lake Allegan, 3 1/2 miles long, was formed by the City of Allegan's 1936 hydro-electric dam on the Kalamazoo River. Further downstream is the Ottawa Marsh, nearly five miles long.

Fishing is varied. Salmon, brown trout, and steelhead are caught in the Kalama-zoo River, and Swan, Bear, and Sand creeks. Silver Creek has trout. Panfish are in Swan Creek Pond and Little Tom Lake, and Ely Lake has bass as well.

Paternalistic peppermint tycoon A. M. Todd developed huge farms in Allegan, Van Buren, and Newaygo counties. Though mint-growing has virtually disappeared in Michigan, the Kalamazoo firm Todd founded is today an important manufacturer of flavorings. Left, a bottle of Todd's peppermint oil. Right, the mint plant itself.

Hiking trails over mostly flat terrain permit loop variations around both the **Ely Lake** area (3 miles; a nearby wild cranberry bog that once supplied Chicago with cranberries is still productive) and along both sides of **Swan Creek**. South of the Swan Creek dam at 118th Ave. (reach-able from Allegan via its Monroe Rd. ex-tension), 7 miles of trail border Swan Creek Dam, leading to an old iron bridge and to the **Old Nursery group campsite**, on the spot where a wealthy Chicagoan once tried to establish a cattle ranch and tree farm on lumbered-over land. Another 4 miles of trail along both sides of Swan Creek leads north from the dam to the **Highbanks Unit** at Koopman Marsh, good for bird-watching. Campgrounds and swimming beaches at Ely Lake and Swan

Cross-Country Trail through oak woods connects the iron bridge with Ely Lake; the 5-mile **Northwest Trail** swings north from Ely Lake along 120th Ave. and back to the dam.

Swimming is encouraged at two day-use beaches, both on hiking trails. The prettiest is on **Swan Creek Pond** just south of the 118th Ave. (Monroe Rd.) dam. A red pine plantation separates the beach and picnic area from the rustic, 21-site Pine Point Campground. The beach at small, round **Ely Lake** immediately adjoins an 80-unit rustic campsite.

Canoeing is popular from the Allegan Dam to New Richmond or Saugatuck.

Camping is at **Ely Lake Campground** (80 sites around Ely Lake, connected to Little Tom Lake by foot trails) and at **Pine Point** (21 sites on beautiful Swan Creek Pond). Both have swimming beaches and access to the long trail system. Campgrounds are primitive — that is, picnic tables and outhouses but no electricity.

Hunting of many kinds is encouraged here: waterfowl, deer, turkey, small game (pheasant, rabbit, and woodcock at the Farm Unit; ruffled grouse, squirrel, and woodcock everywhere else),

Bird-watching here offers year-round events, according to the Audubon Society. **Spring** migrants include the Louisiana Waterthrush, Pileated Woodpecker, Hooded and Golden-winged Warblers, Scarlet Tanager, and Rough-legged Hawk. The Ottawa Marsh is one of the few places in Michigan where large numbers of Prothonotary Warblers can be seen. In **summer,** an unusually wide variety of birds, both northern and southern spe-cies, remain here to nest. **Fall** brings thousands of ducks and geese, including uncommon Ross's, Barnacle, and White-fronted geese which feed with more plentiful Canada and Snow geese. Many remain through the **winter.**

The **M-89 bridge** over the Kalamazoo River marsh offers an excellent view of waterfowl in the marsh to the south and is accessible even in hunting season. 118th Ave. through the Farm Unit also offer excellent waterfowl viewing — birds aren't disturbed by cars. Winter is a good time to see birds of prey hunting there.

Cross-country ski trails, over 22 miles in all, radiate out in a series of loops from parking lots at the game area headquarters and Highbanks Unit office. Stacked loops provide a choice of distances from 2 miles to 14 miles without repeating a trail, and to 18 miles with little repetition. South of Swan Creek dam and 118th Ave. it's hillier; north is generally flat. The trails are right where lake-effect snowfall is the heaviest. They don't open until January 1, in deference to the hunters who pay the bills here. On weekends these trails are often quite crowded; Saugatuck Dunes might be a better choice.

Fenn Valley Vineyards and Wine Cellar   ★

6130 122nd Ave. 3 1/2 miles west of Fennville. From I-196 or the Blue Star Hwy., take M-89 (Exit 34) some 3 1/2 miles east to 62nd St., turn south (right), and turn east (left) onto 122nd. Ave. in one mile. (616) 561-2396. Open year-round, Mon-Sat 10-5, Sun 1-5.

The best all-around winery tours provide visitors with a look at grapes growing in the vineyards, a look at the winemaking process in the winery, and an opportunity to learn about winemaking and taste various wines. Fenn Valley's self-guided tour is among the best. Fenn Valley is a small, family winery that grows all the grapes it uses, unlike the big Paw Paw wineries which buy grapes trucked in from contract growers. The 230-acre property is in a scenic, rolling area four miles from Lake Michigan. **Picnic tables** are outside for visitors to use.

The wine-making equipment is viewed through windows, which isn't quite the same as feeling the drippy, cold air of a fermenting room and seeing bees buzz around pungent grape juice in season.

For game area maps
on cross-country skiing, camping, hiking, and hunting, and an interesting illustrated **brochure on Fennville's geese** and migrating birds, write headquarters, 4590 118th Ave, Allegan, MI 49010., Enclose a self-addressed, stamped envelope.

But to most people, the winery interior is just so many barrels and shiny vats if they don't understand what they're looking at. Fenn Valley's 17-minute video show on grape-growing and wine-making, plus the handling and use of wine with food, is much more informative than many winery tours.

Fenn Valley was established in 1973 by a wine-loving Chicago-area businessman, William Welsch, to shelter the money he'd made in his building-supply business. His son Doug, a biology teacher, is the wine-maker. It was one of the very first Michigan wineries to start growing French hybrid grapes — crosses of vinifera grapes like riesling and pinot noir with American varieties that are more resistant to heat, cold, and disease. In France hybrids are regarded as fit only for table wines; quality-conscious Michigan vintners are working hard to uplift their status as another kind of good wine.

Fenn Valley does well with its hybrids: seyval blanc (a dry, crisp white wine), vignole (a dry white wine, with pineapple overtones when it's from southwest Michigan), and vidal blanc (a crisp, semi-sweet German-style wine that's Michigan's most success-ful hybrid). It also makes a propri-etary, blended wine — Lake Shore Dry White, some premium wines from vinifera grapes, and raspberry wine judged one of the best in the U.S. Prices are from $4.99 to $8.99 a bottle.

In addition to the usual wine glasses, cheeses, and other gift items, Fenn Valley's tasting room sells home winemaking supplies, barrels, and grapes and grape juice in season.

For interesting reading about wine, pick up the Welschs' opinionated *Fenn Valley News and Views* newsletter and two excellent free booklets from the Michigan Grape and Wine Industry Council. (Look for the grey and purple covers.) *Discover Michigan Wines* has some good recipes from winemakers' famlies using their own wines.

RESTAURANTS

Crane's Orchards and Pie Pantry Restaurant ★

6054 124th Ave. (M-89), 2 miles west of Fennville and 3 1/2 miles east of I-196/31 exit 34. (616) 561-2297. **Mother's Day-Oct. 31:** *Mon-Sat 9 a.m.-7 p.m., Sun 11-7.* **Nov. 1-March 31:** *Tues-Sat 10-5, Sun 11-5.* **April-Mother's Day:** *weekends only.*

Of all Michigan's many family farm stands that have become popu-lar visitor destinations, Crane's is the most generally interesting, with the most individualistic per-sonality. The Cranes are fourth- and fifth- generation Fennville fruit farm-ers. They grow all the fruit they sell and make into pies.

They haven't allowed commercial-ism to obscure the basic, simple idea of the place. It invites you to take a pleasant drive in the country to buy fruit (pick it yourself if you like) and then have cider (cold or hot and spicey), a slice of very good pie, or soup and a sandwich. There is a small shop with some honey, apple butter, frozen pies and desserts, and a few gift items, but it doesn't over-whelm the place. Ham, beef, and turkey sandwiches ($2.50-$3) are served on dense, flavorful homemade buns. Soups are also good. Tasty desserts ($1.75) include pies with all-vegetable shortening (apple, peach, blueberry, and cherry), plus dumplings, crisps, strudels, and ice cream.

The restaurant, in the lower level of an old barn, is a cheerful, homey hodgepodge of interesting old things. The odd kitchen and dining room tables and chairs are familiar pieces of Americana. Burlap potato sacks form the ceiling; apples with faces are painted on the concrete floor. A Round Oak stove (the pride of Do-wagiac, Michigan) helps warm things up in winter. Charles Lindbergh

Cider is made at Crane's on Fridays in the fall. Visitors are welcome to watch.

is the star of a the newspaper and magazine stories on the walls. Old tools and machines are on display, explained, in the vestibule.

It takes a good eye and special sensibility to bring this mix off so well and stop just short of being too corny and cute. Lue Crane, wife of fruit-grower Bob Crane, devised and decorated the pie pantry when the continuing crisis in agriculture first loomed large in the early 1970s. (Interestingly, she's far from a farm girl herself, having moved to 12 different cities when she was in school.) Today making pies to freeze has become an extra winter income source for neighbors, and the five Crane children and spouses are involved in the wide-ranging family operation, which also includes a delightful bed and breakfast.

Su Casa Restaurant/ Supermercado Mexico ★★

306 Main, just west of downtown Fennville and next to a Shell convenience store. (616) 561-5118. Daily 8:30 a.m.-10 p.m.

Tucked behind a Mexican grocery store, this is one of the most authentically Mexican restaurants you'll find in the northern U.S. To get to it, you walk through the "Supermercado Mexico," packed with large containers of pinto beans, chilis, and large pieces of fried pork rind. It's interesting to look at all the food and housewares, including mortars and pestles used to mash bean with.

Entering the restaurant, you see a large Aztec-inspired mural of a sacrificial maiden and lots of stained

glass and tiles. At breakfast and lunchtime on weekdays, it feels like you are in Mexico. The convivial customers all talking away in Spanish, and the waitress speaks only some English. The jukebox, a Rock Ola 488, plays only Mexican songs. Evenings brings more Anglos; Su Casa enjoys excellent word-of-mouth, and the food is outstanding.

The chefs are from Mexico City and go all the way to Chicago to obtain imported ingredients. At dinner, a favorite dish is Carne Asada ($5.99) — skirt steak with salad and guacamole. Another specialty is Camorones a la Diabla ($7.99) — shrimp in a very hot sauce. Non-Hispanics often order the Com-

Excellent food and a friendly, authentic Mexican atmosphere have made Su Casa a popular dinner destination for West Michigan fans of Mexican food. Breakfast and lunch customers are almost exclusively Mexican-Americans. Shopping for Mexican foods from plantains, fresh chiles, and cilantro to spices, big jars of salsa, and large pieces of fried pork rind is an added bonus.

bination Plate #1 ($6.99) — a soup, enchilada, hard tacos, and broiled meat. The chicken enchilda ($4.95) is also very good. Hamburgers Mexico City-style are $1.80. Before your order is taken, a basket of delicious, dark corn chips and separate bowls of hot guacamole and salsa are presented.

Breakfasts are also popular. Huevos à la Mexicana (scrambled eggs with chopped tomato, onions, and green peppers) is $2.50. Huevos con chorizo (scrambled eggs with Mexican sausage) is also $2.50.

LODGINGS

Kingsley House
(616) 561-6425.
626 W. Main at the west edge of the village of Fennville.
Bed and breakfast with 5 large rooms. Impressive Queen Anne house with turret and wraparound porch, built by one of Fennville's leading fruit farmers and businessmen. Restored and furnished with antiques, largely oak. Guests use big, sunny living area with games, organ and hymn book, local history books. Location on busy M-89 means occasional road noise in front rooms. Full breakfast. Cross-country skiing in orchards directly behind the house.

J. Paules' Fenn Inn
(616) 561-2836.
2254 S. 58th St. at Lake Land Dr. 58th intersects with M-89 just west of Fennville. Inn is 1/2 mile from M-89.
Bed and breakfast with 6 rooms on 3 floors. 4 share baths. May-Oct. $55/$65 for 2 people. Nov.-April $45/$55. Weekday non-summer rates: $30 without breakfast. Very nice 3rd-floor studio with kitchen, eating area, shared bath: $75/night. 1900 house with attractive living-dining area, near Hutchins Lake (good fishing, primitive swimming

beach). Pleasant, large rooms. 2nd-floor deck.

The Crane House
(616) 561-6931.
6051 124th Ave. (M-89) 2 1/2 miles west of Fennville.
Bed and breakfast with 5 rooms with private or shared baths, $60-$80. The 1872 family homestead of the Crane family, sixth-generation fruit farmers and operators of Crane's Pie Pantry across the road. Outstanding full breakfast prepared by Lue Crane or her daughters. Mix of primitive, farmy antiques, quilts, and Americana makes this like going back to grandma's house if grandma were a social historian with a good eye for arrangements and unusually interesting things. Comfortable parlor with parlor stove. Games in dining room. 2nd-floor deck. Surrounded by orchards.

Kingsley House

Holland

Few if any American industrial towns remained as ethnically pure for so long as Holland. Founded by Dutch religious dissenters in 1847, it remained 90% Dutch for over a century.

Loyalty to home and neighborhood are characteristic of the Dutch. In Holland, Michigan, this was reinforced by the immigrants' strong religious convictions and by their intentional isolation in their own small, self-contained city. As a result, Holland remained unusually homogeneous four and five generations after the first immigrants arrived. Natural blonds are the rule in schools of the Christian Reformed Church. It's still not uncommon to find Dutch-Americans whose families have been in the U. S. for five generations who have *no* non-Dutch ancestors. The phone book is full of Dutch names. Many last names end with the Frisian suffix "-ma, " meaning "man," and fully six percent of the pages are devoted to "vans."

A less Dutch town

Prosperity and suburbanization are now eroding Holland's Dutch complexion as outsiders move here to fill the growing number of job openings. The Dutch, here and abroad, have a long history of self-employment in farms, small manufacturing shops, stores, and services rather than working in factories or large organizations. Now some of Holland's many home-grown industries have become spectacularly successful. They have created a boom that is drawing considerable numbers of outsiders to the city for the first time in its history. This boom is also clogging U. S. 31 in the early morning and mid-afternoon, with commuters from Muskegon.

As more people come to the area to fill jobs, the Dutch may actually become a minority of Holland's residents. The hundreds of high school kids who practice for months to perform as klompen dancers at Tulip Time now come in a very broad range of hair colors and skin tones. Most noticeable are the Mexican-Americans, who now make up a quarter of all public school students.

The tourist draws

Still, it's the city's Dutch heritage that bring visitors to the area — that and the beaches and very popular state park. The big draw is Tulip Time in May, when Holland is jammed with half a million tourists taking in millions of tulips. Other Dutch attractions are in high gear all summer. **Windmill Island**, a sort of mini-

Tulips without tourists
Consider visiting Holland the week before crowds jam the town for Tulip Time, when flowers are already in bloom al over town. **Tulip Lane**, 8 miles of clearly designated tulip-lined streets, starts at 12th and River, by the Herrick Public Library, and winds through historic and suburban neighborhoods. You can hear **klompen dancers** being told how to smile at the 6 p. m. dress rehearsals at Centennial Park (Thurs, Fri, Mon & Tues before Wed's kickoff parade).

The Wizard of Oz books, considered an allegory of Hollywood with its dreams and charming con artists, were partly written just south of Holland in Castle Park, a turn-of-the-century summer colony much favored by Chicagoans like author L. Frank Baum. It is on Lake Michigan west of where 146th Ave. intersects with 66th St. The colony is named after a small castle-shaped hotel (not open to the public) on a central green.

theme park, has one of the few authentic old Dutch windmills allowed to leave the Netherlands. **Dutch Village** (a recreated village out on U.S. 31 by the new Manufacturers' Marketplace) and the **Netherlands Museum** go beyond kitsch to offer some worthwhile glimpses of Dutch culture. Even the two **wooden shoe factories** — tourist traps in the nostalgic style of several decades ago — have a certain charm and sincerity.

Holland's downtown, one of the state's most pleasant, is reorienting itself to feature interesting specialty shops in the face of mall competition. (One mall, a **Manufacturers' Marketplace** outlet mall next to Dutch Village, is a visitor destination of its own.) Architectural details from the Northern Renaissance are in evidence as you walk around the business district. You can take nice downtown walks to Centennial Park, the Netherlands Museum, the attractive Hope College campus, and a lovely historic neighborhood that's especially nice in spring, when block after block is lined in tulips.

Material signs of Holland's Dutch roots have flourished since the late 1920s, when high school teacher Lydia Rogers promoted city beautification by planting masses of tulips, resulting in the Tulip Time Festival. De Zwaan, a 200-year-old Dutch windmill, has been rebuilt as a visitor attraction on Windmill Island in the Black River. It's a majestic sight when viewed in the distance from the walkway in The Window on the Waterfront Park where River St. crosses the river.

The mother colony of Dutch Separatists

The original settlers of Holland were religious Separatists led by their pastor, Albertus Van Raalte. He chose the site on the southeastern bank of Lake Macatawa (originally called Black Lake) largely because of its relative isolation from other white settlements. These Separatists, rural artisans and farmers, had resisted the 19th-century Dutch movement to modernize the state-controlled church. Some were actually jailed by the Dutch government for their belief in a more literal interpretation of the Bible. The opportunity in the 1840s to form their own self-run community in America had the same appeal it had for the Puritans

Private homes house visitors at Tulip Time for $20 a person. Call (616) 396-4221, or just show up at the Visitors' Bureau in the Civic Center, 150 W. 8th, and a room will be found for you.

two centuries earlier. Times were hard in the
Netherlands then, and the success of the industrial
revolution in England had weakened the Dutch
economy. A severe potato blight in 1846 made it easier
to encourage already poor people to pull up stakes and
face the uncertainties of pioneer living in America.

Van Raalte's Kolonie arrived in February, 1847.
They lacked any experience of wilderness life. Few had
ever even cut down a tree. These novice pioneers en-
dured great hardships, including malaria, diphtheria,
and smallpox to carve a little community out of the
forest of enormous virgin hardwoods and pines.

Dutch immigrants began pouring into the young
hamlet right away, boosting its population to well over
1,000 within a year. The local environment encouraged
farming the rich bottom lands of the Black River
Valley, establishing fruit orchards, lumber mills, and
tanneries that used tanbark from the felled timber.

Hard times and religious oppression in the Netherlands led increasing numbers of pious rural folk, an
estimated 250,000 in all, to emigrate to the U. S., mainly in an arc around southern Lake Michigan from
Muskegon to Green Bay and the Fox River valley
around Oshkosh, Wisconsin. Often whole congrega-
ions or neighborhood units arrived together and
established their own communities. By 1849, new
arrivals had founded the nearby villages of Zeeland,
Vriesland, Groningen, Overisel, and Drenthe, named
after the newcomers' place of origin. Graafschaap was
settled by Dutch speakers living in Germany.

Separatist pastor
Albertus Van Raalte
brought a thousand
members of his con-
gregation in Arnhem
and founded Holland
in 1847. It was the first
year of a wave of Dutch
Separatist communi-
ties that eventually
brought 250,000 im-
migrants to the U.S.
Van Raalte, then 35,
financed the move by
selling his brick and
tile factory and bor-
rowing from Dutch
businessmen already
in America.

The Dutch agricultural heritage

Most of the Dutch immigrants were farmers,
familiar with sandy and mucky soils. Dutch farmers in
Michigan grew onions and cabbage for urban markets,
pioneered the American culture of celery (based in
Kalamazoo), and later got into raising, blueberries,
asparagus, and poultry. Poultry is still much in
evidence in Zeeland and other Dutch farm towns in
Ottawa County. Bil-Mar ("Mr. Turkey"), based in tiny
Borculo north of Zeeland, has become the nation's
second-biggest maker of specialty turkey products,
after Louis Rich. And Michigan's big bedding plant and
nursery businesses remain dominated by the Dutch.

But the Dutch agricultural heritage dwindled
somewhat, even in the late 19th century, as succeeding
generations of settlers in Holland and Ottawa County
took up the typical American pattern of leaving the
farm for city jobs. Dutch workers were critical in supplying labor and leadership in the Grand Rapids furniture industry, which became nationally important in
the 1880s. From the vicinity of Holland, some Dutch
moved on to bigger West Michigan cities, to the point
that today they are the dominant ethnic group in West
Michigan, from Kalamazoo to Muskegon and most of

all in Grand Rapids. The Dutch have given the region a unique social and political coloring and a strong non-union work ethic.

A city divided

An important split developed in this highly religious community in 1882 over the issue of membership to unions and secret societies. To outsiders the similarities between the two factions vastly outweighed their differences. But two totally separate denominations, today known as the more traditional Christian Reformed Church (CRC) and the more liberal Reformed Church in America (RCA), resulted. The CRC long held that membership in unions and secret societies put outside organizations between a man and his God. They have a big parochial school system.

The two denominations continue to dominate the religious landscape. There are 28 Christian Reformed churches in the Holland area and 26 Reformed Church in America congregations. By comparison, the Catholics and Presbyterians each have only two churches, the Episcopalians one, and the liberal Unitarians none. Holland's Hope College, established as the anchor of the Reformed faith in 1866, is today related to the RCA. Calvin College in Grand Rapids is the main CRC college and seminary. Together the two colleges have made this region the center for America's four million Reformed Dutch Christians.

Until recent years the effects of this deeply religious community were conspicuous to outsiders. Virtually everything shut down on Sundays. Holland was a place where there were few taverns or restaurants serving alcohol. "The Dutchman loves his beer," but drinks at home with friends. one Dutch woman explained. Even today, there are a few neighborhoods in Holland where the elderly residents frown on outside Sunday activities, especially something as noisily conspicuous as mowing your lawn. When the local newspaper, the *Holland Sentinel*, began a Sunday edition several years ago, dozens of subscribers cancelled in protest.

A more cosmopolitan population

In the past quarter century, the population of this almost totally Dutch city has changed radically to the point where the Dutch are actually becoming a minority. In their place is a growing population of Mexican-Americans, a legacy of the migrant fruit and vegetable pickers who traveled north for the summer from Texas in the 1940s. Gradually more and more of these Hispanics found preferable permanent employment, at first in the big Heinz pickle factory, other fruit and vegetable processors, and in poultry processing. Today Holland, along with Adrian in southeast Michigan, has the highest percentage of Hispanics in

The devastating fire of 1871, on the very day of the great Chicago fire, spared the Hope College campus and the 1856 Pillar Church (above) on Ninth and College. The survival of these important institutions was a great help in re-building the town after most of it, including the business district and factories, was destroyed. Dry timber debris left in cut-over forests combined with hot, dry, windy weather to produce forest fires throughout much of Michigan and Wisconsin that summer.

Waverly stone
After the fire of 1871, many of Holland's buildings were constructed of Waverly stone, a distinctive bluish-grey stone mined from a quarry just northeast of town. Downtown buildings such as the beautiful Tower Clock Building at 8th St. and Pine and the DuMez Building at 31 E. 8th are made of this material. In the historic district, the Queen Anne house at 225 W. 11th is also of Waverly stone.

Michigan, over 15% in 1980 and growing rapidly. The Mexican-American community is growing with Texans coming up from the distressed Rio Grande valley looking for work. For very good food and a fascinating, close-up look at the first stages of Mexican-American migration to Michigan, go to Su Casa restaurant and general store in Fennville, p. 115.

Holland's churches also invited many Vietnamese and Cambodian refugees to settle here in the 1970s, and Asians now make up over 5% of school enroll- ment. But African-Americans have rarely been em- ployed in Holland industries, unlike in Muskegon, whose foundries recruited blacks during World War II. Blacks make up just 1% of the population.

The tone of life in Holland has become far more at- tractive to outsiders who, even ten years ago, found Holland too contained and clannish. Hope College's high-quality theater and art activities have enlivened the local scene. Herman Miller's research unit, which in the 1950s set up shop in Ann Arbor for its more creative atmosphere, recently moved to Holland. Pereddies (p. 141), the popular Italian restaurant and deli started by two former Detroiters, showed that a laid-back 1980s-style cafe could do very well here; now the old neighborhood shopping district around it is coming back to life with specialty shops and an antique store (p. 130).

Holland's large Spanish-speaking community goes back to the World war II bracero pro- gram which alleviated labor shortages here by bringing up mi- grant workers fromTexas at harvest time. Many later found permanent jobs in Holland's growing economy. Spanish- speaking churches are dotted around the central city, but you have to go to Fennville or Grand Rapids for a really good Mexican restaurant.

Just because Holland has become more liberal doesn't mean it's very much less Republican. Virtually *all* the Dutch vote Republican, except for a very few renegade intellectuals — it's one of those natural political affinities that goes back to the Civil War. (Hol-land's first mayor named a son Abraham Lincoln Cappon.) But Republican in Holland encompasses a wide range of the political spectrum. Holland's widely respected state senator Paul Hillegonds, who makes a point of supporting Detroit, is the rallying point for a revival of Michigan's strong tradition of moderate Republicanism, in eclipse since Governor Bill Milliken left office.

Holland's Republicans include plenty of outward-looking, tolerant social activists, centered around the Third Reformed Church, a beautiful Gothic Revival frame building on 12th Street.

The costs of prosperity

The city of Holland, locked in by surrounding townships, has little remaining land for housing developments. This has helped escalate housing costs and further spurred residential growth in the outlying townships.

As the local economy keeps booming, issues of affordable housing and traffic congestion are coming to the forefront. As in Grand Haven, its equally prosperous Ottawa County neighbor to the north, anti-growth sentiment is rising. Together these cities make Ottawa County the state's fastest-growing county.

Home-grown manufacturing giants

Many local plants have steadily grown over the years, though 1990 saw the closing of the 500-employee G.E. plant. In 1896 Pittsburgh-based Heinz established a plant on 19th Street at Lake Macatawa to make pickles and vinegar. It has grown into the largest pickle plant in the country. You can see the many large cypress vats as you drive west along 16th Street to the lake.

Life Saver, the first company to occupy the city's Southside Industrial Center back in 1967, employs 1,000. This is the world's only source for the famous Life Saver candies, sold in the familiar cylindrical package. Also made here is Bubble Yum bubblegum and Beechnut gum. When the wind is right, you can smell some of the wonderful flavors — different flavors on different days, depending on what is being produced — if you drive east out M-40 by the big plant.

While some major Holland manufacturers are branches of outside companies, the city stands out in the number of major homegrown companies. Gerrard Haworth, a shop teacher at Holland High School, started a small company in his basement in 1948 that

Holland's "baby mayor"
In 1988 voters surprised the nation — and themselves — by electing the youngest U. S. mayor, 22-year-old Phil Tanis, a recent Hope College grad with longish hair. He owed his victory, he said, to his good reputation as a city councilman in initiating Centennial Park improvements and to his opponent, the incumbent mayor, not taking his challenge seriously, which irritated voters. Tanis chose not to run again in 1990.

Cheap electricity
One attractive feature about Holland for industries is its inexpensive electricity. The city-owned 77-megawatt power plant on Lake Macatawa produces electricity costing local companies 25% less than private utilities serving the region. The thrifty Hollanders have kept their power plant costs to a minimum by adding on to the existing plant gradually and keeping their debt service low.

A Haworth employee inspecting part of an office panel system. The hundreds of holes absorb sound. In recent years, Haworth has exploded to half a billion dollars a year in sales, much of it due to its innovative office systems which integrate electrical wiring in office modules. It is one of several home-grown Holland firms which have grown to become nationally important in their fields.

has grown into the third-largest office furniture company in the U.S. after neighboring Steelcase in Grand Rapids and Herman Miller in Zeeland. Haworth has pioneered in putting wiring into wall and desk panels to meet the needs of today's high-tech offices. Its giant 1.5 million-square-foot factory can be seen along U. S. 31 in the very southeast corner of the city. Inconspicuous by day, it glows dramatically by night. The Donnelly Corporation, founded here in 1906, has become a major supplier of auto mirrors.

All these homegrown giants except Herman Miller are privately owned, and they are all non-union. Labor relations have generally been excellent, except for a strike at Bil-Mar, in which management was largely Dutch and the workers Mexican-Americans. In a tight community like Holland, there's not the tendency for managers to regard workers as their polar opposites when a good number of them are relatives. Pay is good — $35,000 isn't unusual for furniture makers.

Prince Corporation started making auto visors (still its largest product) in the mid-1960s and patented the lighted visor mirror. Its almost 2,000 employees now make all sorts of parts for cars — map lights, arm rests, door panels. The firm has grown to three plants, a technical center, a lab, and a corporate center.

Concern about downtown

Edgar Prince, the gifted inventor who founded Prince, has also become a major benefactor of Holland's downtown. He even bought a Burger King building in order to tear it down and improve appearances.

Holland has one of the most delightful main streets in the state. It remained the city's retail heart until two major malls were built out on U.S. 31 in 1988. In quick succession, the downtown lost Steketee's department store, Woolworth's, and J.C. Penney's, along with other shops. Serious decline threatened the once-robust

Hope Summer Repertory Theatre is a favorite vacation highlight, with its popular and interesting plays and musicals. 1990's playbill: The Music Man, The Merchant of Venice, I DO! I DO!, Moss Hart's Light Up the Sky, Athol Fugard's A Lesson From Aloes, and Steel Magnolias, plus The Children's Performance Troupe. $8.50-$12.50/single ticket, or a 4-show coupon for $33. 3 or 4 plays are performed each week. Early reservations advised. Call (616) 394-7890 for schedule.

business district. The situation was ironically made worse by Snowmelt, a major renovation project designed to make downtown more attractive in winter. The city built fancy new brick sidewalks and put pipes under the sidewalks and streets. Warm water, a by-product of the city's power plant, flows through the pipes in winter, keeping the entire district free of snow and ice. But for awhile, the area was so torn up that vulnerable businesses couldn't make it. Although a few vacant storefronts remain, glossy new specialty shops are locating downtown, and its future looks promising.

The downtown area also gets a boost from its proximity to the 2,700-student **Hope College**, whose attractive campus is just one block south of the heart of downtown. (See p. 129.) West of the campus and across River Street, many of the attractive historic homes on 12th Street are owned by Hope faculty.

A town without slums

One of the visually striking things about this city of 30,000 is how seldom you see dilapidated housing. Even in the poorer, largely rental district of town centered around 16th and Washington, the homes are well maintained, with only a few exceptions.

Many of Holland's most affluent residents live on South Shore Drive, which begins at the Heinz plant and heads west along Lake Macatawa to Lake Michigan. This is where manufacturing tycoon Edgar Prince has his home and where Amway co-founder Jay DeVos has his summer residence. (Neighbors hate his noisy, self-important arrivals by helicopter.) Scattered incongruously among the newer expensive estates are a number of small, modest summer cottages, relics of an earlier era. A recent trend has been for the affluent to buy up several adjacent cottage properties, remove the little cottages, and build a large home.

Tulip Time,
beginning on the Wednesday closest to May 14, draws some half-million visitors, largely seniors in tour busses. The opening parade of street scrubbers and bands goes into action when the governor officially inspects the street and sees dirt. There are loads of shows (from Lawrence Welk and Christian music to barbershop, vaudeville, and 50s songs), displays, folk dancing in wooden shoes, historic tours, etc. The biggest crowds are Saturday. It's impeccably organized, a real volunteer-powered community event locals go all-out for. Call 1-800-822-2770 or 616-396-4221 for information.

For a year-round visitor packet,
contact Holland Conv. & Visitors Bureau, 150 W. 8th St., Holland, MI 49423. (616) 396-4221.

POINTS OF INTEREST

Downtown Holland ★

Along 8th St. between River and Columbia. Many stores stay open until 9 p.m. Mondays and Fridays; some are also open Thursdays, or every night but Saturday. Closed Sundays.

Downtown Holland today is a mix of stability and change: the stability of turn-of-the-century buildings of unusual craftsmanship and style, now being stylishly renovated and

restored, and the changes brought in 1988 by two big new shopping centers opened out on U. S. 31 that year. Until then, downtown Holland had been the only major shopping area within 25 miles. To remain viable, more of Holland's downtown shops are becoming focused on visitors and college students at nearby Hope College.

Holland's business and government leaders were determined to preserve downtown as the focus of

Parking is free and plentiful
along 7th, just behind 8th St.'s north side. Smaller lots are also along 9th.

their community by getting out ahead of this wrenching change, which saw the exodus of all downtown's mid-priced anchors — Sears, Woolworth's, Steketee's, Penney's — at once. Many physical improvements were already in place by the time the malls opened. Beautiful flower beds along with pleasant benches and seating alcoves, attractive street lamps, paving, and ornamental details line the three blocks of 8th Street that form the core of downtown. Mid-block stop signs keep the street-scape pedestrian oriented. Everything is first-class and picture-perfect, in the same spirit of Old World craftsmanship and pride in which Holland's newly prosperous burgers erected these fine buildings 80 and 90 years ago.

Around 1990, however, downtown Holland looked like it was being kept alive by good intentions and lots of Ed Prince's money rather than a strong market. Today it's remarkably lively, with many interesting and creative new businesses and more to open as we go to press. It makes for great browsing, what with numerous book and record stores and galleries, specialty shops, lots of places to eat and snack, four parks, an art movie theater, two nearby museums (the new **Holland Museum**, p. 128, and the reconfigured **Baker Furniture**

Craftsmanship is a point of pride among Holland's Dutch, and its turn-of-the-century downtown was built most hand-somely. Now facades are being refurb-ished in a historic vein with low-interest loans arranged by Mainstreet Holland.

Museum, p. 134), and even a down-town bowling alley (at 9th and Center). Pick up a store location map at area stores to get the full picture. Downtown Holland has everything but Sunday hours and bars (though beer and wine are served at Alpen Rose, the 8th Street Grille, and Till Midnight).

The good shopping starts around the corner from 8th on River at 9th. (Five parking lots on 9th make it a handy place to park.) At the corner at 213 S. River is the **Black River Gallery** (616-392-7479), an attractive artists' cooperative with some fabulous, fresh watercolor and pastel landscapes and flower pictures, among other media. Next door at 211, **The Highwheeler** bike shop (616-396-6084) has bike rentals and free maps of recommended bike paths and routes. (See p. 119.) **The Country House** (616-392-7620) at 224 S. River, an upscale women's wear store with a big Liz Claiborne section, occupies at picturesque 1920s building with stepped Dutch gables.

Across River Ave. there's a profusely stocked party goods and card shop, a doll shop, and, at 210 S. River, **The Shaker Messenger Gallery of Shaker & Folk Art** (616-396-4588). "We know personally everyone who makes things for our store," says an owner, and that personal touch is evident. For do-it-yourselfers, there are books, supplies, and plenty of inspiration and encouragement. Fans of spare and simple country crafts

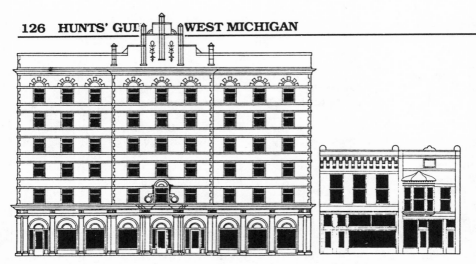

and decor should pick up a newsletter featuring special talks, demonstrations, workshops, and receptions.

Down at River and 8th, **Reader's World** (616-396-8548, open nightly) is an exceptionally well managed and attractive branch of Community News, with a vast array of magazines and a good book section. Across 8th St., **Tower Clock Accents** (616-393-0305) occupies a beautiful space in an 1891 building of Waverly stone, renovated by Holland manufacturing magnate Ed Prince. The downstairs gifts and accessories are much warmer and more affordable than earlier, with lots of sunflowers and punchy cotton afghans. Upstairs are all the big names in china and stemware (Royal Doulton, Kosta Boda, also Dansk), the kitchen shop, and hand-painted, faceted mirrors selling for $1,000 or so and made here in Holland by La Barge Mirrors.

Crossing River and going east on 8th, two upscale, fashion-forward women's wear stores flank the vibrant, active **Holland Arts Council** at 25 W. 8th. (616-396-3278). Its **gallery** typically shows work by several Michigan artists in one medium at a time — recently, photography, weaving, and watercolor. The **shop** is crammed with unusual jewelry, cards, and art-related gifts. The newsletter announces workshops, **performances**, and dances visitors can join in.

Five doors east of the Arts Council, the courtyard park by First

The old Warm Friend Hotel and Tavern (left) on 8th at Central, now a retirement home, gained its name from its chief backer, the Holland Furnace Company, now defunct. "Holland Furnaces Make Warm Friends" was its slogan. Long Holland's leading industry, it helped build the hotel to house salesmen for meetings.

of America Bank has umbrellaed tables that are ideal for takeout food from the **8th Street Grille** across the way, or **Alpen Rose**, the **Nickelodeon**, or **Waalke's Deli**, all across the street and a block east.

Across from the Arts Council at 18 W. 8th, **The Bridge** (616-392-3977) is a self-help crafts store supplied by artisans from 40 developing countries and run by a volunteer ministry of

Western Theological Seminary. It's been a big hit. Textiles, wall hangings, rugs, and jackets especially stand out. Merchandise is very reasonably priced, appealing, and attractively displayed.

The long block of 8th between Central and College has still more good browsing. For the overly organized and the disorganized, **The Holding Company** at 17 E. 8th (616-396-6060) specializes in organizers large and small, stylish and utilitarian. **Booksellers on Mainstreet** at 49 East 8th (616-396-0043) has an attractive mix of books, cards, and some gifts.

Across the street, at 8th and Central, **Alpen Rose** has a genuine

Austrian *konditorei* (the whipped cream pastries, rye breads, and coffee are terrific!) in front of its excellent restaurant. Next door, the bright Guatemalan textiles and clothing at **Tikal** bring something new to Holland. And next to it, **The Tin Ceiling** features folk art and Victorian and Scandinavian crafts from four cooperating owners.

Holland is excited about the arrival of a real deli, **Waalke's Butcher & Deli** at 44 E. 8th (616-395-0998). It's not exactly a New York deli — Jews are rare in these parts — but a branch of the Breton Village Butcher Shop that caters to the Grand Rapids carriage trade. It's a big, bustling place at 44 E. 8th, and there's lots of sunny seating in a light-filled rear dining area. Deli salads, including five or six pasta salads and four kinds of potato salad, are made frsh daily, and much of the sausage is house-made. 90 sandwiches range from $2.50 (for brats and weiners) to $6. Soups and chili and also house-made; bread is from Hempel's and Till Midnight. Imported cheeses and many kinds of seafood are also on hand. Vacationers might make use of party trays and fresh and frozern entrees for takeout; the big, beefy burritos win raves. Open from 7 a.m. to 10 p.m. daily except Sunday.

At 54 E. 8th, **Tewlews Gallery** (616-396-0855) is where Joan Van Leeuw and Jane Van Loo have assembled interesting, bright works by 50 Midwestern artists in various media, including a lot of jewelry. Ask them about still more galleries not yet open as we go to press.

At College and 8th, turn south (right) onto College toward the Hope College campus to find the popular, reliably excellent **Till Midnight** restaurant and bakery with a sidewalk cafe, up from a coin and stamp shop and **Jacob's Ladder** (616-392-3303), which comes close to being a New Age/Punk/Christian music store. (In Holland you come to expect surprises like that!)

East of College, retailing is largely replaced by offices and service businesses. At 86 E. 8th, the Dutch-style **Knickerbocker Theater** is now owned by Hope College and booked with art and foreign films (shown daily at 7 and 9 or so; adult admission $4.50) and occasional performances. Call (616) 395-4950 for program info. Next door, the lower level of the impressive new 100 East office building now houses the **Baker Furniture Museum** of antique furniture studied by furniture designers. (See p. 134.)

Centennial Park ★

Between S. River and Central from 10th to 12th streets.

There's something so sweetly old-fashioned and leisurely about this big, shady downtown square that it lends a special aura of continuity with the past to events held here beneath its canopy of century-old trees. In 1876, Holland, still recovering from the disastrous fire of 1871, marked the nation's centennial by building a central mound here in the original market square and planting trees along winding gravel paths.

Over the years the park has received numerous picturesque adornments — park benches, a rock grotto at the north end, a central circular fountain (illuminated at night), and palm trees and tropical flowering plants, brought out each summer from the Victorian greenhouse the city has out on Central Avenue near 20th Street. There are even old fashioned "carpet beds" of flowers in the

---

Historic walking tours

You can pick up a brochure describing two annotated walking tours of historic Holland at the Herrick Public Library on River at 12th. (Mon-Thurs 9-9, Fri & Sat 9-6, Sun 2-5). Both tours begin at Centennial Park on River between 10th and 12th. One includes downtown and Hope College. The other covers the historic district centered along 12th between Pine and Washington, just west of River.

shapes of a windmill and wooden shoe. Recent improvements, including brick paths and a gazebo, have carefully respected the park's sense of belonging to another era.

It's hard to imagine a better setting for 750 fresh-faced high school klompen dancers at Tulip Time than the streets around the park, across from yards all abloom with flowering shrubs. Another magical event is the **multiethnic, participatory art festival** aimed at children, held Thursday through Saturday over the July 4 weekend.

The park is a good starting point for interesting walks: east along 12th Street to the old part of the Hope College Campus, or west on 12th into the historic district. Just north of the park, don't miss the Michigan Bell Telephone Building from the 1920s, designed to reflect Dutch Renaissance architecture.

Holland Museum
(formerly the Netherlands Museum)

Tenth at River in the old post office facing Centennial Park. (616) 392-9084. Mon-Sat 10-5:30, Thurs to 8, Sun 2-5. $7/family, $3 for adults, $2 seniors & students, under 5 free.

What used to be the Netherlands Museum, the only U.S. museum focused on Dutch culture here and in Europe, has now moved into Holland's grand old post office. Its focus is now on the city of Holland, though it continues to display many artifacts from the old museum: Delftware; a quaint tiled Dutch living room recreated in the Cincinnati apartment of a Dutch emigrant; a large doll house, furnished down to inkwells and cookie cutters; and many things shown in the Dutch exhibit of the 1939 World's Fair. These include an 11-foot clock surmounted by the Queen and her ministers (press a button and it plays the Dutch national anthem) and model glass houses of worship

Few if any peoples in history have lavished more attnetion on the home and its cozy amenities than the Dutch. This rural living room, on view at the Holland Museum, was recreated in a Cincinnati apartment.

representing the Netherlands' many denominations stemming from its tradition of religious tolerance — tolelrance that, ironically, did not extend to protect the fundamentalist rural Christians who emigrated en masse to the U.S.

Many exhibits are incomplete as we go to press. One wall will become a chronology of Holland history, from the hardships of the early years to today. The story of Holland's remarkable economic development is told well, with many products, old and new, and an emphasis on the cultural values that created the climate for growth. A prominent part of the story is the arrival of Holland's Mexican-Americans and Asians and their cultures. One gallery features changing exhibits from the museum's many artifacts in storage. For a more intimate look at the Dutch migration to West Michigan, see the Dekker Huis in Zeeland (p. 146).

Hope College campus

Centered on College Ave. between 10th and 13th streets. Campus maps available at the admissions office, 69 E. 10th St. from 8-5 weekdays. **Events hotline:** *(616) 394-7863.*

The 2,500-student liberal arts college has both a strong faculty and high academic standards for admission. Hope is proud of its reputation for producing future science Ph.Ds. Its theater program is also outstanding. Good teaching and a caring faculty involved with students are big attractions at Hope, like many small liberal arts schools.

Hope's affiliation with the Reformed Church in America (p. 120) gives it a Christian dimension — official literature talks about maintaining an environment in which "students are free [and encouraged] to examine what it means to be a Christian in today's world." But chapel attendance and religion courses are not required, and the faculty and student body doesn't overwhelmingly reflect membership in the parent denomination, as it does at Grand Rapid's Calvin College. Catholic students, in fact, are said to outnumber Reformed Church members. The separate Western Theological Seminary, also affiliated with the Reformed Church in America, occupies the southwest corner of the campus.

Hope's campus is an attractive architectural hodgepodge, including a few Dutch-style buildings, developed gradually over more than a century. Its oldest building dates from 1857, when Hope was only an academy. You can get a look at student life at Hope by walking along **Van Raalte Commons**, a portion of 12th Street converted to a pedestrian mall connecting College and Columbia

Hope's logo, an anchor, goes back to its founding as the anchor of Reformed faith in the New World.

streets. Or you can visit the basement of the **DeWitt Center** off Columbia between 11th and 12th, where there is a cafeteria, student bookstore, and small game arcade. On the first floor you can see the college's FM radio station (89.1) in operation. Behind a plate glass window a student DJ spins rock 'n' roll records which no doubt would shock earlier generations of Hope students.

De Pree Art Center and Gallery   ★

Off Columbia between 11th and 12th, behind the visitor parking lot. (616) 394-7500. Sept through April: Mon-Thurs 9-10, Fri 9-7, Sat 10-7, Sun 1-10. Summer hours: Mon-Fri 9-5.

An old yellow brick factory building has been turned into studio space for Hope's well-regarded art department. There's also a large **gallery** with two-story ceiling, ideal for large canvasses and constructions. The gallery mounts a stimulating range of exhibits, including occasional shows by nationally known artists and contemporary artists from the Netherlands.

The building honors in name and spirit Hugh De Pree, the retired chairman of Herman Miller furniture. A Hope alum, he chaired its board of trustees for 12 years. He, his father, and his brother Max won international admiration from designers, art critics, business managers, and social critics for their application of good design principles to furniture manufacturing (Gilbert Rohde and Charles and Ray Eames designed for Herman Miller) and for their Scanlon Plan, a model of workplace democracy first introduced in the 1950s.

Washington Square

Washington between 18th and 19th Streets.

This older one-block neighborhood retail district has become something of a specialty food center with the success of Pereddies' deli, bakery, and restaurant (see p. 141). **The Leaf and Bean** (392-6260; Mon-Sat 10-6) sells coffees, teas, and related brewing devices and mugs, along with some candies, gifts, cards, and a big selection of simple striped and checked kitchen towels. **Washington Square Wines** (392-4422; Mon-Thurs 8 a.m.-11 p.m., Fri & Sat unitl midnight) is a good wine store. **Pereddies** itself consciously follows the traditions of old Italian groceries and carries all the expected staples: olive oils and vinegars, imported and fresh pastas, and cheeses, plus deli salads and crusty Italian bread and foccacia baked on the premises. (The bakery/deli is open Mon-Sat 10-8.)

Across the street, **Kottage House Antiques** (Mon-Sat 11-9) is a new mall occupying a deceptively large series of interconnected buildings. It's strong on furniture and unusual pieces, very attractively displayed in an uncluttered, quality-oriented environment, and seldom bargain-priced.

Kollen Park

Between 10th and 12th Streets along Lake Macatawa.

This immaculately maintained city park offers a beautiful view of sailboats on the lake, marred only by parked cars along the shore. There's a picnic pavilion, plenty of shade trees, a flower bed in the shape of a cross. The **American Legion band** often performs on summer Tuesdays; call (616) 392-4863 for the schedule. Kollen Park has a boat launch and places to sit and fish, but no swimming beach. It's not far from Pereddies Bakery/Deli, 447 Washington, with great selections for picnics.

Cappon House   ★

9th and Washington. (6160 394-1362. Open regularly in summer (June through August), Wed 1-4 and 2nd and 4th Sundays 1-4. Sept. 22-Oct. 20, 1990: open daily (10-4, Sun 1-4) except Mon. for special exhibit on **19th-century lighting; also open at Christmas.** *Tours at other times cheerfully arranged for groups of any size. $2.*

The 1874 Italianate home of Isaac Cappon (pronounced Ca-PON), Holland's first mayor and one of its richest men, was Holland's most elaborate home in its day, with exceptionally ornate woodwork, an impressively grand parlor, sitting room, and hall, and massive Berkey & Gay furniture from Grand Rapids. By standards of older, wealthier places, the house isn't amazing. But Holland's original settlers in 1847, including the 18-year-old Cappon, had little money, and the house was an impressive testimonial to the success of Cappon's tannery, which once was Michigan's biggest.

The house stayed in the Cappon family for 109 years, well maintained, until Isaac's daughter left it to the city. About three-fourths of the furniture is original, which allows for an unusually authentic look at the life of a prominent Dutch-American family. Isaac Cappon had 16 children, including five with his second, much younger wife, who had been the maid when his first wife died.

His adult children were so upset at his remarriage that he moved into a smaller nearby house for some years. But he and his new family eventually reconciled and moved back into this big, seven-bedroom house. Small children were confined to the big upstairs nursery to save wear and tear on the house. Some younger children lived here as adults and remodeled the house in the 1920s. Lavinia Cappon's 1920s bedroom is especially charming. (A high school home economics teacher, she made sure the costumes at Tulip Time were authentic.)

Gradually the house is being restored to its appearance in the 1870s. The somber dark red and green exterior colors are a step in that direction, but the landscaping is recent and not at all accurate. As the center for city historical events, the Cappon House hosts occasional Victorian teas, barbershop concerts, croquet tournaments, exhibits of Victorian handicrafts, and the like.

Macatawa

Take any north-south street south to 19th St. and go west past the Heinz pickle factory to Lake Macatawa. When it reaches the lake, 16th bends and becomes South Shore Dr. leading four miles out along the lake to Lake Michigan. There is no public Lake Michigan access in Macatawa, but Saugatuck State Park (p. 102) is just 5 miles south.

Macatawa, Holland's oldest and most prestigious resort area, goes back to 1881, when prominent men purchased Macatawa Park on the south side of the mouth of Lake Macatawa. (Macatawa is the Ottawa word

for black, and the lake was first called Black Lake by early whites in the area.) Within a few years it had grown into a cottage colony with several hotels. The huge, arcaded porch of the Hotel Macatawa, built for 300 guests, surveyed the mouth and the point. Today the site is a private park used by cottage-owners and guests of the Point West resort.

Today Macatawa retains some of its cottagey charm, but marinas and Holland's most expensive homes are far more prominent along this scenic drive. Two upscale "fine dining" restaurants overlook the lake. **Point West** (335-3358) has a better view, the **Sandpiper** (p. 142) has better food.

L. Frank Baum spent 10 summers in Macatawa and nearby Castle Park.

A freighter leaves Lake Macatawa and enters Lake Michigan. Holland has made less public use of its waterfront than other West Michigan ports. There is no boardwalk and only a relatively small city park on the water. The Lake Michigan beach on the channel at Macatawa is private, owned by the cottage association and Point West Resort (the building complex above the freighter's bow).

He worked on parts of the Oz books here and also wrote a satirical novel about Macatawa, *Tamawaca Folks,* under the name of John Estes Cooke.

Nob-Hill Country Store ★

1261 Grafschaap Rd. just south of 146th Ave., about 3 miles southwest of downtown Holland and 1 mile west of the Tulip City Antiques Mall on Washington. Take Grafschaap Rd. from South Shore Dr., or from U. S. 31 take Washington St. north, turn left immediately onto Matt Urban Dr. which turns into 146th Ave. (616) 392-1424. Mon-Sat 10-5:30.

This century-old country store, complete with original shelves, drawers, and pot-belly stove, is now an antiques mall. About 20 dealers offer quite a range of old stuff, including jewelry, inexpensive collectibles, and furniture refinished and in the rough. Prices are generally quite reasonable. At the old wooden counter, browsers can enjoy coffee, doughnuts, and pigs in a blanket (frankfurters in biscuit dough, an old Dutch treat). For years this was the Graafschap Hardware Store, now expanded across the street.

Tulip City Antique Mall

1145 S. Washington south of 32nd St., 2 miles south of downtown, very near the Washington north exit from U. S. 31. (616) 396-8855. Mon-Sat 10-5:30, Sun noon-5.

A plain, 12,000-square foot building on a high-traffic commercial street houses about 55 dealers with a wide range of goods and prices. There are loads of collectibles, dolls, books, some Indian artifacts, and plenty of room for furniture.

Nuttin But Puttin Miniature Golf ★

915 Lincoln at 37th St. Lincoln is also M-40 heading southeast from Holland to Allegan. 2 blocks north of U.S. 31. (616) 392-7234. Mon-Sat 10 a.m.-

10 p.m., mid May to mid September. $1.50/person until 6 p.m., $2.50 thereafter.

What a combination, straight out of a 1930s roadside strip! Here is a flower-filled miniature golf course whose first hole is through an alligator's moving mouth. It's next to the **Salad Bowl (396-8328)**, a popular old-time lunch counter in a quaint, Tudor-style building. It serves pizza, pies, sandwiches, and Balken Brij, a fried liver pate served on toast. The Salad Bowl abuts the wildly colorful **Jonker's Gardens (392-7234)**, one of the leading greenhouse/florists of Holland's flower-loving Dutch. It makes for a nice low-key outing or driving break coming north off U.S. 31 onto Lincoln.

Actually, it's not entirely a relic of the 1930s. Garden store owner John Jonkers laid out the miniature golf course in 1961 as a summer showplace for his bedding plants, clematis, hibiscus, cannas, and the like. Now that his sons run the store, minigolf is his retirement project. The course has a covered bridge and waterwheel, and a profusion of potted plants everywhere you look — clearly a high-maintenance labor of love. It's worth the fee just to experience this wonderful, folksy, colorful golf garden from within. And the course is more challenging than the neat rectangular layout would make you think.

Windmill Island Municipal Park ★

Corner of 7th and Lincoln, just northeast of downtown Holland. (616) 396-5433. **May, July & Aug:** *Mon-Sat 9-6, Sun 11:30-6.* **June & Sept:** *Mon-Fri 10-5, Sat 9-6, Sun 11:30-6.* **Oct:** *Mon-Fri 10-4, Sat 9-5, Sun 11:30-5. Adults $3.50, children 5-12 $1.75.*

Visitors seem to love this city park built for tourists. It features **De Zwaan** ("the swan"), the only working antique windmill outside of the Netherlands. The mill grinds whole wheat flour sold at the park, but only

At Tulip Time Windmill Island's formal tulip beds are abloom. Varieties are neatly identified by number so you can order bulbs for fall shipment from Veldheer's Tulip Gardens nearby. Unless the tulips are blooming and the mill is actually in operation on your visit, Dutch Village on U.S. 31 at James Road is a better family enter-tainment value — more attractive, more interesting, more fun for children, with better shopping, and more enthusiastic klompen dancers.

Windmill Island does offer some very pleasant attractions. The 1910 Dutch **carousel,** with its gay barrel-organ music, is wonderful. The shady, canal-side **terrace** between the carousel and the cafe is nice. (Refreshments there are very ordinary, but picnics are permitted.) The windmill and nearby drawbridge are picturesque. Fans of folk art may well enjoy **"Little Netherlands,"** a model of a canal-laced Dutch town in 1847, the year of Holland's founding. It fills up most of a good-sized building with ships and canals, streets and wind-

At Tulip Time Windmill Island provides plenty of photo opportunities like this, neatly indicated with signs. Its souvenir shop sells lots of schlock, and motels up and down the coast are booked with tour groups. But Tulip Time goes beyond commercialism. 1,500 high school volunteers — including increasing numbers of boys — practice klompen dancing 3 times a week from January through May in preparation for the event, and buy and sew their own costumes.

mills. Local artisans built and carved it as a Tulip Festival project in the 1930s, and put in lots of jokey scenes and corny comments.

Scheduled attractions include an overblown but mildly interesting film about De Zwaan and its relocation in Michigan, klompen dancers who were lackadaisical on our visit, followed by a competent, brisk tour of the five-story windmill. Windmill Island's **gift and fudge shop** and few historical displays are mostly uninspired. The landscaping and summer flower beds are less attractive than when they were new, if old photos of spectacular dahlia beds are any indication.

The commercial spirit is so assertive and unrestrained on Windmill Island that it leaves a bad taste in your mouth. Offensive items like

"You're not much if you're not Dutch" are sold in the gift shop of this city park. This place needs a strong manager to fuss over details: to keep plastic garden windmills off the quaint Dutch street, to tidy up the messy causeway, to furnish and accessorize more completely the potentially charming Posthuis Inn, to ban plastic paddleboats from the canal and screen. That way visitors, after shelling out $7 a couple, might really feel they're "two minutes. . . and two centuries. . . from downtown," as the travel brochure boasts.

Baker Furniture Museum

100 E. Eighth St. between College and Columbia in downtown Holland, next to the Knickerbocker Theater. Enter thru middle door, take elevator to lower level. (616) 392-8761. Mon-Fri 10-5, Sat 10-12, closed Sun. Call (616) 392-3181 for winter hours, Nov.-March. Adults $2, children 12-16 $1. Under 12 free.

The collection was moved several years ago to Holland, where Baker also has a plant. Now it is housed in the lower level of a fancy new office building, in air-conditioned quarters. But interpreting the furniture for visitors without previous knowledge of furniture remains haphazard; the museum is recommended for design students and admirers of traditional furniture.

The furniture museum began in the 1920s, when Hollis Baker, the founder's son and a connoisseur of art and antiques, took over the business. He reorganized the operation to produce furniture he personally liked. Lengthy buying trips to Europe resulted in most of this collection of original-state antiques.

A Georgian room setting of some of Baker's current exacting reproductions is part of the most interesting room. There, examples of the original antiques sit alongside the Baker copies. Often it's hard to tell them apart, so cleverly executed is the new "antique" finish. In the chair

hall, chairs are warehoused, in no particular order, on three tiers. Hollis Baker liked 18th-century English, French, and Italian styles best, but prototypes for Baker's contemporary and Chinese lines of the 1950s are here, too. A room of colorful, freely painted 18th and 19th century folk baroque pieces enliven the mix somewhat, as do occasional odd items like wine coolers, commode chairs hiding chamber pots, and an 1800 French bathtub.

The foundation of Baker Furniture's early prosperity, and the kind of mass-produced, middle-class furniture Hollis Baker hated, sits in the corner of the museum reception area: an 1890s golden oak "combination bookcase" with shelves with glass doors alongside a drop-front desk — just the thing that lend an elegant note to the parlor of a modest home. What a contrast to the lushly photographed villas and palazzi in the Baker Furniture catalogs!

Don't miss "The Making of a Treasure," a **15-minute video** showing Baker Furniture craftspeople hand-carving furniture, tying upholstery, and utilizing other custom skills to produce their top-of-the-line furniture. A new book $30 celebrating Baker's centennial is for sale.

Holland State Park

2215 Ottawa Beach Rd. (near Lake Michigan) Holland, MI 49424. (616) 399-9390. 8 a.m.-10 p.m. $3/day; $15/year for state park sticker. Camping fees: $10/night includes electricity and shower; $7/night Oct. 15-April 15 (no shower). Early reservations (Jan./Feb.) imperative for summer weekends; some space usually available weekdays. Reservation forms at all state park headquarters, or through DNR, Box 30028, Lansing 48909. $4 reservation fee.

Michigan's most popular park incorporates some nature in a high-energy urban-resort setting. The Victorian gingerbread cottages between the park's two sections are

Jet skiers zoom past Holland's unusual 1907 lighthouse, across the channel from Holland State Park. The light tower juts out of a roof gable. What once was the light keeper's house has been covered in steel to withstand the fierce Great Lake storms.

part of the Ottawa Beach cottage development going back to the 1880s. The park's Lake Michigan beach was once the site of the Ottawa Park Hotel, with an arcaded porch so long it seems to have rivalled the Grand Hotel's famous porch.

This park is popular not only for its 1,800 feet of sugar sand **beach** but for boating, charter and pier fishing, and windsurfing. (Instruction and rentals are at Surf Shop Windsurfing, 1/2 mile before the park entrance.) The broad **Lake Michigan beachfront** is just at the busy inlet to Lake Macatawa; the big red lighthouse across the channel is a local landmark. There's a large bathhouse and food concession and vast parking areas; this beach is a hot spot for young people, not only from Holland but Grand Rapids. Behind the beach, 147 campsites on the **Lake Michigan Campground** are laid out on blacktop and beach sand. (No ground fires are permitted.)

Many benches and **picnic tables** face the **channel**, which affords good

perch fishing in summer. So does the **pier**. In fall and spring, pier fishermen cast for steelhead, salmon, and brown trout.

The park's separate **Lake Macatawa Unit** about half a mile east on Ottawa Beach Road is somewhat more relaxed. 221 campsites have fire pits and picnic tables. It is just across the road from the boat launch on Lake Macatawa. About half its campsites are beneath mid-size pines; those against the wooded dune are quite private. The other half are on an open, grassy area.

Tunnel Park

Between Lake Michigan and Lake Shore Dr. just south of Lakewood, and 2 miles north of the channel to Lake Macatawa. (616) 846-8117. 7 a.m.-10 p.m. Fee charged between Mem. Day and Labor Day: $2/day per vehicle, $12 annual pass for nonresidents, $8 for residents.

Recent renovations have spiffed up this popular older county park. There's still a tunnel through a sand dune to the beach; it leads to an attractive new platform and stair down to the wide, sandy beach. The children's play area is strategically sited at the foot of a steep stretch of dune, and climbing up the sand is encouraged. A tall, challenging stairway brings you atop the dune, where picnic tables and grills and an overlook platform take advantage of the view.

The small woods in the park aren't anything as deeply mysterious as the majestic beeches and maples at Kirk Park, 11 miles to the north. But there's more level playing area here for sports.

Park Twp. bike paths ★

Along Ottawa Beach Rd. and Lakewood Blvd. to Lake Shore Dr., Holland State Park, Tunnel Park, and Kirk Park. For a free map, contact Cross Country Cycle, 137 N. River (616) 396-7491.

Separate bike paths, sometimes well off the roadway, enable cyclists to bicycle safely out busy Ottawa Beach Road to Holland State Park and along beautiful Lake Shore Drive, through dunes and woods, to beaches at Tunnel and Kirk parks. Other paths parallel interior roads, permitting loops. Another loop goes along South Shore Drive south of Lake Macatawa, starting at 17th Street south of the pickle factory, and goes almost to the channel, returning via 32nd Street.

Poll Museum of Transportation ★

U.S. 31 at New Holland Rd., 5 miles north of Holland. (616) 399-1955. Open daily except Sunday May 1 through Labor Day. Adults $1, children 10-12 50¢, under 10 free with an adult.

Clyde and Ethel Poll started collecting old vehicles in 1940. A tool and die worker, Clyde started this museum in 1954 after selling his business. It's an unpretentious little museum, "just a hobby," says Ethel. But the 30-odd cars, trucks, and fire engines are an interesting assortment of vintage American vehicles, and the collection is continually be-

ing upgraded. There's a 1904 Cadillac, one of the earliest you're likely to see of that important make. Two early Buicks, from 1908 and 1910, are on display. You can see a 1921 Pierce Arrow and a 1931 Packard. A favorite is the bulky 1948 Chrysler Town and Country convertible, in mint condition, complete with wood sides.

Old fire engines take up almost half of the long, cinderblock museum, whose exterior is done up to resemble a Dutch village. One is a 1920 American La France. The ma and pa museum also has collections of old bottles, model trains, toy trucks (greatly expanded), and sea shells.

Ethel Poll runs the rather large **gift shop** up front. She says the museum doesn't get as many visitors as it used to. "It's the young people," she explained. "All they seem interested in is sports."

Veldheer Tulip Gardens★★

*12755 Quincy St., just east of U.S. 31, 4 miles north of Holland. (616) 399-1900. Hours change with the season. Open all year. **May** daily 8-dusk. **June through Oct** daily 8-6. Admission fee (May only) $2 adults, $1 children 6-16.*

In May, tour buses flock here to see Holland's most spectacular mass of blooming tulips at this bulb-grower. There's a very pleasant formal garden, complete with drawbridges and the inevitable windmills; in summer annuals replace the tulips. And there are 30 acres of tulip fields behind Veldheer's warehouses. Beds are numbered to correspond with mail-order catalog numbers, so you can place orders for fall bulbs after seeing the real thing in bloom (about April 20 through May). Veldheer claims to grow the world's largest selection of tulips, 76 varieties in all, plus various daffodils, hyacinths, crocus, and fritillaria. Prices run from $5 to $6.70 for quantities of 10.

Veldheer's garden store offers a wide selection of corny garden ornaments frequently seen around Holland: wooden windmills ($50 for the two-foot size, $80 for four-foot), kissing Dutch couples, and painted wood tulips, along with a parade of plywood skunks, deer, frogs, and cute-as-a-button puppies with long eyelashes.

For a less commercial tulip experience, drive out to see the fields of tulips at dusk, when the tour busses are gone and locals come out after work to enjoy the flowers. (It's remarkable how most everybody in Holland genuinely seems to enjoy the tulips and the accompanying festivities.) Especially on overcast days at dusk, the sweeping masses of tulips seem to glow and shimmer with their own light.

De Klomp Wooden Shoe and Delftware Factory ★

12755 Quincy St. just east of U.S. 31, 4 miles north of Holland. Next to Veldheer's. (616) 399-1900. Hours same as Veldheer's, except closed on Saturdays in Jan & Feb, Free admission.

This unprepossessing metal building next to Veldheer's Tulip Gardens is the only place outside the Netherlands where earthenware is hand-painted in the Dutch style using genuine Delft blue glaze. Blue and white Delft began during the Netherlands' great sea-trading days as an imitation of expensive Chinese porcelains which the middle class could afford.

Clear, interesting signs explain the process of decorating the ceramics and applying glazes. Visitors can see greenware being formed and painted. Painters are happy to answer questions and explain any confusion about what is and isn't handpainted. (Inexpensive looka-likes are decorated with printed decal transfers.) Visitors see the artists freely painting decorations on the soft white bisque before a third and final firing alters the pale paint

Wooden shoes ("klompen" in Dutch, "sabots" in French) are practical footwear for outdoor work on damp ground. They are still made and frequently worn in the Netherlands, but with rounded toes rather than the cute pointed ones made and sold in Michigan. In Europe wooden shoes are made of poplar; Michigan's factories use aspen, which is easily worked when green, but dries hard. Prices vary according to size. Multiple pairs of thick socks are worn to cushion the foot.

to a brilliant blue.

Popular items are personalized wedding and retirement plates ($80 and up when completely painted by hand), mugs ($13 and up), tiny shoes and figurines ($8), house portraits, and wedding or baby tiles. Items handpainted here come in a wider variety of colors than the traditional blue and white: green and gold, red and gold, or multicolor.

"De Klomp" means "wooden shoe", and there's also a wooden shoe demonstration workshop with picture windows, where visitors can sometimes see shoes being made on old Dutch machinery. De Klomp's large stock of plain and decorated wearable wooden shoes comes from the Netherlands, where it is more economically produced. Prices here ($16.45 for a women's size 7) are significantly cheaper than at other local outlets. Other Dutch souvenirs are also for sale — imported sweets, polyester lace valences, myriad forms of windmills and wooden shoes — all the Dutch souvenir shops have pretty much the same stuff.

Dutch Village ★★★

*12350 James at U.S. 31, 2 miles northeast of downtown. (616) 396-1475. **Shops** open year-round 9-5:30, in summer until 8. Free admission when grounds are closed. **Grounds** are open from the last weekend of April through September. Gates open*

at 9 a.m. and close at 6. Admission: $4 adults, $2 children 3-11.

Fantasy, nostalgia, kitsch, and education are beguilingly combined in this recreation of a Dutch Village. It's sandwiched between truck-filled U.S. 31 (noise buffers would be a nice improvement) and the new Manufacturers' Marketplace outlet mall, which picks up the Dutch theme with step-gabled shops and a canal with wood drawbridge.

The brick buildings that line Dutch Village's four canals really do look like they're in the Netherlands, with their careful detailing and imported tile roofs. In summer when the grounds are open, the best part is the operating, antique street carnival attractions, free for the cost of admission: a **carousel**, two splendid, ornately carved Dutch **street organs**, and the **Zweefmolen**, a swing something like an antique carousel. It's just scary enough for older kids to want to ride it again and again—conveniently allowing adults to look longer at interesting exhibits and shops.

High-kicking, adept **klompen dancers** perform at 10:30, 12, 2, 4, and 6 to waltzes and gallops played on the Gauen Engel organ, an oversize 1880 Amsterdam street organ restored by the famous Carl Frey in 1960. For organ-lovers, this

Highlights of a visit to Dutch Village are the sights and sounds of an old-fashioned Dutch street carnival: a carousel, a giant swing, two splendid operating organs (the Golden Angel is pictured here), and street dancing in wooden shoes.

alone is worth the cost of admission. Visitors can go behind the organ to see the bellows, wood pipes, and punched music paper (much like a player piano's) in action. Recordings of street-organ classics are for sale in one of the gift shops.

The kiddie attractions are great. A wavy **slide** descends from a wooden shoe house. **Ducks** can be fed on the pond, and **goats** and **sheep** in the half-scale barn. Attached to the barn is a typical 18th-century **farmhouse**, realistically furnished, with an alcove bed in the stairwell, and a root cellar down below. The nearby garden area has a European-style grape arbor, roses, and a giant stork holding a diaper. Visitors can sit and pose for photos, one of many such planned photo opportunities.

Displays of **Dutch regional costumes** and a well-done **windmill diorama** are tucked within a building across the way, along with a **cheese-making exhibit.** Next to it, in a grisly allusion to medieval superstitions that survived in 17th-century Holland, is a scale where suspected witches were weighed. (If they were unusually light, they were suspected of being able to fly.)

The gift shops at Dutch Village cover an enormous range. The **Souvenir Shop** covers the low end, including the usual Dutchware plus costume dolls, God Bless Our Camper plaques, and some attractive tulip posters. The **Arts and Crafts Building** goes way upscale with lead crystal, Dutch lace valences, a lot of pricey English and French collectibles (interesting carved figures, quaint porcelain villages), beer steins, Delft-trimmed Dutch copper and brass cookware, and cases of stunning Royal Delft, including a $900 plate after a Rembrandt painting. In the same building is a small **wooden shoe factory** (for demonstration only) and shop.

Imported cheeses, Belgian chocolates, cookies, and jams are for sale in the **Gourmet Food Shop** and **terrace** overlooking the Manufacturers' Marketplace pond.

All this 20th-century consumer buzz is artfully concealed from the streets of Dutch Village, where life seems to proceed at an earthy, rural pace. A fiberglass dog pulls a cart. Cheeses are piled on a sled. Fish hang from a fishwagon. The **Bioskoop** (movie theater) shows a free movie on the Netherlands, heavy on local color but intelligent enough.

Manufacturers' Marketplace

On James just east of U. S. 31. Mon-Sat 10-9, Sun 11-7.

An idea born in an empty Muskegon discount store has blossomed into six snazzy, themed, open-air outlet malls with food courts, mostly in areas of high-traffic tourism. The Holland Marketplace is Michigan's third, after Monroe and Birch Run near Frankenmuth. By the summer of 1990, it was up to 65 stores, almost as big as the chain's Monroe mall. Increasingly, stores are outlets for well-known single brands, from **Gitano**, **Evan Picone**,

Vassarette, **Bass Shoe**, **Van Heusen**, **Harve Benard**, **American Tourister**, **Manhattan**, and **Jonathan Logan** to the new **Bugle Boys** store, for men and women as well as boys.

In these days of competitive discounting, the prices (advertised as 20% to 70% off) aren't necessarily rock-bottom at all. You can usually do better at special end-of-season closeouts at local stores. Here the advantage is in having so much discounted merchandise concentrated in one place, for easy comparison shopping, on an ongoing basis. Most merchandise is manufacturers' overruns — current-season items which manufacturers overproduced and failed to sell to retailers.

Fashions won't be as up-to-the-minute as in regular retail stores, but goods are first-quality unless otherwise indicated. Manufacturers' Marketplace promotional literature stresses quality, selection, and brand names as much as price.

All things considered, this is an exceptionally pleasant mall environment. Dutch Village founder Harry Nelis, who sold the site to Manufacturers' Marketplace, made sure that the buildings carried out the Dutch theme in quality style. It comes off very well, with a long, canal-like pond and wooden drawbridge linking Dutch Village with Marketplace shops that look like a quaint Dutch town. The glaring exception is the futuristic design of the adjacent 10-screen movie theater, not on Nelis land and therefore not subject to his approval. This place is planned as the ultimate, self-contained mall destination, what with the movies and the big Country Inn motel right next door. Tour busses bring people for shopping weekends; weekdays are less crowded. **West Shore Mall** (Holland's new regional mall anchored by Penney's, Sears, and Steketee's) is right across James.

Real closeout bargains can be found. **Carter's Childrenswear**,

Socks Galore, Ribbon Outlet (with many crafts and gift wrap items) and **The Paper Factory** are worth checking out. **Pooh's Corner**, the children's division of Grand Rapids-based Baker Book House, has a discount children's book and video store here.

Wooden Shoe Factory ★

447 South U.S. 31 at 16th St. (616) 396-6513. 8 a.m.-6 p.m. daily. No shoemaking demonstrations after 4:30 or on Sunday. 25¢ admission to shoe factory.

This giant, old-timey tourist trap, right on busy U.S. 31, is ideal for a fun, interesting break on long car trips. The wooden shoe factory, Holland's busiest, turns out 10,000 pairs of wearable klompen a year. The novelties and souvenirs are fun for all ages. And the adjoining restaurant, updated and fresh, is as good as most highway chains. Surprisingly, locals patronize it heavily, along with the pine-paneled Wooden Shoe Tap Room next door, one of Holland's few taverns.

Visitors view the wooden shoe factory through large screened windows. It's not a museum, but a highly specialized wood shop, and shoemaker Jim Baker is the only American member of the Dutch wooden shoe guild. The 80-year-old equipment, from France and the Netherlands, makes so much sawdust you want to sneeze. Regional varieties of French and Dutch wooden shoes are on display.

The gift shop has nifty, cheap toys for kids and a wide selection of the usual Dutch souvenirs: placemats, T-shirts, Delftware, and wooden shoes of all sizes, put to more uses than you could ever imagine. Don't miss the cheese, fudge, and baked goods, with lots of free samples, in the last room of this sprawling complex. There are a wide array of imported Dutch cookies, candies, and cheeses, and some attractive European metal tins.

Dutchmasters Minigolf

465 U.S. 31, a little south of 16th St., behind the Wooden Shoe Motel and between the Wooden Shoe Factory and Quad 31 Theaters. (616) 392-8521. Open mid-May through Oct., daily from 11 to 10. $3/game, except $2 on weekdays from 11-5.

This multi-level course is challenging, costly, possibly too frustrating for many children. But on a fantasy level it's definitely fun, with water hazards, windmills, gorgeous flowers and shrubs, and clever uses of wooden shoes.

Brooks Beverages self-guided tour

U.S. 31 on the south side of Holland. Turn east on 32nd St., then right in 1/2 block). (616) 396-1281. 8-5 Mon-Fri.

You get a refreshing notion of the trusting sensibility of West Michigan folks when you tour the company that blends and bottles Squirt, 7-Up, Dr. Pepper, Hires, RC, Vernor's, and Sunglo for the region. Brooks lets you on your on own to see its highly automated lines. To top it all off, you end up at a cooler where you are welcome to help yourself to sample their products.

You view all the action from a second-floor corridor, which gives an excellent bird's-eye view of the complex machinery, beginning with the syrup room where the sugar, syrup, and water are mixed in giant vats. Then it's on to the filling room, and then to the giant production room, where bottles are labeled and packaged.

The tour only takes 10 minutes or so, in which time several thousand bottles or cans have been filled by the sophisticated machinery. It makes for a nice, short diversion from the highway, especially if you have kids.

RESTAURANTS

Till Midnight ★★

208 College Ave., half a block south of 8th in downtown Holland. (616) 392-6883. Mon-Sat lunch 11-2:30, dinner 5-9:30, limited menu 'til midnight. Closed Sun. Full bar. Visa, MC, AmEx.

with saffron, from housemade stock. Add an appetizer like cheese tortellini with Italian sausage ($7) or polenta with feta cheese and grilled chicken ($5) for a meal.

The creative menu changes seasonally. Dinners are in the $12 to $18 range, but you can always order off the excellent sandwich menu — around $5 at lunch, $6 at dinner, which includes a salad or chips and salsa. Burgers or a great grilledl chicken breast with cheese and sundried tomato mayo are always available.

Alpen Rose

4 E. 8th at Central, downtown. (616) 393-2111. Mon-Fri 9 a.m.-10 p.m. (to 10:30 on Fri & Sat), Sat 8:30-1:30, Sun brunch 10:30-2. Full bar. Visa, MC, AmEx.

Austrian and continental cuisine in an atmosphere so authentic, you'd think you were in Salzburg. The 8th St. entrance is to a bakery and *konditorei* with casual booths and excellent rye bread, hard rolls, and whipped cream pastries. The food andgarnishes are authentic too. (The owner-chef's from Austria, via Mackinac's Grand Hotel.)Dining rooms are off Central. Dinner favorites include Sauerbraten ($12.75), smoked pork with kraut and dumplings ($11.75), bratwurst (›9), and caramelized tenderloin tips with orange in puff pastry ($13.50). Fore lunch, lighter fare like pepper linguine salad ($6.75) with grapes, olives, and chicken. Saturday brunch buffet to 11 a.m. is $6, Sunday's buffet $13 for adults, $6 for kids.

Nickelodeon

24 E. 8th between Central and College downtown. (616) 394-4692. Open 9-5:30 except to 9 Mon, Thurs & Fri. Closed Sun. No credit cards.

Lively snack shop with an operating player piano. Serves ice cream and fountain treats, Vienna Beef hot dogs ($1.45, or $1.95 with everything), homemade soups, chili, good coffee, many flavors of popcorn.

Eighth Street Grille

20 W. 8th between River & Central, downtown. (616) 392-5888. Mon-Sat 11-11. Full bar. Visa, MC, Am Ex.

Cool, cavernous old place with booths and tables where customers feel comfortable reading or writing over coffee or beer. $4.50 blue plate special may be burrito with rice, stew on a biscuit. $3 all-you-can-eat soup bar features chicken corn chowder and 2 changing soups. Burgers $5, pastas $7 or so. Kids' menu available.

Pereddies

447 Washington Square between 18th and 19th. (616) 394-3061. Mon-Thurs 10-10, Fri & Sat 10-11. Dinner reservations recommended. Beer and wine. Visa, MC.

Holland's pioneer of casual chic is this bakery-deli-restaurant in the tradition of old Italian neighborhoods like the ones in Detroit where its owners grew up. Homemade breads and pasta sauces are the stars (red or white, with or without mushrooms or clams). So are the signature meatballs ($3.25 as a dinner appetizer, at lunch $4.25 on a sub or $5.95 on pasta with a salad and garlic bread). Sandwiches with chips are $4.25-$5.25 at lunch only (Till Midnight is a much better value), pastas with salad and roll $5-$8 at lunch, $7.50-$11 at dinner. At dinner, 9" x 13" pizzas are $12.50, with many custom options including goat cheese. All the expected favorites are on the dinner menu — lasagne ($8.95), veal saltimbocca ($12.95), lamb chops ($15.50), shrimp scampi ($15.50).

The Sandpiper   ★★

2225 South Shore in Macatawa. From River downtown, go south, turn west onto 16th. It turns into South Shore. The Sandpiper is next to Eldean's Marina. (616) 335-5866. Lunch Mon-Fri 11:30-2, dinner daily including Sun 5:30-9:30, brunch Sat 11:30-1:30, Sun 11-2. Full bar. Visa, MC, Diners, AmEx.

When the Eldean family who owns a big marina here built this attractive, light-filled waterfront restaurant five years ago, they were lucky to land as a chef a graduate of the Culinary Institute who wanted to come back home to west Michigan. He's been here ever since, and the Sandpiper has consistently won awards with its creative food, regarded as among the very best in west Michigan. Lunch is more conventional, with the $4.95 soup, salad, and half sandwich combination the best-seller. The seasonally changing dinner menu is big on seafood. Popular regular items are grilled chicken with prosciutto ($12.95), duck with sausage, apple, and liver stuffing ($14.95), and a $10.95 vegetable pasta plate for vegetarians. All dinners come with salad, a crusty loaf of Italian bread, and the chef's fresh vegetable medley — all very good. Five Michigan wineries are represented on the extensive wine list. Chocolate ravioli with cherries and raspberry sauce and baked custard head the dessert list ($3.50).

The view is more of masts and boats than water; Point West farther out South Shore has a fabulous view from its terrace, but food and service are erratic.

Russ'

3 Holland locations: at 210 N. River on the north side, 1060 Lincoln at U.S. 31 on the south side, and the original Russ' on 361 E. 8th at Chicago. Mon-Sat 7 a.m.-11 p.m. No alcohol or credit cards.

It says a lot about Holland that when you ask about where the old-timers and insiders go for coffee and talk, the answer is usually Russ'. Russ started here at 361 E. 8th and built its reputation on its hamburgers and pies. Now it has expanded to a growing West Michigan chain with breakfast and a 12-item dinner menu, headed by fried or baked chicken or fish. At $4.15, it's quite a deal, with a roll, potato, and salad or soup. The pies — at least half a dozen baked fresh in the commissary each day — are $1.15. The burgers range from $1.10 to $2.95 for the Dutchman Supreme with cheese, bacon, lettuce, and tomato. It's all pretty good, the atmosphere is pleasantly homey, and the service is friendly and efficient. (The Dutch, who built some of Europe's most wonderful towns in the Netherlands, here have embraced shopping centers, chain restaurants, and all the accoutrements of suburban living.)

Candlewick Inn

1136 Ottawa Beach Rd. at Waukazoo Rd. in Waukazoo Plaza on the way to Holland State Park. (616) 399-8468. Tues-Sat 9 a.m.-8 p.m., Sun 11:30-2. No alcohol or credit cards. Out of town checks accepted.

On the north side, you can't beat this family restaurant for good, health-conscious home cooking that's a very good value as well. The popular buffets at lunch ($4.75 with one meat entree) and dinner ($6.95 with two meats, always including baked chicken) outdraw the regular menu with their salads, soup, breads, and fruit cobbler, the house specialty, for dessert. All are homemade. Healthy options are the rule; one owner is a vegetarian, her husband is on a strict diet, and a brother-in-law is diabetic. There's also a Saturday breakfast buffet ($3.95) and Sunday brunch ($6.95).

Queen's Inn at Dutch Village

James just east of U.S. 31. Mon-Sat 11-9, Sun until 8. (616) 393-0310. Full bar. Major credit cards.

Oddly, Dutch cooking hasn't contributed much to the American culinary smorgasbord. Even in Holland, this visitor destination is the only restaurant that serves more than one or two Dutch specialties, along with standards like lake perch fillets ($7.95 at dinner), a salad bar, hamburger, fried chicken, and steak. Recommended: Pigs in a Blanket (pork sausage in pastry dough) with pea soup and Dutch apple pie ($4.15, lunch only); mettwurst with hot potato salad and red cabbage ($4.95 at lunch, $6.45 at dinner); and nasi goreng (Indonesian rice with pork and fried egg; $6.45 at dinner with salad). Pleasant Old World decor with mottos stencilled on beams. Don't miss the real thatched roof on part of the exterior; it's close to eye level, so you can see how thick it is.

> See also The Salad Bowl, Hope College student center, and The Health Connection and Nickelodeon downtown. Takeout destinations: Kollen Park, Centennial Park, and Window on the Waterfront Park, where River St. crosses the Black River.

LODGINGS

Best Western Holland Inn
(616) 396-1424 (800) 428-7666.
482 E. 32nd at U.S. 31, 4 miles from downtown.
114 units on 2 floors. Summer: single person 1 bed $47, 2 persons 2 beds $55. Winter: Single 1 bed $39, 2 persons 2 beds $46. HBO and Showtime movie channels plus basic cable service. Outdoor heated pool.

Holiday Inn
(616) 394-0111.
650 E. 24th at U.S.31, 3 miles from downtown.
168 units on 2 floors. Single $70-$89. Double $80-$95. Call for a variety of weekend packages. Cable service, no movie channels. Indoor pool, whirlpool, exercise room, game room, and deck games. In-house restaurant, Calypso's, includes lounge.

Wooden Shoe Motel
(616) 392-8521.
465 U.S. 31 at 16th St.
29 rooms on 2 floors. Summer (winter) rates: 1 person 1 bed $34 ($28), 2 persons 1 bed $42 ($36), 2 persons 2 beds $46 ($40). Outdoor heated pool. PG movies broadcast from VCR to rooms (2 per evening). Wooden Shoe restaurant next door. Dutchmasters miniature golf in back.

Blue Mill Inn
(616) 392-7073
409 U.S. 31 at 16th.
81 units on 2 floors. Summer: 1 person 1 bed $31.95, 2 persons 1 bed $36.95, 2 persons 2 beds $41.95, king sized room or waterbed $41.95. Winter: 1 person 1 bed $24.95, 2 persons 1 bed $29.95, 2 persons 2 beds $34.95. Waterbed $35.95. Basic cable service; no movie channels. VCR rental with 1 movie $6.49, unlimited movies (20 to choose from) $9.99. No swimming pool. Good sound insulation between rooms. Well maintained.

Country Inn
(616) 396-6677; (800) 456-4000.
12260 James off U. S. 31, in back of Manufacturers Market Place.
116 units on 2 floors. Winter: single $39, double $44, whirlpool room $49 single, $54 double. Summer: single $54, double $59, whirlpool room $64

single, $69 double. Call for special
package rates in winter. Deluxe
continental breakfast included. No
movie channels. Cable service with
30 channels. No swimming.

Point West Resort
(616) 335-5894.
2330 S. Shore Drive in Macatawa,
southwest of downtown Holland.
60 rooms. Half are in a 4-floor
highrise, each with balcony with
views of Lake Macatawa and Lake
Michigan. Half surround a heated
outdoor pool and game area. The best
location in the Holland area. Rates
vary frequently, ranging from $69 to
$129. Cable TV (34 channels), HBO,
VCR rental available. 5 tennis courts,
private beach, fishing, boat slips. In-
house restaurant and lounge.

Lake Ranch Resort
(616) 399-9380.
2226 Ottawa Beach Rd. across from
State Park.
Motel condo with 29 units in rental
pool. Open April 15-Oct. 15. Sample
rates: 2 double beds $37 off-sea-
son/$62 in-season. Queen bed with
kitchenette $52/$83. 2 rooms (sleeps
4): $56/$87. In-season is Tulip Time,
weekends in June and early Sept. and

June 15-Labor Day.
   2 buildings of attached, 1-story
units face Lake Macatawa and flank a
central lawn and activity area with
heated pool, volleyball, shuffleboard,
picnic and BBQ area. Attractive contemporary decor. Fish-cleaning station.

Eagle Drive Resort
(616) 399-9626.
327 Lakeshore Dr. north of Holland.
6 cottages, 5 attached units. In-season rates (Tulip Time, and late June
through mid-September): single-
room units $42/day, $240/week; 1
bedroom, sleeps 4, $54/$340; 2 bedroom, sleeps 6, $58/$380. Inquire for
off-season rates. No smoking, no pets
in season.
   Mature shrubs and trees, beautiful
lawn, six acres. Simple but well-run
and exceptionally pleasant. In quiet
area of nice houses, across from
Lake Michigan dunes. Asphalt bikeway leads to beaches at state park
and Tunnel Park (1 mile away) and
Kirk Park. Room furnishings are
fresh and coordinated. Kitchens are
fully equipped. Small heated pool,
volleyball, badminton, tennis, a
children's play area, and a rec room
with ping pong.

Zeeland

The little town of Zeeland is a most unusual American city. One of the first wave of Dutch settlements in the U.S., it is still almost entirely Dutch, the way nearby Holland was until recently. In keeping with the strict, religious values of its residents, liquor isn't sold anywhere in the city. Nearing 150 years old, Zeeland now has more jobs than people — over 7,000 in 46 industries, including five plants of Fortune 500 companies. Nowhere is the vaunted Dutch work ethic more pronounced than in this old farm town, where plant-growing and poultry-farming are still much in evidence.

Three of Zeeland's many homegrown industries employ thousands: Herman Miller office furniture, Howard Miller Clocks (founded by Herman Miller relatives across the street from it), and Bil-Mar Foods, the second-biggest U. S. maker of turkey products, including Mr. Turkey processed meats.

Home, church, and work

Three streets illuminate three main spheres of life in Zeeland: home, church, and work. A drive along Church Street (one street south of Main) passes huge Dutch Reformed churches, the old-fashioned corner parks at Church and Central, and impressive homes from the early part of this century. This street's air of well-built solidity suggests the Calvinist attitude that worldly prosperity is a natural sign and consequence of devout Christian faith.

Main Street, a compact and pleasant shopping district, is an unusual blend of historic preservation

"People —
Product —
Progress"
The motto on the city seal sums up Zeeland's outlook and values: a real community in the traditional sense, with a practical, down-to-earth style, strong work ethic, and faith in the future.

Distinctive brick houses like this centennial farm on James Street west of Zeeland dot the countryside and Dutch farm villages east of Holland.

and modernism. Bronzed Plexiglass roofs cover the downtown sidewalks, and two lanes of traffic curve between lush plantings and benches. Plaques on refurbished buildings recount their histories. It's remarkable how often the same names crop up in this tight community, where families stay and flourish for many generations. The **Zeeland Bakery**, right on the Main Street mall, offers not only the usual sweet rolls and doughnuts, but Dutch butter cookies and Holland rusk, which locals eat soaked in milk. And in the window of the Zeeland Sport Center, there's a remarkably large, upright **bear** carved from a tree trunk. Zeeland retailing's strength is in furniture and accessories stores with things for the home, usually with a country theme.

Out Chicago Drive

Chicago Drive, along the railroad tracks one street north of Main, offers a glimpse of Zeeland's manufacturing and agriculture. **DeBruyn Produce**, at Washington and Chicago, sells many varieties of bulk vegetable seeds for growers (and to the general public) in a sales room with moderne wood interior from the 1950s. Main Street east of town turns into Byron Road, with the corporate offices of **Herman Miller** and **Howard Miller**. Herman Miller's headquarters are especially interesting because they put into practice the firm's design philosophy (functional and contemporary) and management philosophy (participative management in which executives and workers interact frequently and learn from each other). The building is simple and functional, but a very human-scaled, personal, non-corporate atmosphere is created by the accoutrements: flowering shrubs and ground cover, picnic tables and bike racks, and playful, idiosyncratic art and soft sculpture in the lobby.

Paul de Kruif, author of Microbe Hunters, grew up in the brick Queen Anne house just west of Vande Luyster Park on Church St. His father was a local physician. De Kruif studied bacteriology at the University of Michigan, then combined his humanitarian interest in science and his honest, down-to-earth writing style in many popular books about medicine and science.

Chicago Drive passes along a wide swath of muckland that stretches all the way to Grand Rapids. This spectacular channel is the remnant of a huge prehistoric river that carried glacial meltwaters to an early version of Lake Michigan. It was much used for celery farming by the Dutch farmers of Zeeland, Hudsonville, Jenison, and Grandville, until that specialty crop, first popularized by Michigan farmers, became dominated by California growers.

POINTS OF INTEREST

Dekker Huis ★★

37 E. Main in Zeeland, just west of the downtown business district. (616) 772-4079. Thurs 10-4, Sat 10-1. Closed Nov.-early March. No fee; donation appreciated.

When it comes to conveying the experiences of ordinary people, this small museum, run by the Zeeland Historical Society, is one of the very best around. Dekker Huis (pronounced "HICE") uses objects to effectively illustrate ideas and provides a context for the objects you see. There's a trunk — a very small trunk — displayed with everything the typical Zeeland pioneering immigrant family took to America. The guides are apt to be lifelong Zeelanders who are part of the history themselves.

The museum consists of a house built by a grocer next to his store, and an exhibit space for changing shows in the former store. Permanent exhibits with photographs and artifacts illustrate "The Home Land,"

"The Journey," and "The New Land." The founders of Zeeland all belonged to the same Secessionist congregation in Goes (pronounced "Hoos"), a farm town in the eastern province of Zeeland, and emigrated in 1847.

It is touching to see the photographs of houses in Goes, of very serious churchgoers sitting in their pews, and of the barn where the emigrating congregation met after they broke away from the established church. Emigrants left their cozy kitchens for a harsh environment on the Michigan frontier, where, for awhile, the whole village shared a single handmade shovel. (It's in the museum.) Dutch Secessionist immigrants were among the poorest who left Northern Europe. When they first arrived, they lived very simply indeed, as you realize when you enter the museum's log addition. It's as big as many of the early settlers' houses.

When you step inside the small but comfortable dining room and parlor, furnished roughly as it was about 1920, you experience the material success the immigrants were so proud of, and the bourgeois domesticity for which the Dutch are famous. Lace curtains, dark wood trim, imitation Oriental carpets — it feels cozy but a little stuffy. It's interesting to see the 1920s laundry set up for wash day on the side porch.

Bil-Mar Country Store

8300 96th Ave. in Borculo. From U. S. 31 north of Holland, turn east onto Port Sheldon Rd., go 5 miles east, turn north (left) onto 96th Ave. From Zeeland, take Central north (it becomes 96th Ave.) about six miles. (616) 875-8131. Mon-Fri 9-5:30, Sat 8:30-3.

People drive from far away to this popular outlet store of Bil-Mar Foods, out on a country road near the giant turkey processor's corporate headquarters. Prices on Mr. Turkey products are not reduced, but there are very good values on turkey parts and damaged products that may be

improperly sealed or underweight. Bil-Mar also makes frozen airline dinners (beef, fish, beef, corned beef) which are sold here on the familiar plastic trays for from $1.29 to $5.99 (for the prime rib). Bil-Mar also makes macaroni and cheese, lasagna, stuffed peppers and such for institutional customers like hospitals and dorms. Big 9 by 13 inch trays, popular for parties, sell for from $15 to $19.

RESTAURANTS

The Old Schoolhouse Restaurant

9354 Port Sheldon Rd., just east of the center of Borculo, 8 miles northeast of Holland. From Zeeland, take State St./96th Ave. 5 miles north, turn east onto Pt. Sheldon. From U.S. 31 6 miles north of Holland, take Pt. Sheldon Rd. 5 miles east. (616) 875-7200. Tues-Thurs 8-8, Sri & Sat until 8 in winter, 9 in summer. No alcohol or credit cards. Out-of-town checks OK.

Eating here is a little like going to a rural school reunion. There on the walls of this good-sized country school are many class pictures, maps, teachers' aids, and such from American schools of the 1920s. The effect is charming and authentic, not hokey. Food is quality middle-American basics. Favorite dishes include French toast at breakfast with homemade bread ($2.65 including meat), at lunch Teacher's Choice (a two-patty burger with ham and fries, $3.85), and at dinner Swiss steak and two side dishes ($5.70). Vegetarians could make a meal of the soups, salads, and sides alone. Friday and Saturday there's a $7.45 dinner buffet.

The village of Borculo is in the heart of Dutch farming country, historically an important center of poulry production. It's just a couple minutes away from the Bil-Mar Country Store (p. 146).

Grand Haven

Grand Haven is an unusual combination: an up-scale resort that is also a prosperous manufacturing city. The two roles coexist harmoniously because the city's thriving manufacturing sector is well to the east, separated from town by U.S. 31.

The resort area keeps this city of 12,000 year-round residents packed during the summer. For several good reasons, Grand Haven is a favorite of boaters. The city's harbor, protected by high dunes from Lake Michigan storms, has long had the reputation as the safest on the lake. There are 22 marinas, including Lake Michigan's finest, the Grand Isle Marina, which attracts many big Chicago yachts. And boaters heading up the Grand River can quickly reach several bayous east of Grand Haven and big Spring Lake just to the north.

In most Michigan port towns on Lake Michigan, the business district is several miles inland at the head of a long lake. Grand Haven's downtown is a lot closer to Lake Michigan, within easy walking distance. Boats can conveniently tie up right at the foot of the bustling, attractive downtown, allowing boaters to walk easily to a variety of interesting shops, restaurants, and nightspots. It is an attractive place to browse and shop.

Busy harbor
Unlike most Great Lake ports, Grand Haven continues to en-joy frequent freighter traffic. Page two of the daily Grand Haven Tribune lists arrival and departure times.

The 25-foot-deep harbor is not deep enough to receive most ocean-going ships, which need 27 feet. But the freighters that do arrive are still enormous.

For many decades the singles scene at Grand Haven's beaches has been intense. Families also use the beautiful beaches, but for teens and young adults from Grand Rapids and elsewhere, Grand Haven is the place to be.

Grand Haven is a city that has worked hard to encourage its commerce and tourism. To boost tourism, during the economic doldrums of the early 1980s the city created a long and remarkably well-designed **boardwalk**, enlivened by immaculately maintained landscaping and a variety of other amenities and attractions (see p. 153). Now new bed-and-breakfasts and improved restaurants are taking advantage of Grand Haven's self-described reputation as "Lake Michigan's bright spot."

The south side of the city, near Lake Michigan, has a third identity, that of an upper-middle-class suburb whose breadwinners are independently wealthy or commute to bigger cities nearby. Grand Haven's new mystique as a fun, attractive place to live free of big city challenges has developed to the point that two recent public school teaching vacancies here attracted a thousand applicants.

Problems with success

This old lumbering and commercial fishing town has become so successful at attracting tourists and manufacturers that an anti-growth sentiment is growing. In order to cool things down, in 1990 the city actually got rid of its dynamic city manager, Larry Deetjen, chief architect of its revitalization. As in other popular Michigan resort towns, Grand Haven's quality of life is threatened by traffic congestion on summer evenings. Harbor Drive along the lake is often bumper-to-bumper cars, and the experience of negotiating U.S. 31 over the Grand River drawbridge at rush hour can be harrowing.

It's quite a turnaround from the 1970s, when Grand Haven was such a grimy industrial backwater that Michigan State students from the region called a cribbage hand with no points a "Grand Haven hand." The low point occurred between 1979 and 1981, when the city lost its three largest employers. In a town where half of the jobs are in manufacturing, 30% of these jobs were suddenly wiped out when the locally owned companies were bought out by conglomerates and shut down. But the heavily Dutch city has a skilled labor pool with a strong work ethic and low tolerance for unions. With aggressive recruiting and healthy growth of existing firms, manufacturing employment has

Grand Haven's splendid boardwalk along its Grand River harbor has stimulated a good deal of upscale development such as Harbourfront Place (left). The old Story and Clark piano factory, two blocks long, is now a retail-restaurant-office complex with adjoining condominiums.

Coast Guard Headquarters
Grand Haven is the headquarters of a Coast Guard Group. Located in the city's old Board of Power & Light Building on S. Harbor Ave., the command oversees six stations located in Michigan City, St. Joseph, Grand Haven, Ludington, Manistee, and Frankfort. Their major mission is search and rescue, using 6 44-foot lifeboats powered by twin 185 hp engines plus 22-foot Boston whalers with twin 100-hp engines.

surged 80% since 1984.

Most manufacturers here are job shops, making parts for manufacturing firms elsewhere. The city's biggest employer is actually one of its oldest. Eagle Ottawa has supplied the automotive industry with leather for car seats since early in this century. Today, with the vogue for leather seating in luxury automobiles, the company is booming, having doubled in size within the past decade to 800 employees. Eagle Ottawa is now the dominant supplier to the Japanese, with Honda, Toyota, and Nissan its major customers.

The busy harbor

The same harbor which attracts affluent boaters also handles one of the Great Lake's greatest tonnages of cargo. Freighters make trips in and out daily delivering heavy loads such as fertilizer and road salt and coal. A lot of the coal feeds the city's huge 58 megawatt electric power plant, a familiar sight across the channel from downtown. The city has generated its own electricity since 1896. The present plant was built at a cost of $90 million, a third of which was spent to make its tall smokestack pollution-free.

Just north of the power plant, close to an inlet on the Grand called "the sag," is a Chicago-owned firm that fills a freighter every three and a half days with 24,000 tons of the unusually clean Grand Haven sand. Sand is shipped to GM and Ford foundries around the Great Lakes, where it is used to makes the molds and cores for engine blocks.

Long a tourist mecca

Grand Haven's clean sand has also been a boost for tourism. Popular beaches are on both sides of the Grand River's mouth. The state park just south of the inlet has one of the most heavily used campgrounds in the state.

The first tourist steamer came to town in 1856. On the *Chippewa*, a big sidewheeler from Chicago, passengers enjoyed a remarkable menu of 12 entrees, including venison in Cyprus wine sauce, buffalo tongue, turtle steaks, and passenger pigeon chops.

But Grand Haven's fame as a resort didn't really spread until 1872, with the construction of the five-story Cutler House Hotel at Washington and Third. Famous throughout the Midwest, it had a steam elevator and hot and cold running water in each room. The Cutler was nicely complemented by the "World Sanatarium & Magnetic Mineral Springs & Laboratory" across the street, which treated 2,000 patients a year for such ailments as rheumatism and arthritis. In the 1880s the beautiful Highland Park resort colony, then two miles south of town, was built (see p. 162). Perched on the steep dunes overlooking Lake Michigan, a hun-

Charter salmon fishing on Lake Michigan
Grand Haven has over 50 charter fishing boats, each of which can take up to 6 fisherman for a half or full day's fishing on the lake. The best times for catching the big coho (up to 12 lbs.) and chinook (up to 25 lbs.) are May and early July through mid-August. It's an unusual trip that doesn't end up with at least one big fish, and the captain cleans the fish for you. Costs, tackle included, are $250 and up for half a day and $400 and up for a full day.

Free guide to cottage rentals
The Grand Haven Chamber of Commerce publishes an annual cottage rental guide with descriptions and prices of about 50 local cottages, condos, homes, and apartments. Typical cottages rent for $600 to $800 a week in the summer, and apartments for $300 to $400 a week. For a copy, write Chamber of Commerce, P.O. Box 509, Grand Haven, MI 49417.

dred Victorian summer homes were built and occupied
by residents of St. Louis, Chicago, Louisville, and
Grand Rapids.

Fur-trading outpost

The gentility of Grand Haven in the 1880s was quite
a contrast to the rude trading post of half a century
earlier. The first white resident was the legendary Rix
Robinson, who managed some of John Jacob Astor's
fur trading posts in the region. Born in Massachusetts
in 1789, Robinson was a law student when the War of
1812 began. He fled west after being drafted. Robinson
set up the Grand Haven trading post in 1821 at the foot
of what is now Washington Street. Fluent in several
Indian languages, Robinson married the daughter of
an Indian chief.

But Grand Haven's first permanent settler was
Reverend William Montague Ferry, long a missionary
at Mackinac. He was drawn by the business prospects
of establishing a community in this locale with the
good harbor and plenty of water power. In 1834, he
hired a schooner to take his family and 16 other settlers to this site. (The family went on to successfully
exploit timberlands north of Muskegon.) The original

This 1871 view of
Grand Haven's main
street, Washington,
shows the famous
Cutler House hotel in
the left foreground.
The lavish Cutler first
made the little town
an important visitor
destination. You can
see the town's first
railroad depot just
across the Grand River
from the foot of
Washington. There
steamships to Chicago
and Milwaukee met
trains from the East.

1835 plat of the village, with its simple grid pattern from Elliot to Howard streets, has become the central city today.

The rise and fall of lumbering and fishing

In this region, the choicest variety of white pine, called "cork pine," was especially abundant. Light but durable, it was easy to transport and an ideal building material. When pioneers moved beyond the forested regions of Ohio and Indiana and settled the treeless prairies of Illinois and Iowa, demand for Michigan lumber became great. By the 1840s Grand Haven began to export pine lumber in quantity. Given the huge amount of territory covered by the Grand River and its many major tributaries, it isn't surprising that the city became a major lumber town. Lumber peaked in the early 1880s, when almost 200 million board feet a year were being produced by local mills.

Other important spheres of commerce buffered lumber's collapse when the pine was all cut down. Commercial fishing was long an important industry here. A fleet of steam-powered tugs hauled in huge quantities of lake trout, which was shipped fresh to Chicago, and chub, which was smoked and sent east by rail. By 1915, the supply of fish was also being exhausted by overly zealous harvesting.

Because of its excellent harbor and its connection with Grand Rapids by steamboat and rail, Grand Haven has been a major port throughout its history. Peaches, grapes, and celery were all shipped in immense quantities from here. Equally large quantities of grain, flour, and bacon arrived here from across Lake Michigan and were shipped east by rail. The town's first railroad line was actually laid along the bank of the Grand River opposite from downtown. There a large depot plus dock was built in 1859, and Grand Haven became part of a major route from the east to Milwaukee. Eventually a depot was built on the town side in 1870; it now houses the historical museum.

New hotspot
The new Kirby Grill, housed in the old 1873 Kirby House hotel at the foot of Washington Street, is now a late night favorite. An old style bar & grill, its smoked chicken & lentil soup and baked cajun catfish win raves. The Kirby stays open until 2.

Lighted
downhill skiing
with 130' vertical drip, 6 slopes, and 3 rope tows is at Mulligan's Hollow in Grand Haven (616-846-5590), open weeknights 5-9, Sat. 1-9.

Bicycling around Grand Haven
Flat terrain, scenic dunes, and beaches, make for pleasant bicycling even for the out-of-shape. A separate Lake Shore Dr. bike path to Holland starts 9 miles south of town. Grand Haven's High Wheeler bike shop, 300 N. 7th (open 11-7, 10-5 Sat.) has free route maps of recommended rides from 15-40 miles round-trip.

Lake Shore Dr. is ideal for cycling. For 8 miles into Holland, it has a separate bike path.

POINTS OF INTEREST

Brass River Display ★

On the Boardwalk at the head of Washington at Harbor Dr., between the Chamber of Commerce and the historical museum.

Here, on the spot where William Ferry is said to have first disembarked form his canoe back in 1834 to establish the village of Grand Haven, is a wonderful brass sidewalk map of all the rivers and creeks which feed the Grand River. There are eleven rivers and creeks and 35 communities in the 50-foot display. This splendid brass map vividly shows how immense the catchment area of the mighty Grand River is, all the way to the Irish Hills south of Jackson.

The idea for this instructive map occurred back in 1984 when the city was celebrating its sesquicentennial. Grand Haven's dynamic mayor, dentist Bill Creason, came up with the idea. (Creason also launched the town's boardwalk project.) To get the brass map made, he talked to the head of Grand Haven Brass Foundry, makers of the inner brass mechanisms of single lever faucets. Back then they only had 99 employees (they have 230 now), and 75% of them donated a total of 2,000 hours creating 276 individual sections. Most of them are signed by their individual creators on the side embedded in concrete. They also made the fine sundial at the point on the map where the Grand meets Lake Michigan.

Boardwalk ★★

Just north of downtown along Harbor Drive, extending 2 miles from the South Pier lighthouse along the Grand River east to the foot of 2nd. Parking lots are all along the Boardwalk.

Grand Haven has been in the vanguard of West Michigan ports in creating a continuous walkway along its harborfront. "Boardwalk" is actually a misnomer. Asphalt surfaces much of this interesting walkway, which attracts strollers and joggers from early morning until late evening. It stretches about two miles from the lighthouse on the pier jutting out into Lake Michigan all the way past downtown along the Grand River to across a bridge to Linear Park next to the municipal power plant.

There are many highlights along this pleasant walk, starting with a giant **steam locomotive** at the foot of Second (p. 160); the **Farmers' Market** (p. 160); **Chinook Pier** (p. 159), with shops charter boats, and an adjacent mini golf course; the **city marina;** stands for viewing the heavily-touted, incomparably corny **Musical Fountain** (p. 158); the local **historical museum**; a view up Washington, Grand Haven's main shopping street (p. 154); the **brass Grand River map** (p. 153), the **Chamber of Commerce**, loaded with visitor information; the new **Coast Guard station**; and the **pier with the catwalk and lighthous**e; plus beach novelty and snack shops and gardens along the way.

Of particular interest is the active boat traffic on this part of the Grand River, from large freighters to million-dollar yachts. Many boaters tie up along the boardwalk, giving strollers a close-up view of a good many different types of vessels.

The city marina near Chinook Pier rents slips to visiting boats. Boaters often sleep overnight in their quarters below deck while visiting Grand Haven. Towards dusk it's quite a spectacle to walk along the boardwalk as the crowd of boats in the Grand thickens in anticipation of the nightly musical fountain program.

Midway through June several **ice cream shops** and **eateries** open along the path closer to the pier to serve the strollers. As you walk west toward the lighthouse pier and lake, the view is increasingly dramatic. Across the river you can see the

The Grand Haven pier and lighthouse, a favorite fishing spot, is the climax of a stroll on the city's 2-mile riverfront boardwalk, studded with interesting features. Locals rallied to save the pier's obsolete catwalk, built so the lighthouse could be reached during stormy high waters.

classic old white wooden Coast Guard building, now vacant. The facility is 110 years old and housed two separate units. The lifeboat station is now in new quarters across the channel, with 18 men led by a chief petty officer. The station sends a speedy 22-foot Boston whaler with twin 100 hp engines to help boats in distress. The other Coast Guard group here, the Aids to Navigation Team (ANTs), tends the smaller buoys on Lake Michigan and the Grand River.

Downtown   ★★

Washington between Harbor and Third is the main shopping street; parking is behind stores off Franklin, one street south. Many stores stay open Mon. and Fri. nights; some are open Sun. in summer.

Downtown Grand Haven is a pleasant place to stroll, especially when not congested with cars. Its main boulevard, Washington Street, enjoys a healthy, visitor-oriented re-

tail climate. In the first block past Harbor, the streetscape is a little unsettling — the result of rebuilding after fires with low newer buildings that create a ragged silhouette next to older remaining three-story buildings. Tearing down too many buildings along neighboring Franklin Street to provide parking has left the downtown looking a little bare and isolated.

Pre-tourist establishments

Most stores are clothing or gift shops catering to summer visitors. But you can also find small-town survivors:

• the **Grand Theater** (842-4520) on Washington near Harbor charges $1.49 to see almost-first-run movies

• a good-sized branch of **Steketee's**, the Grand Rapids department store chain, is at Washington and Second.

• kitty-corner from Steketee's, **Hostetter's**, a good, old-fashioned news stand, is well stocked with magazines. It's open from 8 a.m. to 9 p.m. weekdays, until 7 Saturday and 5 Sunday.

Everyday shopping take place out on the commercial strip along Beacon Boulevard and on adjacent Robbins Road on the south side of town.

Contrary to downtown Grand Haven's overwhelmingly resorty image, however, it does have one good hardware store: **Jonker's,** at 210 Washington just east of Second. Across Washington, gentrification has not displaced one of the funkiest, most unusual barbershops imaginable, **Glo Barber Shop** at 209 Washington (appointments only, 616-842-6080). The ancient-looking wood storefront, painted a vivid red, is owned by barber Ron Prelesnik. He took over some 30 years ago from his dad, who had been there 48 years. He has encrusted his shop's walls with a wild profusion of posters, advertisements, and photos that has to be seen to be appreciated.

A block north of Washington on Columbus at Third, there's a cluster of upscale clothing stores in a fairly traditional vein: **Country House** and **Peter Cole Resort Wear** for women, **Boos's** and **Grand River Dry Goods** for men and boys.

The resort carriage trade

Resort wear and summer stuff is Grand Haven's strong suit. The oldest purveyor to the resort carriage trade is **Fortino's** at 114 Washington (open evenings; closed Sunday). It started out just after the turn of the century as an Italian grocery and fruit store and still has an attractively old-fashioned ambiance. Fortino's is famous for its freshly roasted peanuts (8 ounces of redskins for $1.19); it's also the reigning gourmet shop for imported cheese, a big selection of good wine, jams and patés and all sorts of fancy foods.

In its current location in the old corner drugstore at 126 Washington at Second, **Buffalo Bob's** (616- 847-0019) has become part soda fountain, part beach store, part Western wear store, part novelty store, and part skate shop. Surprises are the rule in this fluid, eclectic approach to retailing. Skate rentals for in-line roller skates are $5/hour, $15/day. **Bike rentals** are also available, and it's open until 9 on summer weekdays. Locals enjoy the **soda fountain** for lunch, with salad, soups, sandwiches, and old-fashioned phosphates and shakes.

Also an Uptown

Five long blocks east of downtown Grand Haven is another retail district that's important to visitors because it houses the area's best bookstore, between 7th and 8th a block and a half west of Beacon Blvd. (U.S. 131). **The Bookman** (616-846-3520) is a popular spot because of its comfortable atmosphere. It carries new hardcovers and has good children's, religious, and paperback departments, plus higher-brow magazines,

out-of-town newspapers, and a large room of used books. Special orders are encourages. Open daily 9-9, Sunday from 8 a.m.

The new location of **The Gallery Upstairs** (616-846-3520) is above The Bookman. (Enter off the parking lot next to the bookstore.) has lots of natural woodwork and natural light. Area artists, including many accomplished watercolorists, keep prices reasonable by donating one day a month each to run the cooperative gallery. Hours are Tuesday through Saturday 11-5, Friday to 8.

Big on beachwear

T-shirt design is first-rate in Grand Haven. Beachwear and summer accessories here are right on top of the latest trends. At 121 Washington, **Michigan Rag Company** (616-846-1451) passers-by can watch beachwear being silkscreened (all night long during the week when they're busy), then buy it at the adjaoutlet store. Seconds with minor flaws are a real deal here: $32 50/50 jackets, $12 cotton nightshirts/beach coverups, $24 hooded flannel pullovers. Fabric scraps are used to good effect in bright $2 potholders. Repeat designs of Michigan and Great Lakes lighthouses are popular here.

Michigan Rag's talented owner-designer Richard Sweet designs and manufactures clothes that are comfortable, fun, and long-lasting — the kind of knockabout clothes that become old friends. Michigan Rag's cotton tote bags, hooded parkas, big tops, and loose shorts and pants for men and women are sold nationwide at specialty stores, mostly on the coasts. The styles are simple, and the silkscreened repeat-pattern graphics in motifs like goldfish, flags, sails, coyotes, and swimmers, are fresh and catchy, just like Sweet's fabric wall pictures mounted on stretchers that became phenomenally popular as instant, affordable decorating. Sold under the name Marúshka (Polish for "little Mary," the name of Sweet's wife), they used good design to dish up simple summer themes (sailboats, flowers, fruit, beach chairs, dune grass, gulls) in a fresh, non-cloying way that had enormous staying power — over two decades.

Shops with personality

Another distinctive cluster of interconnected shops with real personality is on the south side of Washington between Second and Third, anchored by **Ad Lib**, a gift and home accessories shop (Mon-Sat 10-5:30, Mon & Fri until 9). Its visually rich but informal and refreshing look plays off a little traditional luxury (paisley shawls, silver trays, and crystal) with a lot of contemporary crafts and Mexican and European imports, often earthenware painted in a folkish vein. American crafts include brass Soleri bells ($100 and up) and glass-enameled plates with nature scenes hand-painted by Michigan's Norman and Judith Brumm ($16.50 and up). Things here may cost a lot or a very little. There are ceramic Italian faience candlesticks, plastic wind-up toys, $4 slip-on silver button covers to customize your plain cardigan sweaters, Mexican handblown glass, Scandanavian posters, and inexpensive folk jewelry from India and Central America.

For years this was just about the only place in West Michigan to find unusual imports. It still bears the inventive stamp of its recently retired founder, Libby Reichert. A Texan and alumna of the Neiman-Marcus staff, she has flair and a good eye and the dedication to search out interesting but not necessarily expensive things all over the world. She married into the family of Grand Haven merchants who had developed a stationery store into a series of sophisticated shops geared to the local resort clientele, selling everything from gifts and housewares to clothing and fancy goods. Forty years ago they decided to make interior doors connecting their shops here — a mini-mall way before its time.

Today the complex extends from **Borr's Bootery** at 214 Washington to the **Basket Emporium** (tableware, cookware, fancy foods and coffees) at 222. Its own little café, **Bach's Lunch** (open 11-4 Mon-Sat), serves sandwiches and salads ($3.75 and under) and pastries in a bright, fresh space looking out onto a charming ivy-covered courtyard. Other interesting interconnected stores with the same hours are **Interior Motives** (a fine decorator's shop with some accessories) and **Whims & Wishes** (with another interesting selection of cards, gifts, and novelties, terra cotta planters, toys, books, notebooks, woven coverlets, and even some antique china).

County offices and a shady, old-fashioned park

Retailing on Washington ends at Third, where churches and government institutions dominate the streetscape. Grand Haven, the first major settlement in Ottawa County, is the county seat, even though it's in the far northwest corner and today eclipsed in size and importance by Holland. These cities' combined success in the 1980s has made Ottawa Michigan's fastest-growing county, with real estate prices rising accordingly.

Shady **Central Park**, an old-fashioned square on Washington between Fourth and Fifth, has a pleasant interior fountain surrounded by benches and flower beds immaculately maintained in the best Dutch tradition. Facing the park on Columbus is the handsome **community center** and **library** (842-5560).

Tri-Cities Historical Museum ★★

1 N. Harbor at the foot of Washington. (616) 842-0700. Summer hours (Me. to Labor Day): Tues-Sat 10-9:30. Off-season: Tues-Fri 10-5 plus weekends 12-4 thru Xmas. $1 adults, 17 and under free.

Housed in the restored Grand Trunk Depot, this local museum displays a wide variety of photos and artifacts from the area's rich history of trapping, lumbering, shipping, railroading, manufacturing, and Coast Guard Service. There is so much here, visitors are well advised to ask to see the 7-minute **video** on the museum and how it relates to Grand Haven history. Other videos available upon request are on the Coast Guard and the beautiful Lake Forest Cemetery (p. 163)

The two-level museum offers a rich store of the usual local museum fare: Victorian furniture and decorative objects in room arrangements, toys, household objects, and tools, war mementoes, and items salvaged from area general stores, drug stores, and hardware stores in the area.

Don't miss the huge and striking painting of a sky-darkening swirl of now-extinct passenger pigeons by Lewis Cross of Spring Lake.

Some of the museum's more sub-

tly captivating items are very wide, crystal-clear group photos of the employees of various area companies in an intriguing variety of poses and expressions. One is the old undated photo of the 93 people who worked at the Peerless Glove Co.

The Coast Guard section is a highlight. The shiny 19th-century French Fresnel lens still sends out a flashing, rotating beam as it once did from Grand Haven's harbor lighthouse, where its beam could be seen 15 to 25 miles out in the lake.

Parking downtown and by the beach can be difficult in summer, even though there are extensive parking areas along the boardwalk and beach, along North Harbor north of Washington downtown, and all along Franklin just south of the main retail blocks. Come early when there's good summer weather; parking may be difficult by 10 a.m. The beach overflow lot is by the cemetery on Lake Ave., half a mile inland.

Harbourfront Place

41 Washington at Harbor Dr., across from the Grand Rapids Boardwalk. (616) 846-7140. Memorial Day-Labor Day: Mon-Sat 10-10, Sun noon-5. Winter: Mon-Sat 10-5:30, Fri until 9, Sun 12-5.

In this imaginative reuse, the big old 1906 Story & Clark Piano Company houses a pleasant mixture of shops, eateries, and offices. Inside, the architects cut a 40-foot atrium through the three floors to open up the space. The original floors, ceiling beams, and old brick walls have been left exposed to retain a sense of the old factory.

There are some interesting shops among the retail businesses on the first two floors. Well stocked shops for toys, embroidery, and needlepoint supplies complement several stores featuring accessories, including one, the **Laughing Dolphin**, that carries items with nautical themes. The **Lighthouse Boutique** and **Dockside** (for men), facing Washington, specialize in nautical casual wear.

In the food court is a **Miller's Ice Cream** shop and a good chicken and burrito spot called the **Original Chicken Co.** (p. 167). On the main floor is a larger full-service restaurant called the **Piano Factory**. Its patio on the upper level off the banquet room overlooks the harbor.

Connected to this complex in another old part of the Story & Clark factory are condominiums with balconies overlooking the Grand River.

Musical Fountain

Waterfront Stadium, off Harbor Drive (downtown Grand Haven), on the Boardwalk at the foot of Washington. Daily at dusk mid-May through Labor Day plus weekends in Sept and first half of Oct. 9:45 p.m in May, June, July; 9:30 Aug-Oct. Schedule of nightly programs available at the Chamber of Commerce just down river.

"Good evening, ladies and gentle-

Fireworks over the world's largest musical fountain and the Grand River is a highlight of the big Coast Guard Festival at the end of July. On summer Sunday evenings an illuminated cross occupies the anchor's place. This spectacle, which seems more suited to the era of Lawrence Welk, still inexplicably packs them in night after night. Adding to the event are the many pleasure boats which jam the Grand River in front of the fountain.

men," intones the penetrating voice coming from the dune across the Grand River, "I am the Grand Haven Musical Fountain." Every summer night at dusk people all over Grand Haven can hear (whether they choose to or not) what is heralded as "the world's largest musical fountain."

For 25 minutes light classical or popular music is pumped out with the help of a 12,000-watt stereo system while changing colored lights play on sprays of water emanting from an unornamented fountain part-way up Dewey Hill. On Sunday the program consists of Christian hymns, accompanied by the slow raising of a huge cross. Other programs range from Sergeant

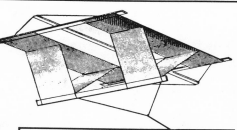

Pepper, operetta favorites, and Hawaiian music to the Grand Canyon Suite. The music is computer synchronized with an elaborate color-lighted water fountain display.

This is supposed to be one of Grand Haven's biggest attractions. Its presence, in fact, is emblazoned on every street sign in town. This claim seems confirmed by the crowds thronging the riverfront area on weekend evenings and virtual flotillas of big pleasure boats cramming the river here.

But the music is rather fuzzy, for all the vaunted power of the stereo system. One person claims it can be heard from Holland to Muskegon if turned up all the way. The display verges on the insipid, notwithstanding the 40,000 gallons of water used and the 125-foot-high, computer-controlled sprays.

Chinook Pier

301 N. Harbor, 2 blocks north of Washington, on the Grand River and the Boardwalk. Parking lot faces Harbor Dr.

Chinook Pier is something of Grand Haven's vacation headquarters. It's the home of its charter fishing fleet, departure point for the Harbor Trolley and Harbor Steamer, and it's right next to the city marina to the west and Farmers' Market to the east. An uninspired mini-golf course is next to it. **Marina Mike's** party store and deli here, a sort of general store oriented to boaters, also has some of the few video games downtown.

Grand Haven's large **charter fishing fleet** is based here. It isn't cheap to go fishing for coho in Lake Michigan; rates are about $75 per

> **For kites, Lake Michigan beaches** are ideal. They provide the updrafts, the space, and the admiring female audiences for mostly young, mostly male kite fliers, who can make two-string stunt kites do amazing loops and dives.
>
> Power kites that block and trap the wind can actually pick the flier off the ground in 30-foot jumps. $16.95 will get a beginner into stunt kites; prices go up to $270 for a 10-foot Flexifoil power kite that goes up to 120 mph. A new four-line "remote control" kite, the Revolution, stops and goes upside down, sideways, backward, and forward. The Mackinaw Kite Company **demonstrates daily on the beach,** wind conditions permitting, and sponsors occasional weekend kite festivals. Call (616) 846-7501.

person for a half day, with a four-person minimum. Nearby at the modern open air fish cleaning station, boat captains in bloody aprons with super sharp knives speedily filet the big cohos caught on the charters.

For reservations to go fishing in Lake Michigan, you can call these Chinook Pier charter services:

Chinook Pier Sport Fishing
    (616) 842-2229.
Marina Jack's Charter Service.
    (616) 842-1343.
Shrimp Boat Charters.
    (616) 842-2812.
Shut R Bug Charters.
    (616) 847-0551.
Whitney Charter Service.
    (616) 846-6640.

Two rows of specialty shops in front of the wharf include a good chili joint (just 95¢ for a chili dog with onions), an ice cream shop, T-shirt and beachwear shops,

Mackinaw Kite Company

116 Washington between 1st and 2nd. (616) 846-7501. Summer (Mem.-Labor Day at least) Mon-Sat 10-9, Sun 12-5. Off-season: Mon-Sat 10-6.

This colorful shop appeals to everyone from the casual visitor to kite fanatics. The kites themselves, appliqued with geometric shapes, stars, and many motifs, come in all shapes and sizes, including tradition-al single-string kites, Chinese box and dragon kites, and the latest pow-er kites. They are visual delights and instant room brighteners. Numerous books explain the history, science, and how-to of making and flying kites. Kite-making materials are for sale here. For casual browsers, there are colorful windsocks and all kinds of air toys (balloons, pocket kites, whistles, gliders, etc.).

Harbor Steamer

Chinook Pier (Jackson Street on the Grand River). (616) 842-8950. Memorial Weekend-June 14: 1, 3, 7 p.m. June 15-Labor Day: 1,3, 5:30, 7 p.m. $5 for adults, $3 for children

This "harbor steamer"really is pro-pelled by a rear paddle wheel, but it resembles an overgrown houseboat more than a traditional steamer. All the seats are in the open air, so trips on any but warm days are likely to be uncomfortable.

The hour-and-one-half trip up the Grand River isn't very scenic. Per-haps it will interest those who enjoy witnessing the remnants of once bustling but now decaying American riverfronts. Once a highlight of the trip was a rusting old freighter whose derelict appearance made if it look haunted. But it has been hauled away for scrap metal.

Our "steamer" (it is actually diesel-powered) also passes Grand Haven's giant coal-fired municipal power generating station. Near the big U.S. 31 bridge is an old and increasingly rare railroad swing bridge, once manned 24 hours a day to pivot the bridge when large boats pass by. Now railroad traffic is so sparse that the infrequent trains operate the bridge themselves. Freighters no longer go up the Grand River past U.S. 31, so the swing and lift bridges only function to allow larger pleasure craft to pass.

The only other major sight on this largely dull passage are the many marinas harboring hundreds of expensive pleasure boats.

Harbor Trolleys   ★

Chinook Pier, 301 N. Harbor Dr. 842-3200. Mem-Labor Day: 11-11. $1 adults, 50¢ children. Trolleys may be flagged down anywhere along the route.

Two "trolleys" take visitors on short guided tours of the vicinity. The red one leaves every 30 minutes and tours Grand Haven. The blue one leaves every 40 minutes and tours Spring Lake and Perrysburg. Both drivers who took us around were quite good — humorous and informa-tive. They give you a nice introduction to the area. In Grand Haven, you learn that Five Mile Hill is named for how far in the lake a boat is when it can just see the top of the hill. In Spring Lake you learn that the big seven-mile-long lake is fed by hun-dreds of springs.

Farmers' Market

Off N. Harbor Dr., just east of Chinook Pier. Open from mid-June through the end of October. Market days: Wed & Sat. from 8 until 2 or so. Open Mondays in July & August, 3 to 7 p.m.

A colorful big awning marks this small but pleasant market that at-tracts farmers with fresh-picked produce.

Pere Marquette historic railroad displays

Near the east end of the Boardwalk, just north of the City Marina at N. Harbor Dr., near Second.

A group of local train buffs has

lovingly restored this splendid outdoor exhibit of old railroad pieces. An
attractive, small children's **playground** separates it from the boardwalk. Overlooking the exhibit in majestic austerity is the huge concrete
coaling tower, 79 feet tall. It was built
in 1925 to drop 300 tons of coal into
the tenders of steam locomotives
back when this was a busy railroad
yard.

At the display's head is Pere Marquette 1223, one of the last steam locomotives made in the U.S. It ran between Chicago, Saginaw, Detroit, and
Toledo between 1941 and 1951. The
101-foot-long engine was too large to
run safely on most Michigan tracks.

Behind the locomotive is the ten-
der, which held 22 tons of coal, followed by a 1946 boxcar. The 1941
caboose, retired in 1981, made the
nightly cannonball run between
Muskegon and Grand Haven. The
older wooden caboose is a vintage
1894 design.

South Pier, catwalk, and lighthouse ★★

*Lake Michigan at the bend in S.
Harbor Drive.*

As one of the few deepwater ports
in southern Lake Michigan, Grand
Haven has been a crucial refuge to
ships caught in Great Lake storms.
The first lighthouse was built here
way back in 1839. The nearer lighthouse was built in 1905. The outer
light, 39 feet high, equipped with a

Fishing from South Pier
Few places are more interesting to
fish from that the long lighthouse
piers at the major Great Lakes ports.
Here in the Grand Haven area you can
quickly get set up with inexpensive
fishing gear at the Meijer's on U.S.
31, which also sells one-day fishing
licenses ($5.25). Live bait is available
at Woods and Waters, across from the
Holiday Inn in Spring Lake (921 W.
Savidge). In April and May you can
catch 15 lb. salmon from the pier. In
summer the main catch is perch.

Piers can be dangerous,
especially when slippery and during
stormy weather. Each year state news
headlines report on drownings from
Michigan piers, usually of unattended small children or thrill-
seeking adolescents.

---

foghorn, dates from 1875.

The long pier's catwalk, once used
to get out to repair the lights during
storms, is no longer considered safe.
But it has great nostalgic value to local citizens, who mounted an enthusiastic "save the catwalk" campaign
and pitched in to restore it.

The pier is a great place to stroll
and observe quite a cross-section of
humanity in an increasingly upscale
town. It's even more popular with
perch fishermen, who say very early
morning is the time to catch the big
ones.

Grand Haven State Park

*On S. Harbor at the Grand River
channel about a mile west of downtown Grand Haven. (616) 842-6020.
To park in the small lot, $15 annual
permit or $3 daily pass required. $10
fee per campsite. Reservations
almost always required.*

This and Mears State Park in
Pentwater are the most booked-up of
the many Michigan state parks. The
48-acre park itself, in a congested
part of Grand Haven and without any
trees, seems the opposite of what a
camper would want. But the
"campers" here are largely people
with big motor homes and trailers
who want to be right on the beach of
Lake Michigan. The 2,500 feet of sand
here and at the adjacent municipal
beach is some of the best quality
you'll find along the Great Lakes.

Another reason for the park's
immense popularity (a million visit it
a year) is the lack of mosquitos and
the opportunity to see the sun set
over the lake. Also, you can walk a

short distance to the pier for good perch fishing, or stroll along the interesting boardwalk to downtown Grand Haven.

The state books 80% of the park's 182 campsites for dates between mid-June and Labor Day by January 1. Still, there's a chance you can get a site if you go the day before to get a priority number and then show up at 8 a.m. sharp to see if you get a spot. The courteous park officials can tell you what your chances are.

For far more scenic camping near the beach, both Hoffmaster State Park and Muskegon State Park not far to the north are much more peaceful and less often booked up.

The Grand Haven beaches attract a lot of teens and young adults, many from Grand Rapids. It's quite a scene, what with the stunt kites, jet skis, windsurfing, and other forms of youthful exhibitionism. Families are also in evidence; there's a playground for kids at the state park and at the city beach just to the south.

Highland Park   ★★

Along and off of Highland Rd., south of Lake Ave., overlooking Lake Michigan. Just east of the Bil Mar Restaurant at 1223 S. Harbor.

This haunting summer cottage colony of 100 cottages sits among dunes overlooking Lake Michigan. Businessmen formed the Highland Park Association in the 1880s to sell memberships and build the romantic-looking Highland Park Hotel with a 200-foot porch. Highland Park has long been a summer retreat for well-to-do families from as far away as St. Louis and Louisville, as well as Chicago and Grand Rapids. The hotel, re-

Boardwalks wind through the treetops in the century-old cottage colony of Highland Park. They provide fine views of spring wildflowers and of chipmunks and other wildlife in the shady back dunes below.

markably, stayed in business until a 1967 fire destroyed everything except the north annex, a delightful pink bed and breakfast which continues the name today.

Today Highland Park cottages, many of them small and plain, command fancy prices — from $100,000 to $250,000. Some, especially those with lake views, have been extensively remodeled and winterized. But many longtime family cottages retain a rather austere simplicity that hasn't changed for decades. Signs with names like Loch Haven and Breezy Rest hang on some porches.

Highland Park lodging
To more fully experience the beauty of Highland Park, you may want to stay either in the **Khardomah Lodge**, which dates from 1873, or the **Highland Park Hotel**, a bed and breakfast. See **Lodgings** for details.

What's special here are the quaint narrow roads, the striking dune environment with steep hills and shady valleys, and the old beech and maple forests.

The best look at Highland Park is from the rambling **boardwalks** that go back and dip through the steep, heavily wooded back dunes. It's dark and cool here, a nice respite from too much sun on the beach. The dunes drop off so dramatically, the boardwalks seem suspended in the treetops as they pass by the cottages' ample porches. From them you can look down on wildflowers and scampering chipmunks. The quainter cottages are back away from the lake, some approachable only via the boardwalk and numerous steps. Most are quite simple, but one is a small frame version of a castle, with crenellations along the roofline.

Finding Highland Park's boardwalks can be a trick. If you are on the beach, look for the stairs climbing the bluff just south of Lake Avenue. They lead to an overlook with benches, a popular place for viewing sunsets, in front of the pink Highland Park Hotel. Walk briefly back along Lake Avenue; behind the hotel, you'll see Lover's Lane. Go down it a ways,

The leisurely atmosphere of plain, rustic summer retreats, before automobiles and air-conditioning opened up so many possibilities, survives at Highland Park's enchantingly simple Khardomah Lodge.

and a little to your left you'll see the white painted railing to stairs that look like a private cottage entrance. This is actually part of the boardwalk, maintained by the Highland Park Association. The boardwalk winds around among the cottages, sometimes ending on a road. (The roads themselves, oriented to parking, not views, are much less interesting.) Eventually you will end up at the lake; turn to your right and get back to your car.

Lake Avenue to Duncan Park and Lake Forest Cemetery ★

About 1 mile from 2nd and Washington downtown to the Lake Michigan overlook at Highland Park. about 1.5 miles back along Harbor Drive and the Linear Park.

Lake Street, the southern extension of Second, is a fine street for a long walk or a drive. The ambiance is lush with foliage in summer, the big houses interesting to look at. Lake Street swings west at **Duncan Park,** a dark and mysterious-looking beech-maple climax forest on the back dunes about half a mile from Lake Michigan. It's for walking, cross-country skiing in winter, and picnicking. There's no through traffic; the auto entrance is off Sheldon Road.

Just west of the park's Lake Drive entrance, entered off Lake, is **Lake Forest Cemetery**, established in 1872 among the hills and dales of the forested back dunes. Few cemeteries can approach this one for the combination of beautiful setting, interesting plants and monuments, and varied strands of local history and American immigrants' experience represented in the dates and birthplaces of people buried here: Yankee, Scotch, and Irish pioneers, soon followed by numerous Dutch.

Majestic beeches, with their deep shade contrasted to the play of light on their elephant-smooth trunks,

Lake Forest Cemetery, with its beautiful landscaping, interesting monuments, and winding paths, reflects the 19th-century tradition of cemeteries as parks for Sunday outings.

anchor the winding paths and are effective natural foils to the elaborate post-Civil War monuments. At the cemetery's southern end is Ferry Hill, which includes the grave of William Ferry, Grand Haven's founder. Ferry was the former Congregational missionary who later attained wealth and prominence as a lumber man and town founder. He wrote his epitaph: "First toil, then rest. First grace, then glory."

In the southeast corner are Civil War and Spanish-American War

---

Cemetery historical map
To get a splendid map and history of Lake Forest Cemetery, complete with 35 identified sites, ask at the Tri-Cities Historical Museum (p. 157).

---

memorials. The Potter's Field, where impoverished and unknown people were buried, is just north of them, and beyond it, a sunken garden. Picturesque cement tombstones are on a lane paralleling Lake Street, which artfully imitate tree stumps, and ferns.

Half a mile farther down Lake, you enter the old cottage colony at **Highland Park** (p. 162). A stay at the **Khardomah Lodge** (see Lodgings) will take you back to the authentic atmos-phere of these summer resorts at the turn of the century — a far cry in their rustic simplicity from the frilly contemporary interpretation of this period.

The walk ends at the overlook in front of the pink **Highland Park Inn**, all that remains of the rambling Highland Park Hotel that once presided over the lake bluff. Plan your walk to arrive here at sunset, and you can join the applause for the biggest daily show on the lake.

Cary Marine

620 N. Beacon Ave., north of Jackson, between Meijer's and the Grand River bridge.

This big, white brick building can be seen as a symbol of the hard times Grand Haven faced in the early 1980s and the kinds of businesses that have helped put the community back on its feet. Until 1980, the building housed one of the town's biggest employers, A&P Parts, which made parts for mufflers. Today, inside part of the building is Cary Marine, a boat manufacturer previously headquartered in Port Everglades, Florida.

Once Cary made a variety of boats, but now it makes high-performance luxury boats — extremely large speedboats that go 60 mph and cost up to $1.5 million.

The 50-foot model has four 420 horsepower Olds engines and four props. Though it sits low in the water, the headroom below deck is over six feet and has six berths, two refrigerators, a color TV, stereo, ultrasuede coverings, and a microwave. The 65-foot model has three 1,000 hp diesels, three refrigerators, and two wet bars.

Grand Isle Marina

East of U.S. 31, just north of the Grand River Bridge

This big pleasure boat facility is said by many to be the best in the Midwest. It is clean. The repair services, though slow, are competent. The food at the **Riverwatch** restaurant is good. The **disco** is considered by some the hot spot of the area ("a fine place for chasing broads," claimed a single 50-year-old boater. And there is a big, indoor swimming pool.

Even for the non-boater, it can be interesting to stroll along the dock and look at the half to three-quarter million dollar boats tied up one after another.

North Beach Park   ★

On North Shore Rd. where it first reaches Lake Michigan. Go north on U.S. 31 until you cross the Grand River, then turn right at the Ferrysburg exit. Turn left onto Grand Haven Rd. (174th St.), go north and turn left again, when you see the fire station, onto North Shore Dr. Park is in about 1.5 miles. $2/car between Memorial and Labor Day. $12 annual pass for nonresidents.

You have to go out of your way to reach this Ottawa County beach. Popular with families, it is less likely to be crowded than Grand Haven's beachfront parks to the south. Not only does the park have a nice long beach along Lake Michigan, but east of the road is a magnificent sand dune with a wooden stairway that gets you most of the way to the top. You'll likely be out of breath when you reach the top, but you'll have a great view of Lake Michigan to the west and an equally nice view of the lush hinterland to the east.

Kitchel Dune Reserve   ★

About 1/4 mile east from Lake Michigan north of the Grand River. See directions for North Shore Park. Continue south on North Shore over 1.5 miles past the park to Berwyck. Turn left, then into the drive of the North Shore Marina, go behind it, and look for the Kitchel Dune Reserve sign.

The paths through the oaks and pines here give a real sense of what the natural dunes are like. The dune-tops also give you wonderful views of the lake, Grand Haven, and the countryside. The 52 acres of undeveloped duneland have a number of habitats representative of sand dunes along the Great Lakes. You can see the horsetails used for scouring by Indians, small ponds with rushes and amphibians, and beanberry, used by Indians as a tobacco. The dune grass is the key sand stabilizing plant in the dunes. Once stabilized, other plants emerge and the dune grass disappears.

The nature trails through these dunes were created in 1980. Stay on them: the dunes are fragile and easily eroded. Also, poison ivy is common throughout the area. The many trees were planted on 40 acres of the preserve in 1941 as community preservation project.

Kirk Park

Between Lake Michigan and Lake Shore Ave. just north of Fillmore, on Lake Michigan 6 miles south of Grand Haven. Operated by the Ottawa County Parks and Recreation Commission (616) 846-8117. $2/day/car between Memorial Day and Labor Day, or $8 annual resident sticker, $12 for nonresidents.

This popular and well-designed new park, 27 acres in all, has 800 feet of beautiful Lake Michigan beachfront. There's no camping, but there's a pleasant picnic area behind the dunes in medium-growth pine woods.

> **A beautiful bicycle trail** winds south through the woods parallel to Lake Shore Ave. all the way to Holland. (Voters in Grand Haven Township north of Little Pigeon Creek have so far selfishly voted down continuing the path to Grand Haven). For more on the path, see p. 136.

A **playground** with nifty new equipment is near the entrance, not far away. From the parking lot and **picnic** and restroom area, a lovely trail leads through the deep shade of majestic beeches and maples to a **lake overlook platform** atop the dunes. The ample beach is now rebuilding after high lake levels cut away trees at the dunes' front. There's a **food wagon** in summer.

From Grand Haven the drive along Lake Shore Avenue goes past attractive homes and cottages, through a deep, sun-dappled tunnel of huge beeches and maples. Half a mile north of the park, the scenic, marshy outlet of Little Pigeon Creek attracts much wildlife.

A scenic drive to Eastmanville and Lamont ★

On Leonard, 13 and 17 miles east of Spring Lake. Take Leonard from Spring Lake. (Turn south onto Lake from Savidge while you're still in town.) Or, from Grand Haven, drive along the south side of the Grand to Eastmanville by taking Mercury east from Robbins Rd., a major street intersecting with Beacon Blvd. at the south edge of town. Cross the river at Eastmanville and continue east on Leonard.)

Settled in the 1840s, these two charming villages were busy little river landings when steamers went up the Grand River to Grand Rapids. But within a few decades, railroads took away their shipping. The main highway, I-96, misses them by miles. As a result, Lamont and Eastmanville still have the leisurely look of pre-industrial America. Handsome Greek

Revival houses, mostly well maintained, have large yards and often, picket fences. Two of the most beautiful riverfront homes are now bed and breakfasts.

The drive along the river valley, past neat old farms that Dutch immigrant farmers have kept tidy, is exceptionally scenic. (It's nice all the way into Grand Rapids, where Leonard becomes a busy commercial street in Grand Rapids' Polish west side. **Ed's Breads** at 1204 Leonard, across from the Burger King, is a fabulous old-world bakery. Phone (616) 451-9100; closed Monday).

Riverside Park, on the south bank of the Grand, is a pleasant shady park with **picnic area** and **boat launch** on an unusually pretty stretch of the Grand. It's on Cedar Street at 104th Avenue, about 7 miles west of the Eastmanville bridge.

Moser's Dried Flower Barn ★

14065 Cleveland (Route 104) in Nunica, between spring Lake and I-96. (616) 842-0641. Mon-Sat 9-5.

It's a pleasure both to smell and see the many dried flower arrangements created by Dutch native Reini Moser from plants grown in the pretty gardens around the rustic sales area, and in the greenhouses you see from the road. Subtle combinations of colors are remarkably pleasing. A medium-sized basket with a wide array of flowers is about $30. The dried flowers will last a good two years (less in Florida, more in the Southwest). Also available are dried materials for making your own combinations.

RESTAURANTS

Official Chicken Co.

In Harbourfront Place, on Harbor just north of Wasington in downtown Grand Haven. (616) 846-7861. Tues-Sat 11:30-8, Mon 11:30-5:30, Sun noon-4.

In the food court of Harbourfront Place, this fast food joint is a good place to pick up a quick picnic lunch or supper to enjoy the Grand River boardwalk nearby. A good choice is their chicken fajita ($3.61). Also good are the barbecue chicken dinners with cole slaw and fresh fries, (3 pieces $5.50, 6 $8.25, 9 $10.90). They also make hamburgers and steak fajitas.

Kirby Grill ★★

Washington at Harbor Drive, downtown Grand Haven. (616) 846-3299. Sun-Thurs 11-11. Fri-Sat 11-1 a.m. Full bar. MC, Visa, AmEx.

This newly renovated space in the high-ceiling first floor of the old Kirby Hotel has become a smash hit, and for good reason. The casual ambiance is pleasant. It's spacious, with a long bar forming a central axis, and the decor is functional, not cute. Some of the booths even have views of the Grand River. The food is quite good. Pasta is big here. The pasta Primavera, with roasted garlic cream sauce, is $6.75. Baked cajun catfish is $11.95. A big half-pound cheeseburger on a kaiser roll is $4.95. At night the Kirby becomes a boisterous, convivial drinking spot. On Sundays, there's a jazz piano with brunch, and eggs Benedict with rattlesnake sausage.

Snug Harbor ★

311 Harbor, across from Dairy Treat, overlooking Grand River. (616) 846-8400. Breakfast 7-10:30, lunch 11-3, dinner 5-11 weekends, 5-10 weekdays. Full bar, Visa, AmEx, MC.

Previously named Dansk Kro, this is one of the better West Michigan restaurants. It's pleasingly located on the south bank of the Grand between downtown Grand Haven and Lake Michigan. Downstairs is the more informal lounge/dining area. Upstairs, plenty of glass windows make full use of the fine location. There's also a deck for outside dining. Danish specialties served with red cabbage include Oxrulader ($8.95); braised beef rolls filled with smod bacon and onion; and Frikadellar ($7.95), Danish meatballs in gravy. Also popular are the stir-fries: shrimp ($10.95 at dinner, $6.95 at lunch) and chicken ($9.95/$5.50). The elaborate breakfasts are well worth trying.

Fricano's Pizza Tavern ★★

1400 Fulton at Hopkins, 4 blocks east of U.S. 31. (616) 842-8640. Weekends 5-1, weekdays 5-midnight. Closed Sundays. Full bar. No credit cards.

Well over 40 years now the Frincaos have been making the same thin-crusted 12-inch pizza at this isolated spot far from Grand Haven's trendy restaurants. It's the only dish on their menu, but it packs them in. There are two lines, one to the front and one to the back room, and sometimes you see 50 people waiting in each to get into the conspicuously austere tavern, where beer cases are stacked against walls. The 12-inch pizza alone is $5.50, and costs up to $6.50 with all the toppings: pepperoni, mushrooms, green peppers, sausage, and anchovies.

Arboreal Inn ★★★

(616) 842-3800 18191 174th. U.S.-31 north from Grand Haven to Van Wagoner exit, west 1 mile to T, turn right onto 174th. 1.4th mile north on west side of road. Lunch Mon-Fri 11-2. Dinner Mon-Sat 5-10. Lunch entrés $3.95-$6.95. Dinner $10.95-$21.95. Full bar.

MC, Visa.

One of the very most delightful restaurants in west Michigan, this classic country inn was actually built in 1981, although it looks like it's been around for decades. The comfortable, unpretentious interior is European in its restrained good taste. The wine list is superb, especially the chardonnays and cabernets. The excellent whitefish from inland Canadian lakes is fresh, never frozen. The Tournedoes Oscar ($17.95) comes with sautéed mushrooms and crab with Bernaise sauce. With 24 hours notice, you can order more elaborate specials such as Chateaubriand ($$42.95 for 2) or rack of lamb ($46.95 for 2).

LODGINGS

Harbor House Inn
(616) 846-0610.
Clinton at Harbor 2 blocks from downtown Grand Haven overlooking the boardwalk and harbor.
15 rooms with private baths. $95, or $115 with fireplace and whirlpool. All have some water view. 2nd night half price in off-season. Brand-new, but looks like an old lakeside hotel with huge porch overlooking harbor. Big continental breakfast. New traditional furniture. Large living room, library. Harbor Dr. can be traffic-clogged and noisy on summer weekends; off-season would be nicer. 10-minutes walk to beach.

Highland Park Hotel
(616) 846-1473.
1414 Lake Ave. in Highland Park, overlooking Lake Michigan.
6 rooms with private baths. May 1-Oct. 1: $75 weeknights, $85 weekends. Off-season $65. The old annex, all that's left of the Highland Park hotel, has a delightful small 2nd-floor porch and enclosed lounge for guests with panoramic view of Lake Michigan. Medium-size guest rooms

have angled lake view. Cheerful, sophisticated country decor with antiques; one of the innkeepers here owns Ad Libs gift shop in town. Continental breakfast, late-afternoon cocktails. Short walk to beach. Beautiful walks in Highland Park.

Khardomah Lodge
(616) 842-2990.
1365 Lake Ave. in Highland Park. (See p. 162.)
16 small rooms on 2nd floor, with baths at end of hall, each sleeps 2-4. (Some have bunks.) Mem.-Labor Day: $49/double, $5/ extra person. Otherwise $39. Rustic and unfussed over, this is what resorts in the old days were really like. Very simple rooms with a huge porch, comfortable common areas, and a big dining room. Carole and Steven Loftis are dedicated to preserving the authentic cottage atmosphere. Original wicker, metal lawn chairs. Chenille bedspreads, accumulated old furniture, old books and magazines along with games, and a melange of artfully assembled old dishes, vintage 1920-1950. Clean and not musty. Mechanical systems, replacement windows are new but unobtrusive. Many overstressed guests love the unpretentious, relaxed effect; it reminds them of grandma on the farm, no fashion colors or matching suites. Added great room overlooks a deeply wooded ravine in back. Coffee provided; kitchen privileges. Occasional street noise; rear rooms quieter. 200 yards from beach. Beautiful walks nearby.

Washington St. Inn
(616) 842-1075.
608 Washington, on a residential block between Grand Haven's two commercial districts., 6 blocks from boardwalk.
Bed and breakfast with 5 rooms, most sharing baths. $60-$70. Comfortable, solid, sunny 1902 house with early 20th-century furniture, pleasant country touches. Large

common area includes entire living, dining, and sitting rooms and front porch. Continental breakfast.

Boyden House
(616) 846-3538.
301 S. Fifth at Lafayette, about 5 blocks from Grand Haven's main shopping area.
5 rooms, all with baths. Interior designer Bernie Snoeyer and his wife, Dutch natives, have turned this place from a memorably decrepit haunted house, full of odd porches and nooks, into a showplace. White walls and rich but uncluttered decor highlight some fascinating antiques and the house's own elaborately patterned surfaces, woodwork, and fireplaces. The house was built in 1874 by a lumberman who lavished patterned shingled and varied woods on the interior. Large guest rooms include sitting area; some have fireplaces. Big front porch, back deck, several large and striking common rooms. Full breakfast. On busy street (Fifth turns into Sheldon Rd., the lakeshore road to Holland) in residential neighborhood; rear rooms are quieter. Walk downtown, to boardwalk, Duncan Park.

Best Western Beacon Motel
(616) 842-4720
1525 Beacon Blvd, 2 miles south of drawbridge over the Grand.
101 rooms, 2 floors. July & August: single $54, double $64. Sept-spring: single $38, double $48. Spring through June: single $44, double $54. Rooms with whirlpools $90 winter, $110 summer. Outdoor pool. HBO.

Days Inn
(616) 842-1999
South Beacon (US 31), 2 miles south of drawbridge over Grand River.
100 rooms. Rates vary frequently through year. Single $47-$75, double $53-$80. Special weekend prices for families in winter. Indoor swimming pool, exercise room, video game room. HBO. Adjoining restaurant,

Trumpets, with lounge. One of the fancier moderate-priced chains in the state.

Holiday Inn
(616) 846-1000.
940 w. Savidge, Spring Lake, just northwest of the drawbridge.
121 rooms, 32 with view of the river. Slips occasionally available ($35-$60). Summer: single $61 ($81 with view), double $71 ($91 with view). Winter $46-$61. Prices vary; call to confirm. Indoor & outdoor pool, whirlpool, steambath and dry sauna. Charter fishing at docks. HBO.

This is a popular place, but the view of a boring stretch of the Grand River full of pleasure boats isn't much to write home about.

Riverview Bed & Breakfast
(616) 677-3921.
4580 Leonard Rd. in Lamont, 20 minutes from Grand Haven beaches and from Grand Rapids, 5 minutes to Grand Valley State University.
Bed and breakfast with 5 rooms, 3 with private baths. $55-$65. 1850 Greek Revival home remodeled to open up in back to a beautiful view of the Grand River. Sunny, big porch/dining area, living room, large patio for guests. Complete breakfast. Very large yard, lushly landscaped. Tasteful country decor with antiques. Nearby fishing, boat rentals, golf. In the quaint village of Lamont.

Boyden House

Muskegon

Muskegon was once the Lumber Queen of the World, then a gritty foundry town, and now a city seeking a future based on recreation and mid-tech industry. It's Michigan's biggest city on Lake Michigan, and historically it's been the least glamorous — despite its beautiful state parks and beaches, wonderful art museum, and some of the better restaurants in the region. Nowhere are the visible disruptions caused by the booms and busts of industrial cycles more apparent and unsettling than in Muskegon.

First-time visitors looking for downtown might react as Gertrude Stein did when she wrote of Oakland, California, "There's no there there." Mini-superhighways named Skyline, Airline, and Seaway sweep you into and out of downtown so fast you hardly know you're there, just blocks from a beautiful lake you never see. The imposing stone castle of a train station looms above weedy vacant land. Much of the historic downtown has been demolished. Four blocks of Western Avenue, Muskegon's main downtown retail street, have been remodeled and enclosed in a mall, in yet another bold attempt to revive a Midwestern downtown.

Energetic changes disrupted the cityscape

Muskegon urban renewal was particularly imaginative, and energetic, but in retrospect misguided. Downtown today consists of parking lots, big build-ings, and little in between that would have given the district a more human scale. On parts of once-bustling Western Ave., you can feel like you're in the ruins of a modern American Pompeii. A handsome tiled floor of a vanished building has become a parking lot, and murals on board fences concealing vacant lots depict for visitors the stores and industries here during the logging era.

Many of the empty smaller storefronts were torn down. Retailing is actually healthier in the downtown of the old industrial suburb of Muskegon Heights than it is in downtown Muskegon outside the mall. It's hard to find the expected downtown coffee shops and taverns. They're actually here, tucked away and marked with inconspicuous signs. In towns like Muskegon, without many visitors, signs are minimal, because it's assumed that everybody who's here already knows where everything is.

More than meets the eye

It's easy to dismiss Muskegon as a Rust Bowl relic, and a lot of people do who live in Grand Rapids and

Sailboats, not smokestacks are the silver lining of the economic cloud of Muskegon's industrial decline. As plants close and warehouses are vacated, views of Muskegon Lake open up that have long been blocked.

A surprising variety of events, from classical music to the big summer air show, are held in Muskegon. Call or stop by the **Tourist Info. Center** *(616-722-3751) in the imposing Hackley Administration Building with the tall tower, on West Webster between 3rd and 4th, across from Hackley Park. (It's open weekdays 8-5.)*

For films, plays, exhibits, lectures, etc., call the **Hackley Library** *(616-722-7276).*

For state-of- the-art bowling technology, stop in at the Brunswick at 441 Western, next to the Frauenthal Theater in downtown Muskegon. Here the Brunswick Bowling and Billiard Division, headquartered in Muskegon, tests its latest gadgets. BowlerVision is an computerized automatic scoring system which shows the speed of the ball you just threw on a video screen, plots the ball's path, and lets you play over 10 different games on a bowling alley. Employees are happy to show bowlers how to use the fancy stuff. Call (616) 722-3489 for hours; sometimes in summer they close for testing.

The splendid Hackley Library was the first of Charles Hackley's gifts to Muskegon, intended to lay the foundation for its transition from dying lumber town to a progressive 20th-century city. Its lavish architectural details make it well worth a visit.

Grand Haven — places that have successfully developed more diversified and prosperous economies. People who want to launch projects in Muskegon today have to fight what they call the "Muskegon mentality" — the prideless defeatism of people who feel they're nothing more than "factory rats." But Muskegon has a lot of less obvious positives. There's its wonderful, cool lakefront location without the congestion other West Michigan ports suffer today. There are beautiful Lake Michigan beaches north and south of Muskegon Lake, and fantastic fishing and duck hunting along the Muskegon River's marshy estuary. The lakes and woods just north and east of here have that "up North" feeling, with good hunting, fishing, and canoeing.

Culturally, the city is blessed — largely a legacy of Chicago industrialists who brought businesses here early in the century. Nearby is the Blue Lake Fine Arts Camp, with its classical music radio station and summer concerts. The art museum, West Shore Symphony, Frauenthal Center (an outstanding conversion of a 1930 movie theater into a high-caliber performing arts complex), and the L. C. Walker Sports Arena (home of the pro ice hockey Lumber Jacks and big pop music concerts) are all first-rate, much better than in most cities of this size.

There isn't the smug piety here so prevalent in many circles in Grand Rapids and Ottawa County. Muskegon High is one of the very few schools in the state which provides good college-prep and vocational educations to a truly representative cross-section of students from all racial and social backgrounds. The city of Muskegon is 20% African-American (1980 figures) and at least 3% Hispanic. Whites represent an unusual variety of ethnic groups drawn by jobs first in lumber and then in industry. There are substantial populations of Poles, Lithuanians, Norwegians, Danes,

The costs and benefits of heavy industry
"For 50 years Muskegon had a charmed life: union-scale jobs and an incredibly low cost of living," says one thoughtful resident. "There was a feeling that you could have it all — fishing, hunting, good schools, plenty of parks, five acres on a lake, and a cabin cruiser. Two months before the 1973 Arab oil embargo, this was a mill town going full-blast. Downtown the sky was brown like Pittsburgh. Muskegon Lake was brown, and oilier than the Grand River."

Today the situation is reversed. Most of the heavy industry is gone. But the environment is quite clean, except for high ozone levels caused by Chicago and Milwaukee auto emissions acarried by prevailing winds.

The Hackley Story

Richest of all Muskegon's lumber barons, Charles Hackley (1837-1905) refused to take his money and run from the stump-scarred north country when its timber ran out. In Muskegon's boom year of 1886, Hackley and his partner, Thomas Hume, were among the few who realized early that Michigan's timber would soon run out. To perpetuate their fortune, they acquired vast acreages of timberland in the West and South. Hackley apparently regarded his great wealth as a trust fund to be administered for society's benefit — though some small-town cynics attributed his generosity to vanity and a wish to rename Muskegon "Hackleyville." At any rate, Hackley decided to invest in Muskegon and try to develop it as a modern and enlightened industrial city.

Hackley had come to Muskegon at 19. He worked two years as a lumber mill hand and one as a logging camp foreman so he could afford a bookkeeping course at a business college. He then became a bookkeeper at a Muskegon lumber mill and soon was able to go in with his father and two older brothers and buy half the mill. Eventually the Hackleys owned it all and developed it into the largest lumber mill in the region (and for awhile probably in the world). Charles Hackley became the sole owner when family partners died. He parlayed its assets into a huge fortune based largely on aggressive and astute acquisition of timber land in Michigan, and later in Wisconsin, Minnesota, the South, and British Columbia.

A retiring and enigmatic personality, Hackley often deferred to the advice of a trusted circle of friends. He started by giving the city a superb library, park, and new school, then promoted the city as a superior place to live and do business.

In all, Hackley's gifts to Muskegon between 1888 and 1912 totalled nearly $6 million — a stunning testimony to the wealth of successful capitalists before income tax was inaugurated. Hack-ley's monumental legacies define Muskegon's historic core, especially now that urban renewal has cleared so much of the rest. In appreciation, Muskegon has celebrated Hackley Day (May 25) as a school and city holiday since 1888.

1990, the Hackley Library's centennial year, offers numerous commemorations, including an **exhibit on Hackley's life and gifts** at the Muskegon County Museum through November.

Swedes, Finns, Germans, and Irish, in addition to the Dutch who dominate other West Michigan towns. Temple B'nai Israel, Michigan's smallest and one of its oldest Jewish congregations, was founded by merchants in the lumber boom. It celebrated its centennial with international attention in 1989.

Things are affordable here, from hotel rooms and boat slips to restaurants and housing. Pleasant neighborhoods of nice homes from the first half of the 20th century (4 bedrooms, 2 baths, $35,000 to $75,000) are along Lake Shore Drive toward Pere Marquette Park.

Reinventing the dying Lumber Queen

From 1850 to 1890 Muskegon was a busy, brawling boom town at the mouth of the long Muskegon River, which starts near Houghton Lake just south of Grayling. Its valley, the narrowest of any Michigan river, was ideal for logging. Logs could be rolled down its steep sides — the so-called "high rollways" from which logs, unjammed in spring, were floated down the river to Muskegon's sawmills. Some 47 sawmills lined five-mile-long Muskegon Lake. The town was at the southeast end. Flanking the channel to Lake Michigan was Pigeon Hill, biggest of all Great Lakes dunes after Sleeping Bear. Sand from this beloved landmark was so completely mined that Pigeon Hill is now a marina.

So efficiently did the lumbermen of northern Michigan learn to clear the vast forests of the Muskegon River valley that by 1893 Muskegon, then a city of some 26,000, faced an abrupt decline as the lumber ran out. Charles Hackley, the wealthiest, most generous, and most civic-minded of all the lumber barons, wasn't willing to see the death of the city that had made him. He gave the city schools, a library, a park, an outstanding art gallery, and a hospital, in order to make the raw boom town an attractive place to live and raise families.

Hackley and other local businessmen organized to attract industries to locate here and lay the groundwork for a sustainable future based on industry. The project bore spectacular success. Sealed Power (now SPX), Continental Motors, Shaw-Walker office furniture, Brunswick bowling and billiards, Campell-Wyant-Cannon and Lakey foundries, and what became the S. D. Warren paper mill — these firms were all recruited while still small, before World War I. They grew and turned Muskegon into a significant industrial city.

Prosperity and stress

The irony was that the industry which powered the city into 20th-century prosperity would also subject it to great stress. The boom of the 1920s was followed by the Depression and then the conversion of industries

Big on beer
In most of conservative West Michigan, the prevailing attitude is that beer and other forms of alcohol are meant for home consumption. At Grand Haven's Coast Guard Festival, people can be ticketed for carrying six-packs or drinking on boat decks. (They seldom are.) But in Muskegon, beer is the great social lubricant. Beer tents are at most local festivals, and taverns are social centers in all spheres of society.

Top employers in Muskegon County:
Howmet. 3,300 jobs, mostly in Whitehall. Makers of precision castings for gas turbine engines. Started here, now owned by a French multinational.
SPX. 1,600 jobs in Muskegon and Muskegon Heights. Diversified corp. making and selling auto components, tools, instruments. The only Fortune 500 firm headquartered in Muskegon.
S. D. Warren. 1,050 jobs. Produces premium coated papers. One of 5 plants in the S. D. Warren division of Scott Paper.
Brunswick Bowling and Billiards. 900 jobs. Makes bowling balls, pins, electronic scorers.
Shaw-Walker. 850 jobs. Office furniture and panel systems. Founded here, now part of Westinghouse.

to war production during World War II. The federal War Production Board recruited thousands of Southerners, mostly black and mostly from two towns in Arkansas and Mississippi, to man the foundries and "keep the fires burning." Their adjustment to city life was compounded by the fact that many were illiterate, the products of inferior education in the rural South. Other workers poured into the city from small towns to the north. Mansions were converted to rooming houses in which three workers shared a single bed in shifts.

High demand and big profits made in rooming-house conversions hastened the decline of older neighborhoods. So did air pollution, which hung over downtown. Both gave extra impetus to the postwar suburban exodus and governmental splintering that is so pronounced in greater Muskegon today.

The central city of about 40,000 is surrounded by no less than five established suburban municipalities and two sizable townships to form a metro area that's unusualy fragmented for its modest population of 80,000. **Muskegon Heights** (population under 15,000) is the old industrial suburb (p. 182) platted and developed by the Muskegon Improvement Company. Today it is over 60% black. **Roosevelt Park** (4,000), a square mile of pleasant suburban ranches, was formed so Cannon-Wyant-Campbell could avoid city taxes. **Norton Shores** (22,000), a sprawling chunk of quintessential postwar suburbia, is centered around Mona Lake, once the site of a large resort hotel. Beautiful, wooded **North Muskegon** (4,000) was long isolated on a spit of land bordered by Bear Lake and Muskegon Lake. Once the bridge and causeway across the wide Muskegon River marshes was improved in the 1920s, the pokey resort and farm village of North Muskegon became accessible by car and developed as a prestigious executive retreat, with large lots and frequent private docks. Its school system, small and homogeneous, is like a private school. Kids there enjoy going to a school that has its own beach.

SPX's new corporate headquarters/luxury marina/restaurant complex on Muskegon Lake, on the site of the huge Lakey Foundry north of the Muskegon Mall, symbolizes local boosters' aspirations for a new, post-industrial Muskegon. It's the first new downtown project oriented to the lake. Business route 31 may be rerouted with a lake view — a nice change from today, when newcomers can drive all around town and never realize Muskegon is on a beautiful lake.

Muskegon's bargain marinas
In small resort towns crowded with boaters, like Saugatuck and Grand Haven, prices of existing berths are increasing. In Muskegon, boating and sailing are cheaper. Slips rent for $1,500 to $2,000 a year, compared with $2,000 to $3,000 in Grand Haven.

POINTS OF INTEREST

Muskegon
Museum of Art   ★★★

296 W. Webster Ave., 1 block east of Hackley Park in downtown Muskegon. From U.S.31, take Bus. U.S. 31 (Seaway) into town, turn left at Third and park by the side of the huge, towered Hackley Admin. Bldg. (616) 722-2600. Tues-Fri, 10-5, Sat & Sun 12-5. No admission; donations appreciated.

Thanks to the beneficence of 19th-century lumber baron Charles Hackley and two astute early directors, this has long been the finest art museum in west Michigan. It's also a very pleasant, easily managed museum, both accessible and stimulating. In the Hackley Gallery is the permanent collection of mostly realistic paintings; they are interesting and complex. The Walker Gallery, in contrast, is a big, open space well suited to changing shows, sometimes very large in scale.

There are some choice classics here, mostly purchased many decades ago. The best-known is the dramatic "Tornado over Kansas," by John Steuart Curry, a prominent proponent of the regionalism that dominated American art in the 1930s, along with Thomas Hart Benton and Grant Wood. Whistler's famous "A Study in Rose and Brown," a simplified, unpretty portrait of a young woman, created such a controversy in Muskegon that the talented first director, Raymond Wyer,

Parking tip: The parking lot on the Third St. side of the huge, towered Hackley Administration Building is convenient to the art museum and other downtown attractions. On-street parking is quite plentiful here — and free. An 8-year-old Muskegon native was mystified when, playing Pictionary, she was asked to draw a parking meter. She'd never seen one!

quit in a huff to direct the art museum in Worcester, Massachusetts, and built it into national prominence. The extraordinary "Tea Time," by Whistler's contemporary William Merritt Chase, was also avant-garde in its day. Edward Hopper, N. C. Wyeth, and Winslow Homer are among the other prominent American painters represented here.

The European holdings, not as extensive, also include some choice works. The most important is "St. Jerome in Penitence," painted circa 1516 by Joos Van Cleve. The saint, in a fascinating, vivid landscape, is surrounded by symbolic and anthropormorphic forms. There are two portraits by Cranach the Elder, of his friend Martin Luther and of Luther's wife, Katharina von Bora. Don't miss another important Dutch painting, Jan van der Heyden's haunting "The Moat of a Castle with Drawbridge."

"We've always been a cutting-edge, open museum, geared to a broader public but ahead of the crowd," says director Al Kochka with pride. Some two dozen **changing exhibits** a year cover topics from printmaking to floral watercolors to porcelain and cross-fertilization between Asian and Western art. The basement **gift shop** has a nice selection of notecards, books, posters, jewelry, and inexpensive gifts for children.

Hackley Public Library ★★

316 Webster Ave. at Third. (616) 722-7276. Tues-Thurs 8:30-8, Fri 8:30-6, Sat 9-5.

The first of lumber king Charles Hackley's many gifts to Muskegon was this splendid 1890 Romanesque Revival stone castle of a library, finished in 1890. To locals, this wonderful library, with over 155,000 volumes, is one of the special things about living in Muskegon. For lovers of Victoriana, it's a treat to visit, starting with the elaborate hand-forged doorknobs and Celtic ornamented hinges on the main doors. Also special is the impressive **main reading room** with its stained-glass windows depicting Shakespeare, Goethe, Longfellow, and the essayist Prescott, Hackley's favorite author. To one side is the huge **oil painting of the library's 1890 dedication** by E. A. Turner of Grand Rapids. It depicts, in a hundred deft portraits, the whole of Muskegon society just before the twilight of the lumbering era. The painting, a compelling blend of impressionism and realism, plays off the dark mass of the school board's dark coats against the shimmer of pastel costumes and parasols in dappled shade. The lifelike portraits, identified in a diagram, provided ample fodder for the town gossip which surrounded the elusive millionaire. Is Mrs. Lee his mistress, or simply a family friend? And who is the mystery woman looking on from a half-darkened window?

Four stone fireplaces with Art Nouveau touches grace various reading rooms; many interior partitions are of sparkling leaded glass imported from France.

Education took top priority in Hackley's gifts to the city. He himself grew up in rural northern Indiana, with few educational opportunities, and as a youth he had to work extremely hard to get ahead.

Hackley spent over $625,000 on this grand library: $100,000 for the building (at a time when an impressive house cost $4,000), $275,000 for books and furnishings, and a $277,500 endowment which has finally dwindled so this library has to scrounge around for funds like most others.

Don't miss the alabaster bust of Hackley and, upstairs, a **mural** of colorful characters from around the world who parade across the barrel-vaulted children's reading room in Muskegon artist Wilfred Berg's 1930s tribute to reading. Today, 55 years later, he's completing the companion mural.

Torrent House

Webster and Third, across from the Hackley Library.

Lumberman and three-term Muskegon mayor John Torrent spent the astonishing sum of $250,000 on this 31-room stone mansion in 1892. In part he intended to show up his rival, Charles Hackley, whose frame showcase seems cozy in comparison. Like many lumber barons, Torrent had extensive holdings: shingle, saw, and lumber mills in Muskegon, Manistee, Ludington, Whitehall, Traverse City, and Sault Ste. Marie.

The city saved Torrent's house from demolition by buying it in 1972. Soon it will house the Hackley Library's research and special collections.

Hackley Park

On W. Webster between 4th and 3rd. ***Hackley Administration Building,*** *349 W. Webster, houses the* ***Tourist Information Center (616-722-3741),*** *Chamber of Commerce, New Muskegon, and Board of Education. Mon-Fri 8-5.*

Hackley Park, Charles Hackley's second gift to his beloved city, is a tree-shaded square with the theatrical 1892 Soldiers' and Sailors' Monument at its center. At a time when monumental public sculpture was much in favor and towns competed to erect impressive Civil War memorials, Hackley was intent that Muskegon go all-out to honor the men who had served their country. As usual, he settled for nothing less than the best in his gifts. First, he acquired and razed houses on the site and erected the central monument. Then he paid $75,000 for the massive 1891 Romanesque **Hackley Administration Building** facing the park. It looks like a courthouse; actually it was originally a school. (Visitors can pick up lots of brochures and maps at the **Tourist Information Center** in the lobby.)

It looks like a grand courthouse presiding over Hackley Park. Actually Charles Hackley donated the Hackley Administration Building as a replacement for an elementary school that burned.

Finally, for Memorial Day 1900, Hackley installed at the park's corners life-size, bronze figures of Lincoln and Admiral David Farragut and Generals Ulysses Grant and William T. Sherman. Perched atop elaborate pedestals, they seem somewhat stuffy today, but their sculptors were considered radical for choosing realistic poses for their subjects. Farragut strides into the wind; Lincoln sits in deep thought.

Hackley Park today isn't the perfectly manicured showplace it was before World War II. The pavement is crumbling, and the park is bordered by too many parking lots and low, single-story buildings to be an effectively enclosed urban space. But if you stand at Clay and Fourth and look across the park at the Hackley Library, Torrent House, and towered

---

Parties in the Park
are held in Hackley Park on Fridays from 5 to 9, from the second week in June through the second week in September. Local groups raise funds by selling food, beer and wine. These popular festivities offer fmusic, from the big local group Beach Bashes to country and ethnic groups.

Hackley Administration Building, the grandest relics of Muskegon's lumber barons, you'll have a clear image of the great wealth once concentrated here. Fund-raising for a gradual restoration is underway; an ornate fountain and exact replicas of the existing original street lights have already been installed.

Mike's Bread and Coffee Shop ★

1095 Third at Houston (entrance on Houston). May move by 1991; call for location. (616) 726-2954. Tues-Fri 8-5:30, Sat 8-3.

This delightful, homey bakery is a little like a French patisserie and a little like a co-op. Mike Canter bakes his own recipes of six European-style whole grain yeast breads ($2.40 a 1.5 lb. loaf),. There's an unusual apple raisin, a dark wheat with bran, and a coarse, hearty pumpernickel. They are all dairy- and fat-free, as this kind of bread often is. His wife, Darma, specializes in party cakes, mousses, and tortes (often baked to customers' family recipes) and in croissant sandwiches, quiches, and a special Russian carrot-cheese pie. A chocolate-cherry-nut cake and a carrot cake are generally on hand. Extras from whatever catering jobs she's doing are for sale at the shop.

For a light lunch, to round out the breads, rolls, and whatever salads and pastries are on hand, there's always coffee, milk, juices, yogurt, cheese, and fresh fruit. This is a friendly place; customers sitting in the three booths often strike up conversations.

There's no co-op in Muskegon, so discriminating cooks appreciate the selection of herbs and spices and baking supplies here. Mike sells organic stone ground corn meal and other flours straight from his inventory, so it's really fresh. The Canters are happy to share their enthusiasm for baking by offering lessons.

Muskegon County Museum ★

430 W. Clay at Fourth in downtown Muskegon, 1 block west of Hackley Park. From U.S. 31, take Bus. U.S. 31 (Seaway) downtown, turn left (north) onto Fourth. (616) 722-0278. Mon-Fri 9:30-4:30, Sat & Sun 12:30-4:30. No admission fee; donations appreciated.

Muskegon's lumber days are the star attraction at this interesting general museum, which includes everything from some excellent, compelling local art to a hands-on gallery of the human body and how it works, to stuffed birds, local industry, and homegrown athletic heroes. It has the potential to be much better if some exhibits were upgraded, with better captions and improved signage to direct you along the confusing corridors.

Interesting **dioramas** of prehistory and early Musekgon County history include the scene at the famous Magdelaine Laframboise's fur-trading post on nearby Duck Lake, circa 1810. Some of the dioramas were made on a shoestring as a Depression-era WPA project, and sometimes they come off more as folk art than current museum-quality displays. But they are interesting and informative.

The dioramas set the stage effectively for the big **Lumber Queen gallery,** off the main hall, full of lumbering scenes and lumber lore. A broader understanding of lumbering in Michigan is conveyed by the outstanding half-hour two-projector **tape/slide show**, which you can request to see in the small auditorium. The lumber barons' business strategy is clearly conveyed, along with the colorful, dangerous daily life in

> **The lumbering era's sights, smells, and sounds**
> are vividly described in *White Lake Reminiscences,* quoted at length on pages 206 to 207.

Like cattle brands, log brands, stamped on the logs' ends, discouraged theft as the valuable logs floated downriver to mills.

lumber camps. It was written by Wendell Hover of Hartwick Pines State Park near Grayling, the home of even better exhibits on logging. After seeing the film, you'll get more out of the museum's dioramas of lumbering scenes. An ingenious game lets you try your luck at lumbering in the Muskegon area in the 1870s, based on the premise that you are an ambitious Easterner who hopes to parlay a few hundred dollars' savings into a fortune by claiming land along the Muskegon River and logging them.

Another highlight is the poignant **passenger pigeon display** in the front entryway, a remembrance of the extinct bird once so plentiful here. Huge flocks of the docile birds once made for easy prey and quick income. There's a dramatically oversized naive painting of a stylized swirl of passenger pigeons being shot at by farmers, done by artist **Lewis Cross** (1864-1951) of nearby Spring Lake.

In the big basement room on Muskegon industry is a series of 19 dreamily impressionistic large murals depicting Muskegon's history. Victor Casenelli, a self-taught artist who settled in North Muskegon, painted them for Lumberman's Bank in 1929. There's irony in his choice of romantic subjects, because now, only

60 years later, none of them have any relation to anything you can see in present-day Muskegon. The first panel, depicting Muskegon before the coming of man, shows Pigeon Hill, the landmark giant dune at the mouth of Muskegon Lake, leveled by sand-mining during World War II. The last vignette, glorifying modern Muskegon in 1929, shows a Chicago-to-Muskegon passenger ship sailing into Muskegon Lake at sunset; today the port is empty except for small pleasure boats.

An attractive **gift shop** has a good selection of publications on local history, as well as interesting, affordable gifts, especially for children.

Hackley & Hume Historic Site   ★★★

484 W. Webster at Sixth, downtown, 2 blocks southwest of Hackley Park. From U. S. 31, Bus. U.S. 31 (Seaway) to Sixth, turn left and go 2 blocks. 616) 722-7578. Open mid-May through September, Wed, Sat & Sun 1-4. Group tours by appt. other times. $2/adults, $1 students, 12 and under free.

Victorian love of ornament may have reached a new height in the 1888 home of Muskegon's great benefactor and richest lumber baron, Charles Hackley. Together with the house of his partner next door and the elaborate, prominent carriage house they share, it forms a remarkable urban ensemble, almost Oriental in its turretted silhouette and rich colors and textures. Houses of this size and splendor were usually made of brick or stone, but Hackley and Thomas Hume, his friend and business partner since 1875, built with the material that made their fortunes. It is said to have taken years for German woodcarvers to finish the Hackley House's fanciful, fascinating carvings of birds, dragons, bats, and a portrait of Hackley himself.

The volunteer Hackley Heritage Association conducts friendly, well-informed tours. After years of hard use as community service offices and a child care center, the Hackley and Hume houses are being slowly and meticulously restored. The surprisingly comfortable Hume House has been furnished with typical rooms of the period when the Hume family lived there, from 1888 to 1942. (Most Hume family furnishings are gone.) The dining room is especially striking, with its clever lighting and interesting set of fish plates.

The Hackley House exterior will

Restoration of the ornate Hackley House (left) includes duplicating the original 28-color paint scheme. Stylish Victorian houses were known for their extremely rich, complex color combinations in autumnal reds, olives, browns, and mustards.

be finished in 1991. Inside it is almost completely restored and fully furnished, often with the Hackleys' own furniture. Most surfaces in the remarkable entry hall are alive with carved or tiled ornament. Light is filtered through many stained glass windows. Each room has a distinctive treatment of fireplace and woodwork. High points include the period bathroom and kitchen, with the Hackleys' fixtures and appliances mostly in place; the library where Hackley held school board meetings and personally issued library cards to the people of Muskegon, and the dining room. Its fireplace shows hunting dogs and deer. The woodwork and built-in sideboard are carved with motifs of corn and apples, crossed forks and knives, and fishing creels.

The gaudy splendor of Hollywood's opulent picture palaces is still alive at Muskegon's 1930 Michigan Theater. Today the Moorish-style theater, complete with original lighting and curtain, is the centerpiece of the Frauenthal Center for the Performing Arts and the home of the Miss Michigan Pageant. The mighty Barton Theater Organ is played at some movie intermissions and as the musical accompaniment to four silent films shown each summer.

Frauenthal Center for the Performing Arts ★★

417 W. Western at Third.
(616) 722-4538.

Behind a severe Art Deco facade, this 1,800-seat theater is a rich Moorish architectural fantasy, complete with most of its original fixtures: velvet curtains, Italian lanterns and tapestries on the side walls, a crest over the proscenium. The cream-colored walls were painted over a much richer scheme some years ago; the original carpet pattern is being duplicated. It opened in 1930 as the Michigan Theater in the Butterfield Theaters' Michigan chain. The mighty, three-rank **Barton Theater Organ** is memorably played at summertime silent film showings every Thursday and Friday evening in July. The Frauenthal is also home of the **West Shore Symphony Orchestra**, the top-notch Muskegon Civic Theater, the Monday-night Kiwanis travel series, and the Miss Michigan Pageant, precursor to Miss America. Broadway touring companies are booked here, too.

The big theater is just part of a top-notch, state-of-the-art complex

that includes the new 169-seat **Beardsley Theater** used for films and plays and the **Clark-Cannon Gallery** (open from noon to 5 Wed-Fri, it shows works by West Michigan artists). Films are shown when the two theaters aren't booked for performances.

For the past couple of years, comedian Pat Paulsen's Cherry Country Playhouse has staged its summer shows here, after its landlords in Traverse City took back their space in renovating the Park Place Hotel. The eight-show season (one week a show) runs from the last weekend in June through the third week of August. Selections from 1993: *I Do, I Do, Annie, A Day In Hollywood, A Night in Ukraine, Nunsense II* with JoAnne Worley, and *An Evening with Phyllis Diller*. Call for ticket information.

Muskegon Mall

At Third and Clay in downtown Muskegon. (616) 722-7243, Mon-Fri 10-9, Sat 10-5:30, Sun noon-5.

It comes as a shock for first-time visitors to downtown Muskegon to realize that the old downtown is *in* a mall. The brick backs of obviously older buildings are the clue. When you walk inside the covered, climate-controlled space, past the plashing fountain and the expected yogurt and cookie shops, you're passing new buildings intermixed with the old marble and limestone fronts of the banks and stores that faced Western Avenue. There's even an entire Victorian building, the ornate Century Club, incorporated into the mall.

In essence, the mall put a roof over Main Street to compete with suburban malls on their own terms, including lots of free parking. It preserved Main Street's mix of goods and services — it has banks, hairdressers, and a big Walgreen's. It's surrounded by acres of free parking, 2,400 spots. In all, 96 buildings were razed.

Once you get used to the weird feeling of being in an old downtown

and a modern mall at the same time, it seems a sensible solution to a dramatic case of downtown decline. Downtown Muskegon in the 1970s offered dim prospects for the kind of specialty retailing that keeps more affluent downtowns like Ann Arbor, Traverse City, St. Joseph, and Birmingham afloat. The mall is quite a pleasant place, now that the city has finally sold it to a new owner from Chicago, who keeps it super-clean, with big palm trees and lots of flowers. Bus routes from all over town converge here; the information desk, with bus information and ticket sales for events, seems like a hub. Thanks to the mall and the Frauenthal Theater, this downtown is busy at night, unlike so many others.

But there are some problems. The parking lots get almost filled up with downtown workers, proving planners' observations that you can pave most of a city and still not have enough parking. The parking lots left big gaps and reinforce the impression that downtown is now dominated by cars and hostile to pedestrians. (Actually it's quite compact and easy to walk around.) And the mall isn't big enough to compete with regional malls. It has two anchors, **Sears** and **Steketee's**, and nine other apparel stores, including **Lerner's** and **Gantos**. Local special-interest shows and bazaars are held frequently to generate traffic.

The mall's new owner is buying up the long-term leases so he can require standard mall hours, causing many locally-owned retailers to leave in the process. He is planning an expansion toward Muskegon Lake, with new specialty stores and possibly a new anchor.

The downtown mall was the brainchild of a young city planner in the 1950s who went on to direct urban renewal in Minneapolis. By one estimate, it cost $33 million (including site acquisition and demolition), of which the federal government paid $20 million.

Deborah's Choice

297 Clay, in the former YMCA across Clay from Muskegon Mall. (616) 726-4747. Tues-Fri 12-5, Sat 10-3.

Deborah Socol, Rhode Island School of Design graduate and a professional artist and photographer, focuses largely on works on paper and often highlights illustrators, and printmakers who use out-of-the-ordinary techniques. Sometimes her shows are planned in conjunction with the Muskegon Museum of Art around the corner. The space itself is memorable. The old YMCA was turned into beautiful condos that retained many intriguing historic features but never sold. The gallery occupies the Y's onetime men's lounge, with 12-foot ceilings, a working stone fireplace, arched windows, and tiled floors.

Downtown Muskegon Heights

Broadway at Peck. From downtown Muskegon, take First/Apple east to Sanford, go south 2 1/2 miles. From Seaway and the south (Bus. US 31), turn north onto Merriam across from the park at Mona Lake. In about 3/4 mile, at a traffic island, turn right onto Crescent and follow the signs to the central business district.

Muskegon Heights is a modern American anomaly: an old industrial community, now over 70% black, with a traditional downtown business district that attracts shoppers and restaurantgoers from a much wider area. The Flamingo Restaurant is one of those memorable holes in the wall treasured by people who like to explore the offbeat crannies of the American culinary landscape.

Most white shoppers are notoriously unwilling to venture into situations where they may be a minority. But downtown Muskegon Heights today is surviving in better shape than most retailing districts from the early 20th century, even if it's not exactly thriving.

Some suburbanites I talked to referred darkly to "crime in the Heights." But it's the only place I can remember where a liquor store has a large plate glass window (Barberini's Beverage Depot at 114 Broadway). Winemaking equipment is prominently displayed there. And a modest Muskegon Heights neighborhood is also the home of the tidiest, quaintest, most cheerful neighborhood grocery I've ever seen in the United States — Boelkins'. (See next page.)

The Heights was planned and promoted in the 1890s as a community of homes built around key industries attracted by the Muskegon Improvement Company, the firm started by Charles Hackley and friends to rebuild the Lumber Queen's economy. For most of its history it was prosperous, if polluted. Today the big industries and the smoke are gone; production has been greatly reduced at the original home of Sealed Power (now SPX), a five-story plant two blocks long on Sanford at Keating. Today SPX uses it mostly for labs and offices and rents space.

During the 1920s, a move to Muskegon Heights' spacious Arts and Crafts houses along streets like Jefferson, Maffatt, and Peck was a step up for successful people from Muskegon. Even the more modest workers' homes have the look of pleasant summer cottages beneath beautiful big oaks. Today downtown Muskegon Heights is the home of successful second- and third-generation retailers founded in that era: **Cohn's Furniture, Sanborn Jewelers,** and **Lockage's Store for Men** — all on Peck north of Broadway. (Lockage's is also home of Mrs. Lackovich's Christmas Shop.)

Vimo's Jeans is owned by a Muslim from Gambia who mixes jeans and Afro-American casual wear with colorful Gambian imports and some traditional leatherwork.

Few retailers here have moved to suburban locations. With a reliable base of established customers and no history of riots during the turbulent 1960s, the prevailing attitude was "if it ain't broke, don't fix it."

First Edition   ★
7 Center, just east of Peck and 1 block north of Broadway. (616) 733-2176. Mon-Fri 7:45-6, Sat 8-6, Sun 8-2 (until 4 in winter).

Pleasantly eccentric, this well organized bookstore is really four retailing genres rolled into one: a sort of expanded newsstand with new paperbacks, some non-bestseller hardcovers, and one of West Michigan's best selections of magazines, from arts reviews to girlie magazines (in an adults-only nook) and comics; a tobacco store; a dealer in stamp and coin supplies but not coins; and a good general used and antiquarian book shop.

Michigan history and Michigan authors are a big specialty here, and American history is pretty good, too. The well-organized used book stock ranges from choice first editions to old magazines to general reading to a lot of science fiction, plus romances (50¢ hardcover, 10¢ paper) and detective stories. Prices are lower than similar stores in Lansing, Ann Arbor, or Detroit. First Edition makes for great browsing or a rainy-day expedition to stock up on vacation reading. (See also the Book Trader, p. 184.) Founder/owner Mary Engen is likely to be up in the U.P. in her similar store in Brevort, 20 miles west of St. Ignace on U.S. 2.

Ron's Books and Comics
2760 Peck between Center and Broadway. (616) 737-2543. Mon-Sat 10-5.

This haphazard operation around the corner from First Edition is quite a contrast. But it's a worthwhile stop for bargain-minded browsers and heavy readers on account of its big stock of used comics, magazines, paperbacks — not just romances and thrillers, but bestselling biographies, self-help, how-tos, and even some more popular scholarly books and literary fiction. The "adult reading" is sequestered in a back room with a

15-minute limit. Romances are available in bulk, in brown paper bags stapled shut — a new concept in book marketing!

Farmers' Market
Center at Baker. Open from first Sat. in May through Sat. before Christmas. Market days: Wed, Fri & Sat, 7 a.m.-5 p.m. Flea market: Tuesdays.

This pleasant little market right in downtown Muskegon Heights features plants for sale in spring and 10 to 12 Michigan growers in the peak season, July through October. The flea market is dominated by full-timers who buy new merchandise at closeouts and used stuff (lots of used clothes) at yard sales.

A browsing drive on and off Peck Street
Start on Peck in downtown Muskegon Heights.

Peck and Sanford are a fast pair of one-way streets between the downtowns of Muskegon Heights and Muskegon. They go through some interesting neighborhoods and along Peck are some shops that make for an interesting, low-key afternoon outing.

Highlights in this vicinity are::

Boelkins' Grocery   ★★
2300 Maffett at Hackley in Muskegon Heights. (616) 733-0611. Mon-Sat 8-6, closed Wed at 12:30 p.m.

From the green and white awning to the brilliant, tidy arrangements of fresh fruits and vegetables visible through the big front windows, this neighborhood grocery is picture-perfect in every detail. It's an almost magical survival of the ideal old-time grocery store from somewhere around World War II. The canned goods on the varnished wood racks look like jewels. Boelkins is cheerful, sunny, neat as a pin, and friendly to all. On our visit customers included a chic woman in African braids and a silver-haired matron from North Muskegon. The butcher's choice meats attract shoppers from all over. There's no alcohol, cigarettes, or penny candy to be had, but this is no gourmet shop, either.

Belasco Antiques

1391 Peck at Isabella, 1/2 mile southeast of downtown Muskegon. From Bus. U.S. 31, take Laketon 3/4 mile east to Peck, turn north (left). 726-3689. Tues-Fri 12-5, Sat 9-1.

In this age of antique malls, when you can seldom meet directly with dealers, it's a treat to find eclectic, rambling private shops like this one, housed in a former garage. Belasco's four very large rooms contain a lot of furniture, more paintings and framed pictures than you usually see, and a little bit of everything else: saddles, toys, kitchen ware, primitives, some vintage clothes, jewelry, and the usual china collectibles. Most of it is over 50 or 60 years old.

The Book Trader

1347 Peck at Isabella (see Belasco's). (616) 728-3181. Mon-Fri 10-5:30, Sat 10-3.

Walk in the front hall of this rambling old house, and you see fairly high-power theology books on your left and horror and suspense on your right— a good indication that this eclectic used book shop touches all the bases. There is lots of room for encyclopedias, slow-moving sets of books, magazines, and other things space-poor shops in higher-rent towns don't often carry. Children's, cookbooks, serious nonfiction, and Michigan history are well represented. The paperback exchange buys used paperbacks for 1/4 their cover price and sells them for just 1/3.

Bob Carr's House of Gifts

1337 Peck, just north of Isabella (see Belasco's). (616) 728-7454. Mon-Sat 9-5:30.

The inside of this beautifully maintained Queen Anne house is a fantasy realm filled with beribboned silk wreaths and floral arrangements, realistic silk plants and trees, and gleaming crystal and brass giftware.

It's completely excessive and beguilingly effective, even to people who would never think of introducing such a degree of romantic artifice into their own homes. Former floral designer Bob Carr now works only in silk and dried materials, which are also available loose. He also carries baskets, country accents, clowns, and Michigan-made Brumm nature pieces. The staff is super-nice, whether you spend a lot or a little.

Don't miss the upstairs bathroom (tiles and fixtures are circa 1900), now luxuriant with hanging plants; or the Dutch-style built-in dining room sideboard; or, in the entry hall, the embossed Lincrusta, a durable antique decorative wallcovering and the remarkable panoramic portrait of this house's former residents in their spring garden in the 1920s.

Muskegon High School and Jefferson Street ★

From Peck and Isabella, make two lefts to get onto Sanford, turn right (west) onto Southern and immediately turn left onto Jefferson. From downtown, take Fifth southeast to Southern. Turn right, then left at Jefferson.

The most impressive houses in the city of Musekgon line three blocks of Jefferson leading to Muskegon High School. The turn-of-the-century school was built as the Hackley Manual Training School, the state's first vocational high school and yet another Hackley gift. It has been sensitively added onto and landscaped to create an exceptionally handsome high school campus. Here's where Jim Bakker first won fame and self-respect as the photographer on the school paper, thanks to a gifted and influential teacher, and where he spun records for sock hops; where football legends Bennie Osterbaan of the U-M and Sonny Grandelius of M.S.U. and pro veteran Earl Morrall played, and where Harry Morgan, best known as Colonel Potter on TV's M.A.S. H., performed in plays.

The homes on Jefferson, built in the post-lumber industrial era of the early 20th century, span many architectural styles, from Queen Anne to Georgian. Many have iron fences, carriage houses, and porte cocheres. Some two decades ago residents organized to keep urban renewal schemes from messing up their stately neighborhood. Today it is a beautiful island of stability in a central city with many frayed edges.

Evergreen Cemetery

On Irwin at Pine, a mile southeast of downtown. From Peck, take Irwin east 7 blocks. Irwin joins Peck just south of Belasco Antiques.

Muskegon's lumber barons set a high standard for funerary splendor, and this flat, rectilinear cemetery makes up in Victorian architecture what it lacks due to its unimpressive landscaping. Not surprisingly, the granite Hackley mausoleum is quite prominent, in keeping with his professed habit of "wanting the best and being willing to pay for it." Hackley erected it in 1887 to bury the remains of his parents and brothers, The 12-crypt structure is open to the public on Hackley Day, May 25.

More famous is the simple granite obelisk commemorating the grave of abolitionist Captain Jonathan Walker, immortalized in John Greenleaf Whittier's 1846 poem, "The Branded Hand." A former fishing captain from Massachusetts, he had tried to sail to the Bahamas with some escaped slaves whom he had befriended as a railroad construction boss in Florida. He became ill and his boat was unluckily washed up on slave-holding Key West. He became the only slave stealer the U.S. punished by branding, followed by 11 months incarceration in leg irons. A Pensacola crowd pelted him with eggs before the branding, but Walker became a hero in the North. As a well-known abolitionist orator, he climaxed his speeches by raising his hand to display the SS brand — for

slave stealer. After Emancipation, Walker felt he could withdraw from public life. He and his wife started a fruit farm on Black Creek south of Muskegon. Abolitionist admirers paid for this monument,

Muskegon Lake Shore Drive, downtown to Pere Marquette Park ★

Begin at Western Ave. and Third. 5 miles one way.

This drive combines a big chunk of Muskegon history with a popular beach and pier and the submarine museum Silversides. Along the way are distinctive neighborhoods and two good spots for a meal or snack.

The section of Western Avenue at the feet of Fourth, Fifth, and Sixth was long dominated by businesses associated with its train station and port (restaurants, hotels, warehouses), which were later joined by car dealers, parts suppliers, and the like. The **L. C. Walker Sports Arena and Conference Center** on Western at Fourth (616-726-2939) was built by the co-founder of Shaw-Walker office furniture, who was an avid hockey fan, as the home for a pro hockey team. In addition to being the home of the International Hockey League **Muskegon Lumberjacks**, the arena is West Michigan's biggest concert venue. It has hosted the likes of Kenny Rogers, Bill Cosby, the Oak Ridge Boys. WWF Wrestling and the Ice Capades are held here, too. **Public ice skating** (Oct.-early April, Sat & Sun 2-4) is $2/adult, $1.50 for kids.

In the next block, the four-story **Amazon Building** with its landmark twin towers was a large knitting factory. It's on a corner; the short side street leads to the deserted docks of the **West Michigan Mart**. Muskegon harbor has the deepest channel on Lake Michigan. This port terminal and big cold storage warehouse, built in the 1930s, boomed briefly after the St. Lawrence Seaway opened in 1958. Volkswagens bound for Midwestern markets were unloaded here. The car ferry to Milwaukee was an integral part of U.S. Highway 16 from Grand Rapids to Milwaukee, and a boon to Muskegon manufacturers and shippers like U.S. carmakers.

By the peak year of 1962, Muskegon had become the 7th-biggest Great Lakes port. But containerized cargo, introduced to cut down expensive handling, killed this budding shipping-related economy. The city of Muskegon couldn't help The Mart's private owners finance modernization to handle the 20'x8'x8' containers. The too. Containerization also led to bigger ships — often too big to fit through the Seaway. By 1969 the port here was virtually idle.

A decade later, car ferry service to Milwaukee was killed by a series of events that began when the Coast Guard required that the aging Milwaukee Clipper ferryboat be overhauled for safety. The McKee family of Detroit, owners of the ferry and the Mart, replaced it instead with the much bigger and newer Aquarama, a World War I Liberty Ship which had been changed into a plush Detroit-Cleveland cruise ship. The McKees counted on Milwaukee making the necessary port improvements to handle the bigger ship. But the city refused; having a ferry didn't mean that much to Milwaukee. So the McKees were left with a beautiful ship with nowhere to go. The Aquarama sat docked by the Mart for two decades. In the popular imagination it remains a symbol of the Port City's faded Great Lakes shipping. It was finally sold in 1988.

Back on Western Avenue next to the Amazon is the empty, impressive Romanesque C&O **Union Station**, a favorite local landmark, built in 1895 of sandstone and brick. Now that its owner, Shaw-Walker office furniture, has been bought by Westinghouse, locals hope its anticipated renovation will serve some more public function than Shaw-Walker's planned furniture showroom.

Across Western, a map of saw-

mills that once lined Muskegon Lake has been painted on a fence by a vacant lot. Near it is the **Muskegon Industrial Heritage Museum,** open to visitors during the Lumbertown Music Festival. Upstairs, rail fans work on their elaborate model layout the first Tuesday of every month.

West of Ninth, **Heritage Landing** is a new county park on the site of an old foundry — another case of regaining lake access as industry leaves. Despite the jazzy entrance, there's nothing to do here yet except picnic. Just west of it is the big Y, followed by the **Hartshorn Municipal Marina** (616-724-6785) with transient marina slips at standard state waterways rates. There's a waiting list for seasonal slip rentals, which cost $1,200-$2,000 compared to $2,000 to $3,000 in nearby Grand Haven. The **Port City Princess** (p. 190) dinner cruise ship is docked here.

Lumbertown, a shopping-restaurant complex in a renovated window-shade factory west of the marina, is no more — a victim of mismanagement more than anything else.

At this point motorists must pay attention and follow the Lake Shore sailboat signs, turning left onto Franklin, then right onto Michigan and Lake Shore Drive. Here in a former brewery, **Cole's Bakery**, inventors of microwavable garlic bread, have built a big new bakery and a private marina.

Between Cole's and the outlet of Ruddiman Lagoon is the quiet, pleasant **Nims neighborhood,** extending along Lake Shore and the three parallel streets some eight blocks. Nims' turn-of-the-century frame houses with big yards are remarkably inexpensive; houses with four bedrooms and two baths sell for under $40,000, or if they're on the bluff with a lake view, for $75,000 to $100,000.

Turn left onto Addison, the first street past the inlet, and you're in beautiful **McGraft Park**, surrounding Ruddiman Lagoon. It has a picnic area and playground equipment. Its free **tennis courts** (lighted at night) are first-come, first-served. Free **evening band concerts** are held most Tuesdays and Thursdays from the first week of July through the second week of August. Call (616) 724-6704 for details. The shady streets of Cape Cods and ranches just south of the park form the upper-middle-class Muskegon neighborhood of **Glenside**.

Back along Lake Shore, another pleasant neighborhood just west of the lagoon outlet is blue-collar **Lakeside**, with its own business district and the inviting **Harbor Theater** (616-755-1937), where recent films cost only $2.

Lakeside's only drawback is that prevailing winds bring the sulfur scents of the nearby **S. D. Warren** paper mill on Lake Shore at Lincoln, built on the site of a Charles Hackley

This lone vestige of shipping in Muskegon is tied up at the West Michigan Docks and Mart, for sale. As M.V. Highway 16, the D-Day veteran of Normandy carried new cars until 1972. U.S. Highway 16 actually crossed Lake Michigan between Muskegon and Milwaukee via regular car ferry service. But the ferry was discontinued. Trucking deregulation made it cheaper for carmakers to transport new cars by truck.

sawmill. As Central Paper, the original plant here was the first in the U.S. to make brown kraft paper, used for butcher paper and the like.. Warren bought it in 1953 and upgraded it to the point that today it makes the Rolls-Royce of papers, the kind of heavy, coated book and cover stock used in publications requiring the best in color and photo reproduction.

This huge paper mill and its stacks of logs extend along Lake Shore for nearly a mile starting. Though it incorporates old buildings, inside it is a high-tech operation with two massive, long paper-making machines, labs and even printing presses to monitor paper quality by printing on the scene. With so much invested in equipment, it's run 24 hours a day, seven days a week.

From the road you can see piles of logs waiting to be debarked in a drum and chopped into one-inch-square chips, which are then stored in open-air piles until needed. Sometimes you can see ships unloading coal and tractor-trailers with wood chips tilted up 60% to empty them into underground hoppers. Four foresters in the northern Lower Peninsula ar-

range to buy logs from landowners for the mill's paper.

Quantities of clean water is a prerequisite for papermaking, a process described as mixing a cake and rolling it between rollers while baking. The mill uses 20 million gallons of water a day — fully half the amount treated by the big Muskegon County Wastewater Facility (p. 197). S. D. Warren's participation was critical in launching that successful new method of wastewater treatment, which returns sewage to the Muskegon River as water clean enough to drink.

Locally, S. D. Warren is viewed as a good corporate citizen and responsible consumer of natural resources. The sulfur smell, much improved in recent years, is not usually noticed in most places.

Across Lake Shore from S. D. Warren, the little blue Mill Inn (p. 199) is a fine place in the daytime to eat and take in a mini-museum of Muskegon history on its walls. Evenings, after a stroll on the beach, you could stop at **Cobwebs and Rafters** (p. 200), a popular new bar with good food in a renovated boat shed.

The pleasant, blue-collar area of former cottages north of Cottage Grove and along Lake Shore by the park is **Bluffton**, an old summer colony favored by vaudeville actors for their summer homes. Joe and Myra Keaton were among the first actor residents, in 1905; their more famous son Buster, star on the silent screen, was just a little boy then. He provided a comic note by being thrown through the air in the family act. Within a few years the Actors' Colony was established, along with the Theatrical Colony Yacht Club (surviving today as the Muskegon Yacht Club on Lake Shore Drive). Based in Muskegon, Max Gruber's well-known animal act (dog, zebra, and elephant) toured the U.S. and Europe for years. Buster Keaton, who was quite fond of Muskegon and maintained his membership in the local Elks Lodge, later started a show

place on Waterworks Road off Lake S Park. (See below). Wind-blown sand totally dominates the environment around the park, year-round. Conventional lawns are impossible; in April, residents put out "FREE SAND" signs in their front yards.

At Pere Marquette Park's northeastern end, **Silversides**, a complete World War II submarine, is docked and on view in summer (p. 189). The **walk along the channel** between Lake Michigan and Muskegon Lake is a nice place to walk and watch boat traffic.

If you follow Beach Drive around to the east along the channel, you'll come to Harbour Towne, a new marina development. Incredibly, this water-filled basin was once the site of the second-tallest sand dune on Lake Michigan, **Pigeon Hill**. (Other dunes also bear this name because people climbed them and caught flying flocks of passenger pigeons in their nets.) To the dismay of many, this cherished landmark was mined for its outstanding sugar sand, ideal for glassmaking, beginning in the 1926. By the end of World War II, it was gone.

Pere Marquette Park

At the south side of the Port of Muskegon channel, 5 miles east of downtown. Take Western and Lake Shore along Muskegon Lake east to the park. Free parking; no fee.

Almost two miles of beautiful sandy beach is the main attraction at this popular city park. It also has a **snack bar**, bathhouse, and unusually fun **playground equipment**, but very few trees. The full-service restaurant, currently incarnated as **Bobbie's on the Beach**, is popular despite mediocre food.

It's not hard to find a convenient

Beach parties at Pere Marquette with live music, beer, food are occasionally held. 1990 dates are July 20-22 and Labor Day Weekend, Friday through Monday. (616) 724-6704.

The Muskegon Coast Guard Station (right) at Pere Marquette Park is on a channel walkway out to one of two piers and lighthouses at the harbor entrance. The walkway is good for fishing and watching the parade of weekend boats.

S. S. Silversides

South shore of the channel between Lake Michigan and Muskegon Lake, at the north tip of Pere Marquette Park. Take Western Ave/Lake Shore Drive to Peach Street. (616) 744-9117. May 1-Sept. 30: daily tours, 10 a.m.-6 p.m. Weekends in April and October. $2.50 adults, $1.50 children and seniors. Overnight stays for youth groups; volunteer activities.

For anyone interested in World War II action, this is a major west Michigan attraction. Often surviving military gear saw little war action, but this big sub was a Pacific workhorse. It sank 23 ships, third highest in the war. The main reason was timing: the vessel was completed just after Pearl Harbor, and Silversides' first mission was just five months later. It went on 14 patrols in all, losing only one man while sinking over 90,000 tons. During one reconnaissance mission, crew members even watched a Japanese horse race by periscope.

For $2.50 you get a competent, if not especially insightful or exciting tour of the sub. The excellent condition of the boat and its near complete furnishings makes the tour worthwhile. As you go below and walk from bow to stern, it looks very much as it did during World War II, with the

Touring the Silversides, you can briefly experience first-hand the claustrophobia of submarine living. Youth groups can arrange to spend the night on the much-decorated World War II workhorse.

parking space here. This is where to watch stunt kites, jet skis, and related beach phenomena. **Volleyball** pros play here several times a summer, including during the Lumbertown Music Festival and Labor Day weekend. Otherwise anyone may use the nets on a first-come, first-served basis.

The **pier** here is the longer of a pair of arms protecting the entrance to Muskegon Harbor. Both have lighthouses on them. Fishermen here take salmon, a lot of perch, and other fish.

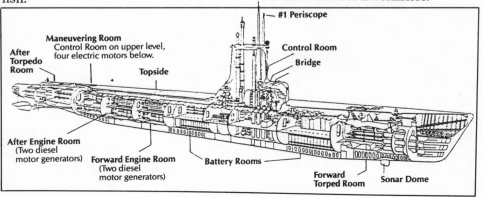

same bunks, sonar equipment, brass torpedo doors, radios, and charting table. It's possible to get a good feel of what it was like in those very cramped spaces to go out on a 45-day tour deep into enemy territory.

After a postwar career as a training sub, Silversides was due to be scrapped when the Combined Great Lakes Navy Association formed to save and restore the boat. The engines and most systems are now operable. It's been in Musekgon since 1987.

Port City Princess

At Hartshorn Marina, 920 W. Western. From U.S. Alt. 31 (Seaway), go left onto Ninth and follow the signs. (616) 728-8387. June-Oct: evening cruises daily , afternoon and lunch cruises Fri-Sun. (Call for times and special events like casino, rock & roll, and murder mystery cruise.) $6 for 1 1/2 hour cruise to $29 for Mon-Sat night dinner/dance cruise.

This 65-foot former Mackinaw Island passenger ferry is now a major new part of Muskegon's effort to develop tourism. The big 79-ton boat carries up to 208 passengers and is popular for group celebrations such as birthdays and weddings.

As an outing for families, however, it isn't all that exciting or comfortable. The boat retains its bare metal utilitarian appearance. At some speeds it vibrates quite noticeably. It would improve matters if the boat's owner invested in decor to soften its harsh appearance and upgraded the seating (currently park benches). The cruise would also be improved by an easier-to-hear PA system and a friendlier, more informative captain.

Moreover, most of the 1 1/2-hour

Cruise tip:
take one of the longer cruises and be sure to go when the weather isn't blustery. About 25% of the time weather doesn't permit the Princess to go out on Lake Michigan, which is the trip's major attraction.

---

cruise is spent in Muskegon Lake, and it's not all that scenic. You do get a swell view of the submarine Silversides and the prim Coast Guard Station and red lighthouse at the pier leading into Lake Michigan. But the time spent on the big lake is disappointingly short, and only a small amount of coast line is glimpsed.

St. Francis de Sales Catholic Church

2929 McCracken south of Sherman, in Norton Shores, about 1/2 mile southwest of McGraft Park. (616) 755-1953. Ask at the church office to see inside: Mon-Fri 8:30-noon, 1 to 7:30. Mass : weekdays 6:30, Sat. 5 p.m., Sun 8, 9:30, 11:30, 1.

Famed architect Marcel Breuer designed this suburban church, which was finished in 1966. Breuer was Walter Gropius's student at the Bauhaus, that crucible of austere, functional modernism, and later practiced with him in Cambridge, Massachusetts. But in his mature career Breuer moved to a much more emotionally powerful style. As seen in this church, it blended modernist simplicity with soaring concrete forms and dramatic use of natural light that recall the glories of Gothic stone architecture in simplified form.

Pleasure Island Water Fun Park

Pontaluna Rd. at Martin Rd. on Little Black Lake, 7 miles south of downtown Muskegon and 1 mile west of Hoffmaster State Park. From U.S. 31, take Pontaluna Rd. exit 1 1/2 miles west. (616) 798-7857. Open Mem. Day through Labor Day, 7 days a week. Opens at 10 a.m. Through the first half of June, it closes at 4 p.m. weekdays, 6 p.m. weekends. Thereafter, it closes at 9 p.m., except weekdays in the last week of August it closes at 6. Ticket prices: $11.95 admission and all rides for anyone over 48" tall. $8.95 for kids 2-4 or under 48". Spectator: $4.95. Discounts after

4:30: $6.95, or $5.95 for kids 2-4.

This attractive, new-style water amusement park is built around three lagoons and a stretch of shoreline on Little Black Lake. The waterslides range from the long (410 foot), gentle corkscrew (it starts from Michigan's tallest slide tower) to the rather terrifying Black Hole. In the latter, you plunge straight down a green translucent tube into the side of a hill and make several harrowing loops before you are deposited at high speed into a bank of water. It's all over in just a few seconds, but it's exciting. Almost as scary is the Rampage water slide, which hurtles you in a small sled steeply down a slide and sends you skidding across a pond.

The bumper boats are a change of pace. You have your own little rubber boat, complete with small outboard motor. For five minutes you can bash into the other boats in the pond to your heart's content.

Calmer activities include 18 holes of miniature golf, a **kiddie water play area**, pedal boats, and a sandy beach for picnicking and swimming.

Warning: this place is a good deal if you visit early in the morning or after 4:30 on a weekday. On weekends in the past, you could spend most of your time waiting in lines. Expanded facilities may reduce waiting times significantly.

Hoffmaster State Park ★★

Six miles south of Muskegon. From U.S. 131, take Pontaluna Rd. 6 miles west. (616) 798-3711. State parks sticker required: $3/day, $15/year. Maps available at the contact station off Pontaluna Rd. or at the office, just past the Gillette Visitors' Center.

Part of the magic of established dune environments is the contrast between sunny, windswept sand and dune grass on the foredunes and the dark and cool back dunes, mysterious beneath the canopy of huge maples and ancient beeches with their elephant-gray bark. Hoffmaster

State Park, more than most dune parks, invites you to explore and experience *all* the dunes' fascinating ecosystems, not just the 2.5 miles of beach and foredunes. There's the **Gillette Visitors' Center** (below) an outstanding campground, wooded picnic spots, 2 miles of **horseback trails**, and 10 miles of wonderful **hiking trails** through beech-maple forests, up dunes and down on to fairly remote beaches. In winter three miles of intermediate **cross-country ski trails** through the forests begin by the picnic shelter at the end of the drive past the Visitors' Center.

The most crowded **swimming beach**, with refreshments and a bathhouse, is convenient to large parking lots and an unshaded **picnic area**. You can escape the crowds by parking at the nature center and

Light filters through the leaves of the beech-maple forest behind the dunes for beautiful color effects. Guided nature walks are regularly held by the first-rate naturalists at the Gillette Visitors' Center.

BEACH		Pioneer Dune Grass	FOREDUNE	
Wet Beach	Storm Beach		Cottonwood	Sand Cherry

taking its beautiful boardwalk for 15 or 20 minutes to another, **quieter beach**. Deeply shaded, relatively private **picnic areas** convenient to hiking trails are off the road to the nature center.

The 333-space **modern campground** is in a separate part of the park, off Lake Harbor Road, beneath a shady canopy of pines and hardwoods. It's very popular because of its beautiful setting and nearness to a campers-only beach. Half of its spaces are reservable, and reservations are advised for all summer weekends; weekdays, there's usually space except during special events. It's open all year, but the water and showers are off from mid-October through mid-April.

Gillette Visitors' Center and Sand Dunes Interpretive Center ★★★

In Hoffmaster State Park, 6 miles south of Muskegon. From U.S. 131, take Pontaluna Rd. exit west 6 miles. (616) 798-3573. Winter hours: Tues-Fri 1-5, Sat & Sun 10-5. Mem. Day-Labor Day: Tues-Sun 9-6. Monday summer hours possible depending on seasonal staffing; call. No charge beyond state park fee.

This top-notch nature center provides one of the best views of Lake Michigan's dunes, the longest stretch of freshwater dunes in the world. And tells their story in an unusually compelling way that makes you respect their fragile ecology and grandeur. The best part of the story is told out

Hoffmaster State Park's varied trails let you explore all the dune habitats, not just the familiar, relatively desolate beaches and foredunes, but interdunal ponds and deeply shady forests.

doors, on the dunes themselves, through excellent diagrams and explanations that explain the very view you are seeing.

A **boardwalk** and 200-step stairway with frequent seats for rest and observation lead visitors up through a beech maple forest so towering, dark, and shady that it seems to have been there forever. At the summit is a spectacular 180-foot high **overlook** with a bird's-eye view of a vast landscape. The stairway was built first, then lifted in place by helicopter. To the west and north you see Lake Michigan and the two lines of dunes paralleling it. East you see the sandy, flat blueberry terrain and pretty Little Black Lake.

On the walk up the stairway and back down and out to the beach, you see how the back dunes vary from desert-like conditions to virtual rain forests of perpetual dampness. These diverse biologic zones are fascinating to naturalists; the basic principles of plant succession were, in fact, based on observations of Lake Michigan sand dunes by University of Chicago biologists.

Another branch of the boardwalk leads through the forest to a gorgeous **beach.** Because you have to walk 15 to 20 minutes from the parkng lot, it attracts a quiet crowd of nature-lovers.

The excellent interpretive signs along the boardwalk and stairs give

TROUGH
Conifer Zone /Interdunal Pond

BACKDUNE
White Pines   Black Oak

Barrier Dune/ Climax Forest

much more insight into the dunes than the elaborate display in the **Exhibit Hall** of the very attractive nature center building. This indoor display was prepared by a professional museum display firm who hadn't learned to communicate with the general public with plain language and clear conceptual overviews. Instead it relies on opaque scientific jargon.

If you're rushed, opt instead for the outstanding multi-image slide show, **"Michigan Sand Dunes and Hoffmaster State Park,"** shown in the comfortable, 82-seat theater. (If it happens not to be regularly scheduled, you can request it.) Written and produced by the center's talented park interpreters, it tells the sand dune story from their formation through the 19th-century logging and resort era, up into the present time. Every hour on the hour, another beautifully photographed slide show features seasonal wildflowers and other subjects.

Downstairs in the **hands-on classroom**, a great rainy-day destination, kids genuinely seem fascivited to cuddle a stuffed owl, to see how soft and plumped-up its layers of feathers are. Visitors can request to see videos on moose, loons, bluebirds, and shoreline erosion — all species at risk due to increased development of their natural habitats.

The excellent **bookstore** focuses on nature publications for all ages, nated with the exhibits. They are in-levels, and budgets, and has an interesting selection of posters, note-

esting selection of posters, note-cards, and nature-related gifts, too. It is run by local volunteers from the Gillette Natural History Association, which also funds and builds many exhibits here.

Trails and picnic areas are off of the road to the nature center. (See Hoffmaster State Park, p. 193.)

Muskegon Race Course

4800 Harvey just south of Hile, just south of the intersection between U.S. 31 and I-96. From northbound U. S. 31 , take I-96 east, exit immediately onto Harvey St. From westbound I-96 at Fruitport, take Airline north to Sternberg, turn west to Harvey, north to track. From B. R. 31 and Muskegon, take Hile Rd. exit, follow signs to track. (616) 798-7123. From May into the first week of October. May & Sept: Fri-Sun. June-August: Thurs-Sun. Gates open 5:30, post time 7 p.m.

This brand-new harness race-track is the only pari-mutuel track in West Michigan. Overhead TV monitors show replays, slow-motion stretch drives, betting odds, and behind-the-scenes views of the horses. Ask about nightly prerace handicapping seminars to help visitors learn about betting on the horses. The grandstand, clubhouse, and restaurant are air conditioned.

Snowmobile racing on ice is featured at the race course on two February weekends in the Muskegon Winter Spectacular. (616) 722-3751.

Downtown Muskegon Antiques Mall ★★

East Clay and Cedar, in the warehouse district 1/2 mile northeast of downtown Muskegon. (616) 728-0305. Mon-Thurs 10-5, Fri & Sat 10-7, Sun 1-5.

About 50 dealers now occupy this new mall in an old factory. The standards for dealers don't seem rigorous — there are a few displays of new country crafts. But the space is so well lighted and organized, and the dealers so satisfyingly varied and mostly reasonably priced, that this mall is unusually pleasant and fun for browsing. There's a lot of furniture and framed prints, loads of salt and pepper shakers, some jewelry and fun dresses from the 1940s, old instruments, military items, and more antiquated handcrafts and unusual things than you often see. at antique malls. The prices and variety make this place a real find for buyers accustomed to prices around Chicago and metro Detroit. For a convenient nearby meal or snack, try Capt'n Hook just north of Clay.

Along Clay from here up the hill to Pine, just east of Muskegon Mall, was an area of weather-beaten shacks called "Sawdust" or the "Bottoms." They were demolished by a Federal Slum Clearance Project in 1938. Its passing removed "the last tangible evidence of the frontier," noted the WPA guide to Michigan two years later.

Muskegon Farmers' Market and Flea Market

Just east of Seaway (Bus. U.S. 31) northeast of downtown. Turn east onto Eastern just north of the bend. (616) 726-4786.

Market sheds mark the scene of this popular market. The abundance of area fruit farms make it especially attractive from asparagus and blueberry season through fall. Declining numbers of local farmer/vendors have led to new rules allowing the sale of out-of-state produce. From May 1 through the end of October, **farm market days** are Tuesdays, Thursdays, and Saturdays, roughly between 6 a.m. and 3 p.m., with the **flea market** on Wednesdays, 6 a.m to 3 p.m. The rest of the year, the flea market is on Saturday and the farm market is closed. Nowadays, flea market vendors are mostly full-time dealers who sell on a circuit.

Fishermen's Landing/ Giddings Park

Off the Causeway (M-120) between downtown and North Muskegon, on the north bank of the Muskegon River. (616) 726-6100. April 15-Oct. 15.

This flat, open city park is right at the mouth of the Muskegon River. It includes 200 spots for boats and trailers (the daily launch permit is $4) and 39 campsites with outdoor showers. There's some interesting-looking playground equipment. Docking facilities are reservable. Fishing tournaments are scheduled on many summer weekends, and this place is packed. Muskegon Lake is great for bass and walleye.

Muskegon State Park ★

Just west of North Muskegon (take Ruddiman Dr. west from U.S. 31) at the end of Memorial Dr. and along Scenic Dr. by Lake Michigan. (616) 744-3480. Maps always available at headquarters, 3560 Memorial Dr. opposite Snug Harbor, and at campgrounds when open. State park sticker required: $3/day, $15 year.

With its three miles of Lake Michigan beach, its busy boat launch and boaters' campground by the channel to Muskegon Lake, and its quiet Snug Harbor bay beach and playground area, Muskegon is a satisfyingly varied destination for those who want to escape the crowds of Grand Haven and Holland's super-popular state parks. Campers here can easily drive to Muskegon's top-

It's not an authentic military blockhouse, but this picturesque lookout on Scenic Drive in Muskegon State Park is a favorite local landmark.

notch sights (its art museum, submarine, Hackley House, and the Gillette Sand Dune Interpretive Center are outstanding) and its two amusement parks.

The park extends along the north shore of Muskegon Lake to Lake Michigan and then north along beautiful Scenic Drive. Scenic Drive ends up near the White River lighthouse and Whitehall — a delightful excursion by car or bicycle. Activity here centers on the windswept **beach** area north of the busy channel to Muskegon Lake, an ecosystem of shifting sand, beachgrass, and shrubby oaks. The unshaded Lake Michigan beach here has huge parking lots and a big refreshment/bathhouse facility. The Muskegon teen beach scene is at the Ovals at Pere Marquette Park; this is more of a family beach. To be by yourself, you need only walk a ways north up the beach.

South of the bathhouse is a long **pier**, popular with strollers and fishermen. It leads to a blinker light that marks the channel to the Port of Muskegon. A walk out the pier offers a dramatic view of the coastal dunes, two harbor lights, and the Coast Guard Station across the channel at Pere Marquette city park. Fishermen on the pier take some salmon, a lot of perch, and a little of everything else. The pleasant **channel walkway**

along the ship canal lets you see boats up close.

The 177-space modern **South Campground** on the ship channel's Muskegon Lake side is next to the boat launch and an attractive wetlands. Concrete pads big enough for trailer and boat rigs make it extremely popular with boaters and fishermen. Low trees and beach shrubs afford varying degrees of privacy between campsites and soften the look of this busy campground. It's open from mid-April through October, depending on weather.

Perched atop wooded dunes on Scenic Drive is a log **blockhouse** with scenic overlook of Lake Michigan. Built in 1935 by the Civilian Conservation Corps, a make-work Depression-era project for the unemployed, it was rebuilt in 1964 after a fire. A steep climb up the hill and into the blockhouse lets you look out of tiny windows, but trees block much of the summer view. A few hundred feet north on Scenic Drive, a turnoff and parking lot is near the trailhead to five miles of looping woodland **trails**.

On Scenic Drive at the park's north entrance is the modern, 180-site **North Campground**, nestled in a hilly grove of towering maples and young beeches. The forest setting and the easy walk across the dunes to the campers-only beach make this one of the very nicest state park campgrounds. Some higher campsites even have a lake view. It's open all year, with electricity but no showers or toilets. (Pit toilets across the road are available.) *Parking is limited to campers; no visitors of any kind are allowed.* Across Scenic Drive, a **rustic campground** has 22 camp

---

Camping availability
varies. In 1990 70% of campsites are reservable. Times around holidays are always full and require advance reservations. Normal summer weekends may fill up if water levels are high for good fishing, or if there's a nearby festival or boating event. Normal summer weekdays there's usually space.

Dunes view off Scenic Dr. in Muskegon State Park.

sites arranged around a grassy central meadow; some back up to woods and are quite private.

Snug Harbor, on the west end of Muskegon Lake, is a pleasant, quiet bay, a perfect place for children to swim and fish. Here a **sandy beach** and **picnic areas** with grills are flanked by cattail marshes. Water quality here, and in similar river-outlet lakes on Lake Michigan's east coast, is now good, but when water levels are low, this beach is weedy. The nearby **playground** is shaded. A spit of land separates the beach from the nearby **boat launch**.

Muskegon Winter Sports Complex ★★

*Off Scenic Dr. in the Muskegon State Park rustic campground. Take U.S. 31 to Ruddiman/ Memorial Drive and go west to Scenic Drive, then north. For information, contact **Muskegon Sports Council**, (616) 744-9629. Season from mid-Dec. through mid-March depending on weather. **Cross-country skiing:** Mon-Fri 3-10 p.m., Sat & Sun 10-10. $2/person, $6/car. **Luge run:** Thurs & Fri 5-9 p.m., Sat & Sun 2-9 p.m. $10/day.*

Snow is plentiful here, just a few hundred yards from the shore of Lake Michigan — it can be snowing a few inches here with no snow at all in central Muskegon four miles inland.

To take advantage of that, to promote Muskegon as a winter sports destination, and to recruit new participants for U.S. Winter Olympics teams, the Muskegon Sports Council has established this remarkable facility, with the longest lighted cross-country ski trails and the only luge run in the Midwest. (Call for information about the council's speed skating program and snowmobile races.) A first-rate facility, it's also inexpensive.

Luge (pronounced "loozh," it's French for sled) is a high-tech form of sledding down an iced chute — something like a controllable roller-coaster. Average time down the 600-meter Muskegon luge in its one-man sleds is 43 seconds; that's about 40 mph. The chute's width, recently redesigned by a three-time luge Olympian, varies from two to six feet.

For the regular $10/day fee, beginners can use one of the Complex's helmets and sleds, and receive hands-on coaching and instruction on the lower course; with demonstrated proficiency, they can be licensed for the upper course.

Lighted **cross-country ski courses** are 2.5 kilometers and flat, and 5 K through hilly pine and oak forests. A new **ski lodge** offers hot soups, drinks, and foods.

Pioneer County Park

Scenic Drive at Giles Road, 2 miles north of Muskegon State Park. (616) 744-3580. Vehicle permit: $2/day, $10/season pass, $5 for seniors 62 and over.

Two thousand feet of **Lake Michigan beachfront** connects with an extensive **picnic grove** and 210-site modern shaded **campground** with everything but sewer hookup. The park store has video games, and there are sports fields, basketball hoops, and play equipment. A very attractive **dune boardwalk** leads to the beach, with scenic overlooks and benches. Recent erosion has chewed up dune fronts, but the beach is now fairly broad and pleasant. Maintenance is not up to state parks standards. This campgrounds ($10/night) has no limit on the length of stay, which makes it popular with long-term campers, largely seniors. It's run on a first-come, first-serve basis, and it fills up by Thursdays for summer weekends. Reservations are for the group camping area only (minimum of 10 campsites). No alcohol.

Michigan Adventure   ★

8 miles north of Muskegon; take Russell Rd. exit from US-31. Open weekends from mid-May; daily mid-June to Labor Day, Mon-Fri, 11-6; Sat-Sun & holidays, 11-7 (616) 766-3377. $12 admission.

None of the rides here are thrilling enough to approach world-class status, but some are pretty good. The big wooden roller coaster, called the "Wolverine Wildcat," is the most exciting ride. The white corkscrew roller coaster was surprisingly unscary, despite its two upside down twists. The log plume's single plunge into water doesn't justify the considerable expense of creating a long meandering stream way up in the air.

This amusement park, however, has exceptional bump 'em cars. Fast and highly maneuverable, they deliver deliciously robust collisions. There is a smallish ferris wheel and a number of standard rides such as the tilt-whirl. Warning: watch out for the innocuous-looking black contraption they call the "Spider." Its attendant said it creates more attacks of nausea than any other ride.

The park also has picnics tables, a game arcade, concession stand, and a number of smaller rides for the kiddies.

There is a big new water park, with wave pool and other attractions.

Muskegon Wastewater Treatment Facility/ Observatory/ Birdwatching   ★

8301 White Rd. From central Muskegon, take Apple east about 12 miles, turn left at Maple Island Rd. Go 2 miles north just past White Rd. Entrance is on east. From I-96, take Nunica Exit (10), turn north onto 112 St. which becomes Maple Island Rd. After 13 miles, you'll pass White Rd. and see the entrance. (616) 788-2311. Daily passes and grounds maps are available at the office weekdays between 8 and 5, or call with pass and map requests for specific weekend days. Small and large group tours available. No charge.

The lagoons and ditches of this ingenious, internationally known wastewater treatment area are an outstanding place for birdwatching, snowmobiling, hunting, and stargazing by the general public. And the much-imitated water treatment facility itself attracts ecologists and sanitary engineers from all over the world. Thanks to it, Muskegon County has dramatically advanced from having a dismal history of polluting its own environment to being a leader in inter-governmental and industrial cooperation in solving serious environmental problems.

By the 1960s, water quality had deteriorated to the point that the lakes and rivers, once known for outstanding fishing, boating, and waterside living, were often smelly, choked with rampant weed growth, and generally not fit for swimming. Poor water quality threatened to stall any hopes for improving the local economy.

The county got in touch with a University of Michigan researcher on wastewater treatment who devised a "freshwater farm" based on the principle that "wastes are potential resources out of place." Nutrient-rich, partly treated wastewater is sprayed as fertilizer onto huge fields of corn. Potentially dangerous bacteria are eaten by other bacteria in the soil. This usually poor, sandy soil yields up to 100 bushels an acre and acts as a "living filter" for the wastewater. When the irrigation water is finally collected and tested before being returned to waterways, it's clean enough to meet all standards for drinking water.

The 17-square-mile facility takes up roughly half a township. The water settles in two huge clay-lined storage lagoons, each nearly twice the volume of four-mile-long Mona Lake south of Muskegon. (These lagoons have to store wastewater over winter, when crops aren't grown.) Corn is grown on 5,500 acres — half the total area. Farm income now pays for a fourth the cost of treatment, down from half when farm prices were higher.

This is one of the most popular birding spots in western Michigan. Many rare birds have been seen here, including gyrfalcons and peregrine falcons. Migrating waterfowl stop at the ponds and cornfields in spring and fall. In spring and summer, the grassy areas have field birds like Eastern bluebirds, bobolinks, and upland sandpipers, with yellow-headed blackbirds nesting in cattail marshes east of the lagoons. Fall brings unusual shorebirds, followed by winter flocks of many kinds of gulls at the landfill and center dike. *Note: birders can't go up on the dikes*

until the current round of construction is completed in 1991.

The **observatory**, with a 12 1/2 inch telescope, was built by the Muskegon Astronomical Society (616-722-4351). On any clear, moonless weekend night in spring, summer, or fall, someone is likely to be there, and visitors are welcome to stop by and observe the sky. **Directions:** from the Maple Island entrance, follow the main road 2.1 miles and look for the reflector

Two summerttime trolley-busses make daily circuits between town and outlying beaches and campgrounds. The **North Towne Trolley** circles Muskegon Lake every 1 hour and 10 minutes between Muskegon State Park, North Muskegon, downtown, and Pere Marquette. The **South Trolley** goes between downtown Muskegon Heights, Hoffmaster Park, and Pleasure Island every 1 hour 20 minutes. Both are handy for families with one car who want to do a variety of things.

Fare: 25¢/person. Hours: between 11 and 6 from Memorial Day to Labor Day weekend, except for 6 special event s that usurp trolleys. Call Muskegon Area Transit at **(616) 724-6420** weekdays 8-12 and 1-5 for schedule and routes.

RESTAURANTS

Rafferty's

601 Terrace Point Blvd. in downtown Muskegon. On Muskegon Lake at the end of Apple (M-46), west of Muskegon Mall. (616) 722-4461. Lunch Mon-Fri 11:30 a.m.-2 p.m., dinner 5-10 p.m., to 11 Fri & Sat. Sun brunch 10-2. Major credit cards. Full bar.

Swank new waterfront development on giant foundry site symbolizes Muskegon's hopes for transition. Overlooks luxury marina; transient slips for boating diners. Outdoor deck. Nice sunsets. Current restaurant operators are owners of Hearthstone. Recommended from extensive dinner menu: prime rib ($14 & $17), potato-encrusted salmon with citrus cream sauce ($17), nut-crusted lamb chops with rosemary butter $20), 4 kinds of pasta $12-$17. Entrees include salad, appropriate starch, vegetable, bread. Ribs, pastas ($7 or so) at lunch. Sandwich, salad menu ($6-$7) and wonderful Hearthstone soups available at lunch and dinner. Brunch buffet $8.

Salvatore's on the Lake

1050 W. Western in the former Lumbertown complex on Muskegon Lake, 1 1/2 miles west of Muskegon Mall & downtown. (616) 726-5392. See hours below. Major credit cards. Full bar.

The Pine-Apple Caffe, an old and excellent Italian restaurant downtown, has relocated to a larger place on the water. The menu's largely the same. The pizza joint has become the casual **Gondola Garden & Grill**, live jazz Fri. and Sat. and extra outdoor seating. All dinner entrees are available here, plus pizza ($8 for 12" with 2 items) and calzone ($4). The house red sauce, liberally used, is distinctive, full-flavored, but somehow light. The **upstairs dining room** has the better lake view. Veal dishes ($14) stand out on the dinner menu. Baked Italian chicken ($9), pasta ($7 and up) and a big fiesta sampler ($10) are also popular. Dinners include OK salad, spaghetti side, and wonderfully crusty round bread loaves with sauce for dipping. Reservations recommended for weekend dinners.

Mike's Kro ★

1384 W. Laketon Ave. across from Catholic Central High. About a mile southwest of downtown Muskegon. From Bus. 31/Seaway, turn west onto Laketon and go 1/2 mile. (616) 755-4800. Mon-Sat 8-8. Coffee and rolls, no breakfast. Lunch 11-2:30, dinner 5-8. No alcohol or credit cards.

This popular Muskegon cafeteria has good, inexpensive food and specialties that reflect much of Muskegon's ethnic makeup. Classic Upper Peninsula pasties ($1.85) are favorites at lunch and Monday and Tuesday evenings. Tuesday night is Dutch night, when a favorite is roast pork and potatoes mixed with kale. Wednesday night they quickly sell out their baked pork chops and pot roast with vegetables. In many ways this is a classic, old fashioned American cafeteria with the familiar carrot and raisin salad, the standard entrees like macaroni and cheese ($2.60, or $1.90 for smaller portion) and baked chicken ($2.95). Everything here is baked; there are no unhealthy deep-fried dishes at all.

"Kro" means "place" in Danish (the current owners are actually Dutch), and the homey decor is full of wonderful bits and pieces of mostly Scandinavian folk-inspired art, with front doors carved with flowers and birds. After your meal, go a few blocks west on Laketon and you can see Muskegon Lake on Lake Shore Drive. It's not far to McGraft Park or Pere Marquette (p. 190).

Mill Inn

2441 Lake Shore Dr. at Lincoln about 3 miles west of downtown Muskegon. From Bus. 31/Seaway, go west on Sherman 2 miles, turn north (right) onto Lincoln, then right again. Inn is a small blue buildings. (616) 755-7263. Daily including Sun 5:45 a.m.-9 p.m. No alcohol or credit cards.

Named for its location across from the huge S. D. Warren paper mill (p. 188), this attractive little spot offers good service, superior diner fare with good homemade bread, a veritable museum of local history on the walls, and a chance to observe a big cross-section of Muskegon people, from mill hands across the street to the country club set up the hill to the west. The Mill End is known for its burgers and coney dogs. Daily specials ($3.50 at lunch and dinner) may include lasagna, ham and cabbage, and beef pot pies. Friday and Saturday's there is a fish fry.

Cobwebs and Rafters

3006 Lake Shore Dr., past the paper mill and Lincoln. (616) 755-5305. Mon-Thurs 11-midnight, Fri & Sat until 1, Sun 12-12. Full bar.

This bright, airy, casual place overlooking Muskegon Lake just down from the Muskegon Yacht Club has been a hit since its recent opening. The owners gutted and opened up an old restaurant from the 1930s. The deck seats 150 and overlooks a marina and open water. There's superior live entertainment (vintage rock, blues, jazz) on weekends from 8:30 to 12:30. Food ranges from a huge burrito ($5.95, or $3.95 for half) and burgers (a half-pound burger at the build-your-own burger bar is only $4.25) to seafood and steaks. The popular steak and perch dinner is $10.95. A full range of bar appetizers includes not only fried clams and nachos but a veggie tray.

The Hearthstone ★

In the Cornerhouse Motor Inn just off Bus. 31/Seaway where it turns north. Turn east onto Norton and immediately right onto Glade. (616) 733-1056. Full bar. Visa, MC, AmEx. Mon-Thurs 11-12, Fri & Sat 11-1, Sun 5-12.

The former psychologist and his wife who started the Hearthstone here have found a successful groove, much appreciated locally, with their creative approach to hearty soups, sandwiches, and pasta salads. The soups (about $2/cup, $4/bowl) could be any of a hundred recipes — on one day, Hungarian goulash and Kentucky burgoo (a southern stew of corn, okra, pepper, pork, and chicken). Sandwiches are more standard, led by a sub special, heavy on meats with antipasto salad fixings, on a crusty French roll ($6, or $3.50 for half). Pasta salada ($6.25-$8) may be linguine with pesto, cream, cappicola, and walnuts, or with brie and herbed olive oil, or with marinated vegetables, tomato, and bacon.

The Brownstone ★

In the Muskegon Co. Airport just south of Mona Lake. From U.S. 31 or I-96, get off at Hile or Airport roads, go west on them to Grand Haven Rd. Turn south 1 mile, then west onto Ellis. Terminal is off Ellis. From downtown, take Henry south a mile past Mona Lake, turn east onto Porter, follow signs to airport. (616) 798-2273. Mon-Thurs 11-9, Fri 11-11, Sat 10-11, Sun noon-5. Full bar. Visa, MC, AmEx.

Food prepared by The Hearthstone (above). Good views of planes and airport activity.

Flamingo Restaurant

108 E. Broadway in downtown Muskegon Heights, across from Rowan Park clock tower. From downtown Muskegon, take Apple to Sanford, go south to Broadway. From Bus. 31 at Mona Lake, follow signs to Muskegon Heights business district to your right (north). (616) 733-4189. Mon-Sat 11 a.m.-3:30 a.m. No alcohol or credit cards.

All sorts of people come from all around to this homey, unpretentious Mexican restaurant, which also serves as a friendly local gathering spot. The portions are large and the food is milder than at El Camino Tacos, Muskegon Heights' other popular restaurant about a mile west at 2818 Henry. The Flamingo's atmosphere is definitely different, homier. It's more of an expanded lunch counter. A picture of the Blessed Virgin joins a photo of a local Mexican-American softball team in the place of honor. Notices in Spanish advertise local appearances of conjunto bands up from South Texas. Big menu includes huevos rancheros with beans ($3.55) menudo (tripe soup), $2.75, six kinds of burritos in two sizes ($2.20-$5.50), a barbacoa (barbecue) plate ($4.40). various forms of chips and cheese, a some as big as a meal, taco salad ($2.50/$3.50), and many combination plates with rice and beans, in addition to all the usual tacos ($1.40-$1.75), tamales, enchiladas ($1.85), and such. American grill favorites also available.

U.S. 31 Barbecue ★

151 W. Muskegon (Bus. 31) in downtown Muskegon. (616) 722-3948. Mon-Thurs 11-7, Fri & Sat until 9. Takeout available. No alcohol or credit cards.

The menu at this 50-year Muskegon landmark is short: soup, chili, fries, and three barbecue sandwiches: pork ($1.89) and ham or beef ($1.99). Meat — 1,000 pounds a week — is roasted in the big brick and glass rotisserie on view in back. This is not southern-style barbecue, but something lighter, with bits of cole slaw, devised by owner George Burris's father. It has quite a following. One fan wanted to open a franchise in Tokyo, but those plans have fallen through.

Service is efficient and the atmosphere friendly. The dramatic contemporary decor was up-to-the-minute in 1962 and hasn't changed a bit since, which makes it pretty special: big windows, an angled ceiling and simple hanging lights, with lots of wood and orange accents.

Bear Lake Tavern ★

360 Ruddiman at the Bear Lake channel in North Muskegon, about 6 miles from downtown Muskegon and 2 miles from Muskegon State Park. (616) 744-1161). Mon-Fri 11:30-10, Fri & Sat until 11, breakfast Sat & Sun at 7. Drinks served later. Full bar. No credit cards. Out-of-town checks OK.

This rustic tavern from the 1920s

glows with varnished old wood that reflects light from big windows overlooking willow trees and small boats on the channel between Muskegon and Bear lakes. Walls display pictures from champion local teams over several decades. This place is a North Muskegon institution for all ages, and it's often crowded. Service is very competent, but it helps to come early at dinner, when fresh fried perch (about $10) packs them in. A good, juicy burger with slaw and fries is around $5 (1/2 lb.) and $4 (1/4 lb.).

LODGINGS

Muskegon Harbor Hilton
(800) 456-8829.
939 Third at Western in downtown Muskegon.

201 units on 8 floors. Upper stories have good views of downtown area, narrow views of harbor. Mall and theater across the street. $79 single, $85 double. Weekend packages: $99 "Escape" includes $40 toward food, drink, and gifts. "Bounce back" $75. Small indoor pool, whirlpool, weight room, dry and steam saunas, gift shop. Good in-house

restaurant, Emeralds, includes lounge.

Best Western Park Plaza
(616) 733-2651.
2967 Henry at Summit, 3 miles south of downtown Muskegon. Take I-96 to Bus. U.S. 31/Seaway, then west on Summit to Henry.
111 rooms on 4 floors. Summer $62-$65, winter $55. Basic cable service; no movie channels. VCR rental available. Large indoor pool, sauna, game room. Recently renovated. In-house restaurant, Silk's, includes lounge. Henry is the area's main commercial strip.

Cornerhouse Motor Inn
(616) 733-1056.
Just off Bus. 31/Seaway where it bends north. Turn east onto Norton and immediately right onto Glade. Glade on Business U.S. 31 and I-96, 4 miles from downtown.
23 units on 2 stories. Winter: $34 single, $40 double. Summer: $36.72 single, $43.20 double. No views. No pool. Basic cable service, no movie channels. Excellent in-house restaurant, Hearthstone, specializes in soups, sandwiches, and pasta, includes bar.

Days Inn
(616) 739-9429.
150 Seaway/Bus. U.S. 31 at Hoyt in Muskegon Hts., 3 miles south of downtown Muskegon.
152 units on 2 floors. Winter: $39-$45 single, $44-$52 double. Summer: $44-$55 single, $50-$61 double.

Rates slightly higher on weekends. No views. Small indoor heated pool and whirlpool. Showtime movie channel (free). In-house restaurant, Daybreak, family style, no alcohol.

Holiday Inn
(616) 733-2601.
3450 Hoyt, Muskegon Heights, just off Bus. U.S. 31/Seaway.
198 rooms on 2 floors. Across from Mona Lake Park. Single $56, double $64. "Great Rates" available in limited quantities except for summer weekends: $52 single, $56 double. Special Sunday and Monday night rates: $39 single or double. Outdoor heated pool. Cable TV, no movie channels. In-house restaurant, Holly's Bistro, serves alcohol.

Blue Country B & B
(616) 744-2555.
1415 Holton Rd. (M-120) at Russell just outside North Muskegon. 1.7 miles west of M-120/U.S. 31 interchange, 3 miles from downtown Muskegon.
3 rooms with shared bath. $30 plus $10 for each extra person, or $5 for family members. Alcohol not permitted. Guests can use entire downstairs of sunny big bungalow-style house, play organ and hammered dulcimer. Complete breakfast. Country decor with some antiques, Avon products. Road noise from busy intersection. One innkeeper, a former preschool teacher, enjoys renting whole house to a family and babysitting.

Whitehall and Montague

When you get up past Muskegon to the twin towns of Whitehall and Montague, it begins to feel like you're entering the more remote, slow-paced pristine north of Michigan. The two old lumbering towns are located at the head of White Lake, by the marshy outlet of the White River. The sense of getting away to a quieter time is especially strong if you avoid U.S. 31 and take the aptly named Scenic Drive along Lake Michigan to White Lake, through the pine woods of the beautiful Duck Lake area to the south. In summer, picturesque sailboats are out on White Lake. The prosperous Chicago and St. Louis families who have come here for generations are sailors, not power boaters.

The White River Lighthouse (p. 208), tucked away beyond huge beech trees at the channel to White Lake, reinforces the out-of-time quality of the area. The white lightkeeper's house and light tower look out from a deeply lush green setting over Lake Michigan. The scene is so pastoral and simple and picturesque, it seems straight out of *Anne of Green Gables*.

Civilized simplicity

Driving from the ship channel along White Lake into town, you pass trim cottages on shaded green lawns, interspersed often with deep woods. No fancy condo developments, giant marinas, or pretentious, slick restaurants here. Civilized simplicity still reigns. Many cottages are white with green trim, as they have been for decades. Just south of Whitehall's main drag are streets of comfortable Victorian homes with big

*Visitor information for the White Lake area is especially ample, thanks to the most helpful **Chamber of Commerce,** in the old train depot on the causeway (it's also Business Route 31) between Whitehall and Montague. **Chamber hours** (Mem. Day-Labor Day): Mon-Fri 8:30-5, Sat 10-4, Sun 12-4. Call (616) 893-4585 for a visitor's packet.*

*Weekly summer events include musicals at the Howmet Theater (p. 211), band concerts and other performances at the **Blue Lake Fine Arts Camp** (p. 216), and free **band concerts** at Lions' Park on Lake St. in Montague (from the causeway, turn west at the boat launch).*

The White Lake Yacht Club, prestigious, prim, and extremely unpretentious, typifies the low-key, anti-trendy style of White Lake resort life.

lawns, shaded by maples planted for the nation's centennial in 1876.

North past the old industrial city of Muskegon, the population falls off so much that a town the size of Whitehall (1980 population 2,900) seems big. People here seem down-to-earth and unusually friendly, even by West Michigan standards. Across the White River inlet in the rival town of Montague (population 2,300), two drugstores still have soda fountains — popular places to meet and eat.

The summer residents, and those cottage-owners who decide to stay year-round, add a cosmopolitan element that makes for a sprinkling of better-quality goods and services than most small towns offer. Traces of affluent suburban Chicago's influences are everywhere. For instance, two early (1902) Frank Lloyd Wright cottages are one White Lake. There are two good bakeries, summer jazz and classical music concerts at the Blue Lakes Fine Arts camp (p. 216), and some year-round artists' studios (p. 209).

The legacy of Hooker Chemical

It's not really true, of course, that White Lake is unaffected by the modern world. When Hooker Chemical of Love Canal fame came to town in 1956, it was hailed as the kind of progressive, technology-oriented industry the area needed. But by the early 1970s, polluiton of White Lake by Hooker and by residential sewage was so bad, it threatened the entire local economy. Today, thanks to a new wastewater treatment facility, the lake is clean enough for fishing and swimming. The infamous Hooker plant, now closed, sits behind a barbed wire barrier.

Whitehall is today the home of Howmet Turbine Components Corporation, Muskegon County's largest employer. Howmet makes castings for jet engines plus ingots of titanium and superalloys. An increasing number of White Lake area residents commute to jobs in Muskegon, and year-round residences are now intermingled among the cottages. But the ambiance remains that of a summer camp.

The frenzied lumber boom

White Lake's lumbering era began in 1837, when Paw Paw storekeeper Charles Mears left with a party for White Lake, to beat out eastern speculators in claiming stands of virgin pine. It took their skiff two weeks to get from St. Joseph to White Lake, then occupied by Indians. Mears's party built a cabin, returned to Paw Paw to bring back equipment for a water-powered sawmill. His mill pond remains in Whitehall, a town he platted in 1859 and called Mears. It's a scenic spot three miles south of downtown on Mill Pond Road between South Shore Drive and Mears.

Mears built the first White Lake lumber schooner to ship his lumber and went on to build a much bigger mill across the mouth of Duck Lake in 1846. Mears' sawmills and other business interests were key in the development of Ludington, Pentwater, Mears, and the ghost town of Lincoln.

In White Lake's lumbering heyday in the 1880s, this tranquil lake was a busy, noisy, unlovely place. The 1897 *White Lake Reminiscences* vivid captures that boisterous scene:

> From dawn's first light, the high, piercing whistle of the whirling seven- and eight-foot in diameter circular saws of some 24 steam-powered sawmills were shattering the silence that had prevailed for thousands of years. Every few seconds the sharp whistle was punctuated with an explosive screech as the whining blades bit deep into a huge pine log and reduced it in seconds to a stack of clean, fresh board.
>
> The sharp, sweet smell of pine sawdust rides the wind for miles, and an offshore breeze carried that resinous smell far out over the wide waters of Lake Michigan. It has been said that many a sharp-nosed skipper of a fog-bound lake windjammer followed his nose to a safe anchorage by riding the sawdust trace.
>
> Lumber was king, was everywhere. Floating on the surface of the lake were great rafts of logs, towed from the booming grounds in the lower reaches of White River to the many mills scattered down the length of the lake, each raft with its huffing-puffing, cocky little steam tug bullying and snorting at its charge, five times its size. Along both sides of the lake were the mills: sawmills, planing mills, shingles mills, each with its small cluster of workers' homes close by, each with its long docks reaching like fingers out into the lake.
>
> Docks [were] crowded with the graceful, tall-masted Lakes lumber schooners and wooden-hulled, steam-powered lumber hookers, each vying with the other for more speed, more carrying capacity, for these were the peak years of the lumbering era. . . .
>
> It took a good man to work 12 hours a day at the mill, go home, take care of a garden plot, do his chores, and spend some time with his family. But if you asked a riverman, who spent his waking hours riding and fighting, bucking and charging logs in swift water, he'd say a

Some two dozen sawmills lined White Lake during the lumber boom. Rebuilding Chicago after the great fire of 1871 stimulated lumbering all over northern Michigan. To handle all the lumber schooners, like the ones shown loading here at White's Mill in 1880, the White Lake channel was straightened and improved.

Why lumbering brought foundries and tanneries
"Every sawmill town had at least one foundry," says lumbering historian Daniel Yakes. To obtain equipment for their mills and logging operations, lumbermen often helped machinists establish shops and foundries. Top-quality foundry sand in Lake Michigan dunes was why so many foundries survived beyond the lumbering era. Tanneries that used leftover tanbark from sawmills in the tanning process were among the earliest industries in lumber towns. They continue to operate in Grand Haven and Whitehall.

mill hand had it easy. And a woodsman who swung a ra-
zor-sharp double-bitted axe, hour after hour, or man-
handled 18- and 20-foot logs five feet in diameter onto
sleds in the dead of winter, or forced a two-man saw
through logs until his arms felt dead on his shoulders —
ask him, he'll tell you that mill hands and rivermen
don't know what work is.

Then there were the sailors. Each trip on the lake was
an adventure into the unknown, for Lake Michigan is
famous for sudden, vicious squalls.

After the lumber ran out

Suddenly, after the peak year of 1887, almost all
these jobs were gone. After so much furious cutting, the
White River timber had run out. So many families left
Whitehall and Montague that they couldn't sell their
houses for any price. Many simply abandoned them. Of
White Lake's two dozen mills, only a shingle mill and
box factory and two seasonal sawmills survived into
the 20th century.

The salvation of the local economy turned out to be
fruit and resorts. Raspberries were grown in the Duck
Lake area, and apples and peaches north of White
Lake around Montague. Astute investors like lumberman and sawmill owner Charles Henry Cook of
Hillsdale had already realized that cut-over pine lands
close to Lake Michigan made outstanding orchards.

Except for fruit, farming on this sandy soil produced
no big profits. But as the mills shut down, farmers
found they could do quite well taking in summer board-
ers escaping the humid heat of Illinois, Indiana, and
Missouri. In 1894 three vacationers from Moline, Illinois, undertook a successful cottage subdivision venture, named Michillinda for the origins of its cottagers
(MICHigan, ILLinois, and INDiana). It was the first in a
wave of cottage associations and small resort hotels in
the next two decades.

As the area became known to Chicago people, so
many summer camps were established that in 1967
Muskegon County had the second-largest number of
summer campers of any county in the U.S. The oldest
Boy Scout camp even has a scouting museum (p. 216).

Resort life:
leisurely and placid
*Once families arrived
in early summer, ac-
cording to Montague's
centennial history,
they "stayed put until
it was time to leave in
fall," socializing with
other guests, boating
and bathing and tak-
ing occasional outings
by boat to other re-
sorts and into town.
Roads then were "mere
sand ruts." "Resort ho-
tels were popular be-
cause they meant a
real vacation for the
wife and mother: no
meals to cook, enter-
tainment more or less
the responsibility of
the resort-keepers,
and a number of other
families around for
sociability. . . . People
came early and stayed
late, to the profit of local merchants and re-
sort-keepers."*

**Before automobiles
quickened the pace of
resort life, White Lake
vacationers arrived on
the Goodrich Transit
Company's imposing
lake steamer, the S. S.
Carolina. A former
hospital ship during
the Spanish-Americ-
an war, it had cabins
for overnight passen-
gers from Chicago.
Steam launches fer-
ried them from the
Goodrich Docks
located in Whitehall
to their hotels.**

An old rivalry

These pleasant, placid-looking towns have waged a long rivalry which has its roots in old resentments. Historically, Whitehall was more populated by Swedish ex-loggers, Montague more by German farmers. Whitehall developed stronger tourism, which buoyed its commercial district and attracted more Chicago people. Though Montague also had beautiful estates and resorts and its share of wealthy retirees, its business district was more farm-oriented, with feed stores and the farm bureau. Whitehall, in comparison, had the toney places: the White Lake Yacht Club, the playhouse, the golf club, and more refined and expensive cottages along the lakes.

It has taken the twin towns a long time to cooperate on areas of mutual concern, and the influx of new blood hasn't helped as much as you'd expect. They still have separate school districts, each with graduating classes of about a hundred. Voters recently rejected consolidation again.

*Annual events include the big juried **arts & crafts festival** on Father's Day weekend, a **Fourth of July** parade, circus, and fireworks in Montague over White Lake, and the 4-day **White Lake Maritime Festival** with a Venetian Parade, water ski show, and kids' games, at the Whitehall municipal marina on the last weekend of August.*

POINTS OF INTEREST

Scenic Drive/ Murray Road/South Shore Drive

North and west of Duck Lake State Park. Reachable from U.S. 31 by following signs to park, continuing west on Michillinda Road to Scenic Drive and following the lakeshore north.

This is a most attractive, low-key area of old-fashioned cottages with big green lawns, intermixed with magnificently shady beech-maple forests by the shore and pine plantations farther inland. Summer residents have been coming here since before the turn of the century, originally via Great Lakes steamers from Chicago, to stay at inns and cottages. The oldest cottage association, Sylvan Beach, on Murray Road facing Lake Michigan, goes back to 1883.

A number of old inns have survived the difficult transition to the Automobile Age and motels. The Driftwood Inn (formerly Murray's Inn) and the adjacent Galleon restaurant enjoy fine views of White Lake near the channel, studded with sailboats based at the nearby White Lake Yacht Club. The Michillinda Beach Lodge, a remodeled 1904 estate on Lake Michigan with numerous rental cottages, reflects in its name the origins of its clientele (MICHigan, ILLinois, and INDiana), leaving out only the area's numerous Missourians escaping St. Louis" humid heat.

A very pleasant drive starts on the aptly-named Scenic Drive along Lake Michigan, beginning in North Muskegon at the state park, or further north at Duck Lake. Going north on Scenic, past the Michillinda Beach Lodge and the White Lake Golf Course, take a left onto Murray Road when you get to White Lake. Past cottages and resorts and steep, shady back dunes, it dead-ends at the White Lake Lighthouse Museum, tucked away and very special. Though there's no developed beach park here, quite a few people get to the beach by walking along the channel seawall and limestone rip-rap in front of the lighthouse.

Backtracking, Murray Road becomes South Shore Drive at the T-intersection where Scenic Drive ends. It follows White Lake and passes by turn-of-the- century cottages on the way into town.

A trip up to the tower makes a visit to this picturesquely situated lighthouse-museum really special.

At Mill Pond Road, turn right (east) along the pond, then turn left (north) into town along Mears Avenue, Whitehall's nicest old residential street.

White River Light Station/ Museum ★★

At the south side of the White Lake channel, at the end of Murray Rd. Murray Rd. goes west from the junction of Scenic Dr. (along Lake Michigan from Muskegon) and South Shore Rd. (along White Lake from Whitehall). (616) 894-8265. Museum open Mem. Day through Labor Day Tues-Fri 11-5, Sat & Sun noon-6. Sept.: weekends only. 50¢ admission 12 and over. Tours of museum and dune ecology available by arrangement. Grounds and channel walk are a public park open year-round.

Tucked away behind huge beech trees at the channel to White Lake, this limestone and brick lighthouse looks so simple and homey, it seems the lighthouse-keeper could still be there. Today it's still a home, of the curator of this delightful museum owned by Fruitland Township. The low-key displays include photographs and maps about White Lake's maritime history: logging, resort cruises, and fishing. Then there are nautical artifacts and navigational devices, a ship's helm, and the station's original Fresnel lens, which

reflected the light in the tower.

You can climb a beautiful wrought iron stairway, tightly spiraled in the narrow tower, for a somewhat spooky, claustrophobic ascent to a fine view of Lake Michigan.

Year-round, people come here to walk along the channel wall and get to Lake Michigan. (The beach up past the water line is privately owned.) This "Government Channel" was so called because the federal government cut it through and built the light to aid navigation when lumber schooners created intense traffic. The "Old Channel" (p. 213) was a circuitous route to White Lake.

Duck Lake State Park ★

Between Michillinda Rd. and Duck Lake at Lake Michigan, 5 miles southeast of Whitehall and 7 miles north of Muskegon State Park via Scenic Drive (highly recommended as a scenic route. From U.S. 31 10 miles north of Muskegon, take the Lakewood Club/White Lake Rd. exit and follow the signs. (313) 744-3480. 8 a.m.-10 p.m. daily. $3/day or $15 annual state park sticker.

Michigan's newest (since 1988) state park is one of the nicest, in an unspectacular, uncrowded way. Camping won't be available until sometime after 1994, but the park offers day users 3,100 feet of sandy **Lake Michigan beach** along sand-swept Scenic Drive, frequently lined with illegally parked cars. (The beach parking lot is a short walk to the Lake Michigan beach, but you have to drive to the distant park entrance and clear through the park to get there. Parking is legal along designated parts of Scenic Drive, too.)

The public Lake Michigan beach flanks the **channel** to unspoiled Duck Lake, the small, two-mile long "drowned mouth" of Duck Creek.

This park gives users a convenient choice between Lake Michigan and the small, warmer Duck Lake, depending on the weather. Bathers can go to Lake Michigan if the water isn't too cold. The pleasant **Duck Lake beach** is less than a mile away via a scenic path along Duck Lake's north shore. (It takes over two miles to drive there.)

The setting for this short, sandy swimming beach is most picturesque. A big grove of pines and large oaks rises above it, with a large, attractive picnic pavilion surveying the scene. Several miles of asphalt drives, a favored destination for joggers and family bicycle outings, wind through the woods to the Duck Lake beach and the separate **boat launch,** near the Lake Michigan parking area. Boaters are limited to Duck Lake; the water's too high to get beneath the Scenic Drive bridge onto Lake Michigan. **Fishing** is good for bluegill, pike, bass, and crappie.

On the south side of the Duck Lake channel, overlooking Lake Michigan, is **one of West Michigan's oldest historical sites,** commemorated by a marker. Around 1790 a log cabin was built as the fur trading post of Joseph Laframboise, agent for John Jacob Astor's far-flung fur empire. After his death, his widow, a beautiful half-Indian woman, French-educated and a shrewd trader, took over, followed by the legendary trader Rix Robinson, whose son was born in the ramshackle cabin.

At this same channel in 1846, Charles Mears, who founded Whitehall and developed for lumbering much of the area between it and Ludington, built a dam across the mouth of White Lake to power a sawmill. A general store, boarding house, and large barn for the operation's horses once stood nearby.

Off the beaten path, Duck Lake attracted few summer cottagers and more small farmers, urban refugees with dreams of raising raspberries, chickens, and mink.

Boy Scouts from Illinois, bought 100 acres north of Duck Lake from Mears's daughter. Today the old scout camp has become Duck Lake State Park.

Fruitland Township Park

On the south side of Duck Lake on Scenic Dr. just north of Duck Lake Rd.

This simple park is a rustic roadside picnic/swimming area on the south side of peaceful Duck Lake.

Terrestrial Forming pottery studio

5385 Lamos Rd. between Michillinda Rd. and South Shore Dr., just north of Duck Lake State Park. (616) 894-2341. Usually open Mon-Sat 10-5, Sun 1-5. Call first to be sure. Call ahead to see the potter at work mixing, throwing, and firing clay.

A fair number of summer people, including potter Peter Johnson, have liked White Lake's small-town, outdoor lifestyle so much they stay. Visitors can see his owner-built studio, picturesquely tucked away in the woods. It's impressive in a rustic sort of way. Johnson, just out of art school in 1970, spent a year house-sitting for his mother-in-law, also an East Coast transplant, and decided to stay and try to support himself on his craft. Defying predictions, he has succeeded.

His showroom is full of functional, reasonably-priced pottery in warm earth tones, contrasted with grey-blue. Dinnerware ($45/place setting) and nesting batter bowls ($6-$35 a piece, $120 for a 7-bowl set) are quite popular as wedding gifts.

Shops in Whitehall

Along Colby (business route 31) at Mears. Stores stay open until 8 in summer.

The **Ben Franklin** variety store (which has an excellent, big crafts department) and **Pitkin Drug and Gift Shoppe,** a big, gifty corner drug store geared to visitors, are the heart of the two-block old business district. **Morat's Cafe** (p. 217) is a fine place to take a break and enjoy the view. Other noteworthy shops, dispersed along residential streets,

are:

First of America Muskegon ★★

119 S. Mears. (616) 893-1715. Mon-
Thurs 9:30-4, Fri until 5:30.

Inside this bank is a remarkable series of **paintings** that dramatically and accurately depict the White Lake lumbering industry, from cutting the logs and piling them on the steep riverbanks to processing them at the sawmill and sailing out the White Lake channel by the lighthouse. Frederick Norman, an English immigrant and Civil War veteran, was fascinated with painting and with capturing the soon-to-vanish lumbering industry he saw as a house painter and sign painter in Whitehall in the 1880s.

American Sampler

124 S. Mears at Spring. Late June-
Labor Day: 9:30-6:30, otherwise
10:30-5:30. Call for winter hours.

A fresh, imaginative, and somewhat upscale version of the country look is reflected in this attractive shop's gifts, decorator fabrics and pillows, some with Oriental touches, and home accessories — for example, Kennebunk super-soft afghans; funny practical beachbags; Waverly

Painter Frederick Norman observed and recorded scenes from the lumber boom in a remarkable series of paintings in the Whitehall branch of the First of America Bank-Muskegon. (Color photographs of them are sold here for the historical society.) This painting depicts logs waiting to be unlocked on a rollway of the steep-sided White River, without showing the ultimate devastation of forested lands.

fabrics; soft sculpture and accessories for children. Jay Christopher dresses, Cambridge Dry Goods, and Nordic House flowered raincoats are part of what's in the expanded women's clothing section.

Slocum Street Antiques

116 W. Slocum, 1 1/2 blocks west of
Mears and 2 blocks south of down-
town. (616) 893-0798. Fri-Mon. Call
for winter hours.

This rambling old house was long the home of The Pack Rats, a large, independent shop. Now that its owner has retired from running a shop and sells her stock in malls, Jean Bronsink has started a new private shop with a general line. Antique toys are one specialty. Ask about the new antiques mall in downtown Whitehall.

Timekeeper's Clock Shop ★
303 Mears, across from the Howmet Theater. (616) 894-5169. By appt. or by chance.

Michael Bronsink, a co-owner of this hospitable bed and breakfast, has turned his hobby, refurbishing antique clock, into his principal vocation. He repairs movements and restores antique cases, and he's been so busy that retail sales of new and antique clocks has taken a back seat to restoration. The public is still welcome to stop by or make an appointment to see the showroom, in the front parlor of this mellow lumber baron's mansion.

Robinson's Bakery ★
1019 S. Mears, .8 miles from downtown Whitehall. (616) 894-5979. Mon-Fri 6 a.m.-5 p.m., Sat 6-3.

Despite the English name, Robinson's is a Swedish bakery featuring limpa bread (a light rye flavored with fennel, anise, and orange peel, baked Wednesdays), heavy, robust rye and pumpernickel, many other breads, and a big assortment of Danish-style (i.e.,made with butter) coffee cakes and sweetrolls.

Everything here is baked from scratch, even doughnuts. Unusual cookies include Swedish dreams and cinnamon diamonds. In addition, Robinson's bakes all the old and new American standards, including chocolate chip and peanut butter cookies and a 1 1/2-pound multigrain Whole Earth bread

Klinefelter's Gallery
1124 S. Mears about a mile south of downtown Whitehall. (616) 894-5650. Mon-Sat 9-5:30.

Limited-edition prints, including many by local and regional artists, are sold at this attractive gallery.

Howmet Playhouse
304 S. Mears at Slocum, 2 blocks south of downtown Whitehall. Season: early July-late August. Wed-Sun. Box office: (616) 894-2540. $10 for operas, $5 for plays.

The Michigan State University theater company no longer is involved in the summer theater program of Blue Lake Fine Arts Camp. Instead, the Piccolo Opera Company of Detroit performs two operas (in 1993, Mozart's *Cosi Fan Tutte* and two short operas by Gian-Carlo Menotti) and the cream of the crop of Blue Lake's talented high-school age summer students stage three musicals. Call for details about the expanded children's theater program.

At Robinson's Swedish-style bakery, everything, even doughnuts, is made from scratch. Scandinavians, descended from loggers and millhands, are numerous in former logging towns like Whitehall and Muskegon.

Causeway/Depot/
Boardwalk/
White River Marsh

On Business Route 31 between Whitehall and Montague.

With the sweeping expanse of marsh to the east and White Lake to the west, the causeway offers some nice views: the hillside houses and churches of Montague peeking above the trees, the much-touted world's largest weathervane behind the Montague village hall on the lake; resident swans and other birds swimming among the marsh reeds.

A wide walk- and bikeway begins at Montague's main four corners and crosses the causeway, then goes up to Whitehall's business district or stays low and ends in a **marsh boardwalk** at Lions' Park. The Montague **Dog & Suds** is blessed with a wonderful river view. **Covell Park** on the causeway has parking and a **boat launch**. The C & O train tracks used to be here; the depot is now occupied by the **White Lake Chamber of Commerce** (p. 203), a helpful source of visitor information open daily in summer.

The whole scene can be viewed from above on the deck of **Morat's River Walk Cafe** (p. 217).

The world's largest weather vane

Just past the causeway in Montague, on White Lake.

Probably half the weather vanes in the United States are made in Montague by two rival companies. But their presence was largely overlooked even by locals until the owner of the original and larger manufacturer, Whitehall Metal Studios, decided to draw attention to this local specialty by building the world's largest weather vane on the lakefront

entrance to town. The arrow is 26 feet long. The ship atop the weather vane commemorates a White Lakes schooner. At night, when the weather vane and the landmark Ferry Memorial Church on the hill behind it are illuminated, it's a dramatic sight.

The showrooms and factories of competing weather vane makers are across the street from each other a few blocks away at 8786 and 8939 Water Street in Montague. Their aluminum castings, in black or plain aluminum, finish, include all kinds of exterior home ornaments, from initials to put on chimneys to flying ducks for the garage door to name and address signs by the mailbox.

Downtown Montague

Along Ferry and Water north of Dowling.

Though its historic business district is fairly minimal (a landmark hotel was destroyed by fire), Montague may well be unique in having *two* drugstores with functioning soda fountains in the very same block. **Lipka's**, on the corner of Ferry and Dowling, is more old-timey; it's been there in some form since 1879. But **Todd's**, a very large, modernized drugstore down the block on Ferry, has the lunch counter that's quite a social hub for all sorts of people. It's open from 8:30 a.m. to 9:30 p.m. weekdays, until 1 p. m. on Sunday.

Montague Historical Museum   ★

Corner of Meade and Church. Take Dowling up the hill to Meade, turn left. Contact: (616) 894-6813. Open Mem. Day through Labor Day every weekend 1-5. Group tours for 10 or more, other times with 1 week's notice. Free; donations appreciated.

This former Methodist church is a community attic on a grand scale. Its several thousand square feet of collections and clutter include Dorothy Gritzner's extensive collection of salt and pepper shakers, Shipibo Indian artifacts from Muskegon newspaperman Lex Chisholm's trip to Peru, one shelf full of old skates and another of milk bottles.

Highlights are the log marks and tools from White Lake's busy logging past and the Miss America Room, featuring Nancy Ann Fleming of Whitehall, Miss America of 1961. Here are her gown, her portrait, and several scrapbooks of clippings kept, apparently, by adoring younger fans. Fleming is "just as sweet as she was when she won the contest fresh out of high school," say locals. "She hasn't really changed" — though she does live in California, hosts a talk show, and is married to a man who is not her original husband.

Like any good attic of an old family homestead, this museum yields its rewards to those with the patience and knowledge to find things interesting, and with the good humor to appreciate the impulses that make people deem some objects historically significant.

All sorts of things turn up in Montague's historical museum, from logging equipment to Miss America's gown to a 7th-grade class scrapbook about chemistry and all the wonderful science opportunities Hooker Chemical promised the area. Postcards of Nancy Anne Fleming, Miss America 1961, are still available.

A wooden doll made of a bedpost, a fake fireplace that opens into a bed, a tree-fork alphabet, a helmet-like electric hair-curling contraption — they're all here, with little or no explanation. A more coherent history of the White Lake area is provided by many well-captioned photographs and clippings on swinging panels. Look for it in the former church sanctuary, just down from the display case of beaded evening bags, over by the old-time doctor's office.

The Old Channel and Old Channel Trail

Drive starts in downtown Montague. As Dowling goes up the hill, turn left onto Old Channel Trail.

The scenic Old Channel Trail in Montague goes along the north shore of White Lake, out past homes and small resorts (some quite distinguished, some modest) and along Lake Michigan, past the original channel of the White River to the attractive Old Channel Golf Course.

The Old Channel of the White River emptied into Lake Michigan about a mile north of today's more direct outlet by the White River Light, which was dug by the federal government in 1875 to accommodate the big increase in lumber schooners.

Once a bustling lumber village was at the old channel mouth, where only a beach and a few houses are today. The Reverend William Montague Ferry, the Mackinac missionary-turned-businessman who founded Grand Haven, had bought extensive pinelands north of White Lake and erected a steam sawmill, the first on White Lake, here at the mouth in 1850. Irish fishermen eventually joined millworkers living in the hamlet, which flourished for nearly 40 years.

But as many lumber mills were built along the lake, this village was surpassed by Whitehall and the newer town of Montague at White Lake's head. (Noah Ferry, mill manager and son of Reverend Ferry, named the new town after his father's middle name.) After the present, much more direct channel was opened, the village at the old mouth died. Today

Of the busy lumbering village at the old mouth of the White River, shown here in 1850, only a few buildings remain. The onetime general store is now the Old Channel Inn, a popular destination for a scenic drive.

its general store has become the popular **Old Channel Inn** (p. 217).

Little **Medbury Park**, in a sandy, windswept beach and cottage area, is on the site of the White Lake Life Saving Station, built in 1875 at the "new" channel opposite the White River Light. Parking is limited. You can get there by turning south onto Lau (left if you're driving out from Montague) and following signs.

At the end of Old Channel Trail is the beautiful, well maintained **Old Channel Trail Golf Course** (616-894-5076), an 18-hole public course overlooking Lake Michigan.

Weesies Brothers Plant Farm

10126 Walsh Rd., about 2 miles northeast of Montague. From Bus. Route 31, take Fruitvale Rd. east and follow the signs. (616) 894-4742. Retail sales from about April 20 through June. Mon-Fri 8-6 (until 8 from mid-May to June), Sat 8-5.

This longtime celery farm is now a grower, wholesaler, and retailer of bedding plants, herbs, perennials, and roses, with about 5 acres under glass. They grow six shades of geraniums, varieties of newer and non-patented roses (including climbers), 10 herbs, vegetables, and many perennials in 4-plant trays (75¢/tray, $7.95/flat of 48). After the bedding plants are gone, they grow a late celery crop.

Hart-Montague BicycleTrail State Park   ★

South trailhead in Montague is on Eilers Rd. just east of Bus. Route 31 on northeast edge of town. North trailhead is on Bus. U.S. 31 on the west edge of Hart. Park on north side of road. Administered by Silver Lake State Park. Call (616) 873-3083 for trail info. Trail pass: $2/day, $10/year, or $5/$25 for families.

The old C&O railroad tracks between Montague and Hart go through unspoiled landscape of fruit farms and woods and surprisingly spectacular topography. The peaceful flatlands of Muskegon County give way to the high hills, blue in the distance, and the long vistas of Oceana County inland from the Lake Michigan resort areas around Pentwater, Silver Lake, and Stony Lake. The asphalt trail is smooth enough for **rollerblades** and **wheelchairs**.

There's a wonderful variety of trailside sights, from thick pine forests and views down onto glacial lakes and wetlands to river valleys to the trailside factory in Shelby that produces manmade sapphires for jewelry. The town center of **Shelby**, a block or so east of the trail, is worth a look. The trail also passes through the small towns of **Mears, New Era**, and **Rothbury**, passing by canning factories and enough other interesting things to make for a lively ride. The whole area exudes a pleasant sense of being back in the 1940s or 1950s, when farms were predictably neat, trim, and modestly prosperous. The orchards are beautiful at blossomtime and harvest time.

Biking from north to south takes best advantage of the long views and gently declining slope. **Hart**, the pretty county seat of Oceana County, is worth riding around for some attractive historical buildings and its beautiful, shady **Hart City Campground** northeast of downtown, overlooking Hart Lake and beach.

Bicycles can be **rented** at McKay's Bicycle Rental just south of Mears (616-873-4271) and The Bicycle Depot at the trailhead in Montague (616-893-2453), where child trailers and jogging strollers are also rented.

Meinert Park

On Lake Michigan at the end of Meinert Rd. From Montague, take Whitehall Rd. (which is Bus. U.S. 31 as you go north) 1 mile north past Fruitvale Rd., turn west onto Meinert Rd., continue 6 miles.

There's no fancy picnic pavilion or wood play equipment at this family-oriented Muskegon County park — just a nice stretch of Lake Michigan beachfront and a low dune. Flower Creek flows into the lake, making a shallow, protected wading area for small children. There are restrooms, and a refreshment wagon is often here on weekends.

White River Canoeing/ Happy Mohawk Canoe Livery   ★

735 E. Fruitvale Rd., 5 miles east of U.S. 31 northeast of Montague. (616) 894-4209.

Famous as a logging river, the White River today is a designated Wild-Scenic River, good for bass, northern pike, and salmon and steelhead runs. It is less canoed, less fished, and more remote in feel than some better-known, longer rivers up north. According to Jerry Dennis and Craig Date's *Canoeing Michigan Rivers,* the lower part is fine for beginners and families with small children, except when water is high. The canoeable part begins at the Hesperial Dam at Hesperia; the first 8.5 miles are shallow, with riffles — sometimes so shallow they can't be canoed.

Though much of the river goes through the Manistee National Forest, there aren't many public access points. The Happy Mohawk Canoe Livery rents canoes, tubes, rafts, and kayaks. (The adjacent White River Campground is under the same management).

White River Campground★

735 E. Fruitvale Rd., 5 miles east of U.S. 31 northeast of Montague. (616) 894-4708. Season: May 1-Oct. 31. Family rates per night from $13.50 (no electricity or water) to $16.50 (electricity and water).

Pretty little Sand Creek curls though this heavily wooded, exceptionally picturesque valley campground that abuts the White River in the Manistee National Forest. There are actually 180 campsites here, but they are arranged to respect the topography, usually with a shrubby wooded buffer to the rear, so sites aren't too close together, and the place has a pleasantly rustic feel. There are showers and a sizable camp store. Extra recreational amenities include a small heated pool, video arcade, sandy beach, fishing, volleyball, playgrounds, nature trails, and canoeing from the Happy Mohawk Canoe Livery, under the same management.

Blue Lake Fine Arts Camp★

On Little Blue Lake 6 miles east of downtown Whitehall. From Whitehall, take Colby/Holton-Whitehall Rd. east to Russell Rd., go south a mile to the entrance. From the south, take U.S. 31 to Russell Rd., go 6 miles north to entrance. Call for concert information: (616) 893-7303. Camp session: 3rd week of June through 3rd week of August.

What started in 1966 as a youth summer camp for fine arts has become one part of a year-round operation that includes a **classical music public radio** station (WBLV, 90.3 FM), an arts school and Montessori school in Muskegon, an international music exchange program, and the Howmet Playhouse summer theater. The eight-week summer camp, now enrolling 3,600 over four sessions, remains at its heart and offers the general public **concerts** nearly every night of the week. All are free but the Saturday

Highlights Series. Faculty, students, and visiting musicians from Europe perform in the **free concerts**. The **Saturday Highlights series** (from $5 to $35) reflects the range of camp programs, with one major symphony orchestra, a children's act, a jazz festival (for 1990 virtuoso drummer Louis Bellson and the legendary Cab Calloway), drama (John Chappel as Mark Twain), ballet, and pop music (song and dance with Ben Vereen).

The Blue Lake approach to arts education is more wide-ranging and relaxed, less intensely competitive than the elitist, pre-professional, prep school atmosphere of older, better-known Interlochen. Camp programs cover classical music, jazz, art, photography, dance, and theater; faculty include many Michigan State professors, and the camp shares the inclusive, "get people excited about learning" enthusiasm of the M.S.U. land-grant approach.

The **camp store** offers a great selection of nifty gifts for musicians, including some very funny cartoon T-shirts for each instrument.

Boy Scout Museum

9900 Russell Rd. at Silver Creek Rd. in an old town hall. 4 miles north of Blue Lake Fine Arts Camp. From U.S. 31 and Whitehall, go east on the Holton-Whitehall Rd. from the main Whitehall exit, turn immediately north onto Silver Creek Rd., go about 5 miles. (616) 894-4062. Open July & August Mon-Fri 9-5. Free.

Old Scouting memorabilia and photographs are displayed in a former town hall on the huge, 5,000-acre Owasippee Scout Reservation east of Whitehall, said to be the first Boy Scout camp in the U.S.

RESTAURANTS

Todd Pharmacy

8744 Ferry 1/2 block north of Dowling in downtown Montague. (616) 894-4573. Year-round hours: Mon-Fri 8:30-9 p.m., Sat until 7, Sun until 1. No alcohol or credit cards.

Just about everybody shows up at this large soda fountain and grill with booths several times a week. For summer people, the nostalgic attraction is malts and sodas ($1.65) and old-fashioned fountain treats like cherry and vanilla phosphates. Soups, salads, and sandwiches are served from 10:30 on. Most of it's homemade — the potatoes start the day in their skins, and pies are fresh daily — and the prices are low: $1.55 for hamburgers, $1.60 for a chef salad in a soup bowl, $3.10 for the hot specials (meat loaf or casserole, salads, potatos, and roll) served Tuesday and Thursday at lunch.

Old Channel Inn

6905 Old Channel Trail, about 5 miles west. From Bus. 31/Dowling in Montague, turn left onto Old Channel Tr. as you climb the hill, go 5 miles west. (616) 893-3805. Mem.-Labor Day: daily noon-10, until 11 Fri & Sat. Winter hours: Wed-Sun noon-9, Fri & Sat until 10. Visa, MC. Full bar.

This beat-up old tavern with a big stone fireplace has always had a certain casual mystique, thanks to its picturesque location and history as a surviving remnant of the original settlement of Montague (p. 213). Now a new owner has improved the food, which now goes beyond hamburgers and fried fare to include soup ($1.75 a bowl), salads, and chargrilled chicken and steak. It's still known for the basics: fried perch ($8.95) and ribs ($10.95) at dinner (salad and starch included) and a half-pound burger ($3.95) any time.

A gated road just south of the inn leads to a small **public beach** on Lake Michigan.

Morat's River Walk Cafe & Bakery

N. Mears overlooking the White River marsh, just north of Colby in downtown Whitehall. (616) 893-5163. Mem. Day-Labor Day: Mon-Sat 6 a.m.-5:30 p.m., Sun 8-1. Otherwise Mon-Sat 7-5:30.

This busy, full-line bakery also carries American Spoon preserves and coffee beans for making your own special breakfast. Morat's is known for its English muffin bread, round cinnamon bread, and specialty cakes. The breads (mostly $1.99/loaf), coffee cakes, and cookies, while good, to us aren't the equal of the hearty European-style breads at Robinson's (p. 211). But the pleasant eating area with big windows and the outdoor terrace looking out onto the White River marsh, the Montague hill, and the big sky, make this a delightful place to linger on a jaunt to downtown. In addition to pastries and coffee, there are soups ($1.75/bowl), chef, chicken, and pasta salads (about $3.25), deli sandwiches on fresh-baked bread ($3.65), and hot dogs.

Pekadyll's Ice Cream Parlour ★

503 S. Mears, 5 blocks south of downtown. (616) 894-9551. Summer hours: 11:30-10 daily. April, May, Sept. hours: 11:30-8. Winter: 11:30-3.

This spiffed-up red-and-white former grocery store is simple and fresh, trim and button-cute without being overdone. The front part is a quintessential ice cream parlor, with a black-and-white checked floor and an old radio and ads from the ice cream parlor's heyday in the 1920s. Hudsonville ice cream (a regionally popular non-premium ice cream) is served in cones ($.85 a scoop, or $1.10 with a homemade cone), you can get splits, parfaits, shakes ($1.99), Colombo yogurt, sodas, and 11 kinds of sundaes. Flavorful homemade soups ($2.29/bowl) and outstanding submarine sandwiches ($2.50 for 4 inches, $4.50 for 8 inches) are served cafeteria-style on the sun-dappled terrace, beneath big pines, or in the plain, cheery rear rooms.

Morat's at the White Lake Golf Club

6777 South Shore Drive west of Lamos Rd. and across from the Yacht Club, about 6 miles west of downtown Whitehall. Open daily Mem. Day-Labor Day: 9 a.m.-7 p.m.

At the charming green-and-white clubhouse of the private White Lake Golf Club, Morat's Cafe and Bakery offers its usual good soups, salads, and deli sandwiches (p. 217) plus grilled hamburgers. You can enjoy them on the pristine screened porch overlooking the golf course. The sign over the clubhouse door says, "The Burial Place of Old Man Gloom," but the portraits of club presidents inside the clubroom reveal are a pretty staid lot.

Lakeside Inn ★

5700 Scenic Dr. at South Shore, 6 miles west of downtown Whitehall overlooking White Lake. (616) 893-8315. In July & Aug: open daily for breakfast 7:30-10 and dinner 6-9. From Mother's Day to Labor Day open Fri-Sun for dinner 6-9. Full bar. Visa, MC.

Many locals think this resort's public dining room has the area's best food, considering quality and value. Breakfasts are basic. At dinner the inn is known for prime rib ($11.95/$13.95), shrimp and scallops ($10.95), and fried perch ($10.25). All include salad bar, starch, and homemade rolls and muffins. Dining room and patio have nice lake view.

The Galleon

On Murray Rd. at the White Lake Channel. Take South Shore Dr. 5 miles west of Whitehall; it ends at Murray Rd. (616) 894-6300. Open May-Sept. Daily Mem.-Labor Day: Mon-Sat 5:30-10, Sun until 9. Lunch Sat & Sun only noon-4. In May & Sept. Fri & Sat only, 5:30-10. Full bar. Visa, MC.

Part of the former Murray's Inn turn-of-the-century resort, The Galleon is another frequently mentioned White Lake finer dining choice on account of its good seafood and steaks and lake view. Diners can come by boat. Dinner favorites: shrimp and beef tips ($12.95), seafood stir-fry ($12.95), and fettucine with crabmeat in a wine sauce ($10.95). All include vegetable, salad, and potato. At lunch the 1/2 pound Galleonburger with bacon and swiss cheese ($5.95 with fries) and French dip are popular.

LODGINGS

Timekeeper's Inn
(616) 894-5169.
303 Mears at Slocum, two blocks south of Colby (Whitehall's main street) and across from the Howmet Playhouse.
Bed and breakfast with 4 rooms, 2 with shared baths, 2 with private baths. Season rates (May-mid Oct.) $50-$60. Winter rates: $35-$45. Continental breakfast.

Comfortable but not fussy, this big, beautiful house, built by a lumber baron in 1881, is one of the very pleasantest B & B's we've encountered, thanks to the thoughtful hospitality of Michael and Marjorie Brunsink. It's full of antiques and elaborate woodwork (and his clock shop fills the front room), but it doesn't feel like a decorator's showcase. The rooms are big. The floors don't squeak. There's an upstairs kitchen with pop in the refrigerator, and sherry in the reading alcove of the upstairs hall. Comfortable chairs on the big front porch look out onto on Whitehall's shadiest, most attractive old residential street.

Ramada Inn of Whitehall
(616) 893-3030.
Colby Rd. just east of U.S. 31 at Whitehall exit. 1 1/2 miles to downtown Whitehall.
64 rooms on 3 floors. Standard rooms $66 in season (June-mid-Sept.), $55 off-season. Whirlpool suites $76/$65, kitchenettes $91/$80. White Lake area's most luxurious lodgings. Outdoor heated pool covered with air-dome in cool and cold weather. Restaurant, exercise room, game room, saunas. VCRs & movies to rent. BBQ pits, bonfires, playground, volleyball, badminton, horseshoes. Spacious grounds, adjacent to woods.

Super 8 Motel
(616) 894-4848.
3080 Holton-Whitehall Rd. between U.S. 31 and Whitehall.
68 rooms. 2 people, 1 bed $40, 2 beds $42. Whirlpool suites $72. 10% senior discount. Winter rates a little less.

Lakeside Inn
(616) 893-8315.
5700 N. Scenic Drive at South Shore Dr. on White Lake west of Whitehall.
27 units, half with lake view. Doubles $40-$65, $5/extra person. Open May through Sept. Some rooms in remodeled 1900-vintage building over the good Lakeside Inn restaurant, which served breakfast July & Aug. Other rooms in attractive single-story motel-like building overlooking lake or a lawn. Tennis, heated pool. Early reservations advised for July & Aug. Beautiful setting, with common lawn with lake view. Good opportunities for bicycling and walks to channel, Duck Lake Park beaches on Lake Michigan and pretty Duck Lake. Dock for sitting on lake, fishing. Big common rooms, 1950s feel in lodge. Clubby, convivial atmosphere. No air-conditioning or phones.

INDEX

Helpful resources

A great deal of high-caliber, free, information may by obtained from the Michigan Travel Bureau, Dept. STG, Box 30226, Lansing, MI 48909. Call (800) 7432-YES. Ask for the specific publication you want.

State highway map
Summer, Fall, and Winter Travel Guides and Calendar of Events
Bed-and-Breakfast Directory
Boat and Travel Directory
Campground Directory (includes private campgrounds)
Canoe Directory
Fishing Guide
Golf Directory
Lodging Directory
Michigan Travel Planner

❶❷ Two downtowns. Unsettling & dramatic contrast between trim white city and poor black one. **Benton Harbor's** downtown (**❶**) almost became a ghost town, while adjacent St. Joe (**❷**) thrives. Don't miss **St. Joe's** Krasl Art center, band concerts in Lake Bluff Park; Benton Harbor's Wolf's Marine.

❸ Curious Kids Museum. Outstanding small hands-on museum, more kid-centered and playful than most. Zany cartoon decor.

❸ Mama Martorano's. Real Italian home cooking, redolent of garlic and wine, shines at this simple spot. Excellent food for little money.

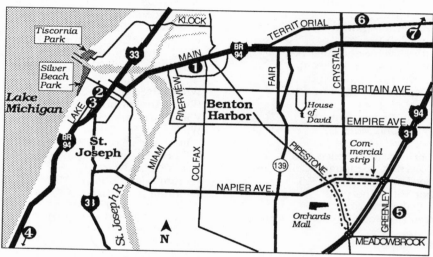

❹ Snowflake Motel. Frank Lloyd Wright conceived this once-luxurious motel which now caters to truckers and construction workers. Friendly staff, budget rates.

❺ The Herb Barn. A fragrant natural world a minute from I-94. Good prices on plants; lots of ideas for uses. Pretty display garden and dried arrangements.

❻ Benton Harbor Fruit Market. Watch the action at world's biggest cash-to-grower fruit & vegetable market. Good retail produce stand. Free posters, recipes.

❼ Sarett Nature Center. Bird-watcher's paradise, thanks to river wetlands, 5 miles of trails, boardwalks, and elevated viewing seats. Good gift shop, excellent talks & outings.

Highlights of
St. Joseph/
Benton Harbor

0   1/2   1
mile

❶ Saugatuck Dunes State Park. Wild, pristine dune country, 2 mi. of uncrowded beach, 14 mi. of hiking trails. Dune tops offer nice lake views.

❷ Downtown Saugatuck. Lively mix of quality galleries, gift & clothing shops along with delightful town common and gardens.

❸ Queen of Saugatuck. Informative cruise on fake steamboat highlights marine geography of Kalamazoo Lake and Lake Michigan shoreline.

❹ Wicks Park & boardwalk. Civilized little park with benches looks across river to Mt. Baldhead. Evening concerts with dance orchestra in gazebo.

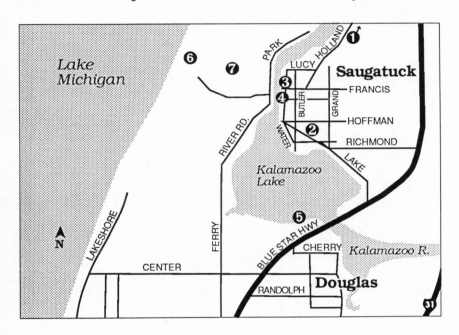

❺ S.S. Keewatin. Bygone glories of elegant Great Lakes cruise ships live on in this 336-foot steamship, now a museum.

❻ Oval Beach. Costs $5 a car on weekends to join the crowd at this popular beach. Well-stocked concession stand.

❼ Mt. Baldhead. Reward of short but strenuous climb is splendid views of city and lakes. Pleasant picnic site below on river.

Bed and breakfast inns. Outstanding quality & variety; over 12 in area, from elegant to casual.

Highlights of
Saugatuck

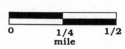

0   1/4   1/2
mile

❶ Kirk Park.
Area's best beach combines natural scenery, pretty picnic spots, good playground, splendid beach backed by high dunes and dark beech woods. Bike path from Holland.

❷ Veldheer Tulip Gardens.
Costs $2 in May to enter the formal garden, but the 30-acre tulip field out back is more magical. Visit at dusk, when tulips glow. Next door is only Delftware factory outside Netherlands.

❸ Dekker Huis.
Splendid local museum illuminates lives of impoverished rural Dutch immigrants of 1847. Vivid displays of early austerity, eventual prosperity.

❹ Dutch Village.
Beguiling mix of history, nostalgia, and storybook kitsch. Small theme park; 18th-19th c. village theme. Wonderful antique carnival rides, street organs. klompen dancers.

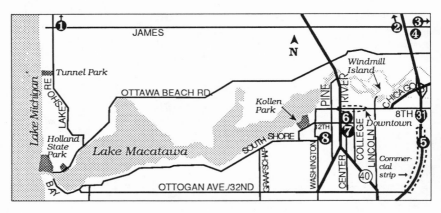

❺ Wooden Shoe Factory.
Fun, old-timey tourist trap has Holland's best demonstrations of wooden shoe making. See antique French sabots and Dutch klompen; sample Dutch sweets and cheese.

❻ Centennial Park. Old-fashioned park with lighted fountain, rock grotto, windmill-shaped flower beds, potted palms from city greenhouse, all beneath canopy of century-old trees.

❼ Netherlands Museum. Dutch bourgeoisie were the Western World's first to create cozy, private homes. See their cheerful 18th-c. sitting rooms, outstanding collections of Delftware, pewter.

❽ Pereddies.
Authentic Italian bakery-deli started by transplants from metro Detroit. Typifies the new Holland: easygoing, pleasant, and multi-ethnic. Mexican neighborhood just south of here.

Highlights of
Holland

0   1   2
miles

❶ North Beach Park. Nice, less crowded beach and terrific dune to climb, with splendid view of town and lake.

❷ Arbcreal Inn. Out of the way, but worth the drive. Good food, great atmosphere in quaint, rustic setting.

❸ Boardwalk. Lively and scenic, with lots of boats, views, strollers, snacks, Snug Harbor Restaurant.

❹ South Pier. Dramatic walk out to two old lighthouses. As popular with strollers as fishermen.

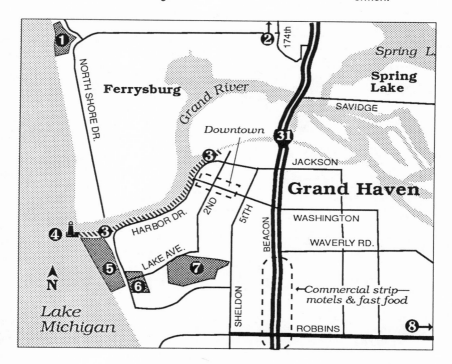

❺ Lake Michigan beaches. Trees are scarce, but these beachside parks are packed with swimmers, kites, and RVs.

❻ Highland Park. Haunting Victorian summer colony in wooded dunes. Scenic boardwalk winds through it.

❼ Lake Forest Cemetery & Duncan Park. Beautiful 19th-century setting with hills, dales, majestic beeches.

❽ Idyllic drive along the Grand to historic East-manville, La-mont, mid-19th-century river villages.

Highlights of
Grand Haven

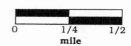

0   1/4   1/2
mile

❶ Muskegon S.P./Scenic Dr. Beautiful park, uncrowded 3 miles of beach, dunes, inland beach & campgrounds.

❷ Winter Sports Complex. Learn to use 40 mph sled. Scenic lighted x-c ski trails, warming lodge. In beautiful state park.

❸ Museum of Art. Outstanding small museum geared to a refreshingly broad public. Don't miss Curry's "Tornado over Kansas."

❹ Hackley House. Exuberant, spare-no-expense Queen Anne fantasy built by Muskegon's great benefactor.

❺ S. S. Silversides. Tour big WWII sub that sank 23 Japanese ships. Looks ready to head out again to sea.

❻ Gillette Visitor Center. Compelling slide show of Michigan's dunes. Sensuous walk thru damp dune woods to spectacular overlook.

❼ Pleasure Island Water Fun Park. Scary "Ram page" Water Slide & "Black Hole"; kiddie water play area; plus attractive picnic area, sandy beach.

Highlights of
Muskegon

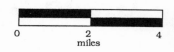

0   2   4
         miles